澳大利亚文化研究

Australian Cultural Studies

第2辑

主　编　王光林
副主编　陈　弘

上海外语教育出版社
外教社 SHANGHAI FOREIGN LANGUAGE EDUCATION PRESS

图书在版编目（CIP）数据

澳大利亚文化研究. 第2辑 / 王光林主编.
—上海：上海外语教育出版社，2016
ISBN 978-7-5446-4284-2

Ⅰ. ①澳… Ⅱ. ①王… Ⅲ. ①文化—研究—澳大利亚 Ⅳ. ①G161.1

中国版本图书馆CIP数据核字（2016）第040363号

出版发行：上海外语教育出版社
（上海外国语大学内） 邮编：200083
电　　话：021-65425300（总机）
电子邮箱：bookinfo@sflep.com.cn
网　　址：http://www.sflep.com.cn http://www.sflep.com
责任编辑：梁泉胜

印　　刷：上海叶大印务发展有限公司
开　　本：787×1092 1/16 印张 9.75 字数 190千字 插页 8
版　　次：2016年6月第1版 2016年6月第1次印刷

书　　号：ISBN 978-7-5446-4284-2 / G · 1364
定　　价：29.00元

编委会名单

主编寄语

《澳大利亚文化研究》创刊以来，得到了中外学者的高度重视，颇有受宠若惊的感觉。惊喜之余，又深感压力重大。这一方面反映出国内学者在澳大利亚文学、文化研究方面已逐渐形成一股不可小觑的力量，另一方面也反映出国外学者对中国澳大利亚文学、文化研究的关注，更重要的是体现出全球化语境下文学、文化研究同行相互学习、彼此沟通、深入对话的趋势。

在本辑的编排上，我们延续了上辑的“学者访谈”、“作家作品”、“文坛纵览”和“社会文化”四大板块，新增了“书讯书评”一栏。“学者访谈”是我们隆重推出的一个栏目，成语有云：“栉风沐雨，薪火相传；筚路蓝缕，玉汝于成。”前辈学者对澳大利亚文化的研究给我们打下了良好的基础，对他们的访谈就是要继承和保持这个活的历史，给后辈更多的引导。本辑的胡文仲教授访谈录相信会给读者很多启迪，而澳大利亚著名作家米勒在访谈中所涉及的很多中国轶事也一定会引起读者广泛的兴趣。“作家作品”中讨论的三部作品都是澳大利亚文学中的名家经典，这些研究体现了中国学者对澳大利亚文学的把握和了解。“文坛纵览”中陶乃侃的译诗体会和陈贝贝研究的澳大利亚华裔文学新进展都会给读者带来耳目一新的感觉。“社会文化”一栏展现了对澳大利亚社会文化各个方面的研究，以使读者对澳大利亚能有更加深入的了解。“书讯书评”是新增的栏目，通过这个栏目，我们希望及时向读者推荐介绍一些国内外澳大利亚文学、文化研究最新的优秀成果。

王光林

目 录

“九人帮”及其他
——胡文仲教授访谈录[1]

李建军

李建军（以下简称李）：在中国的澳大利亚研究发展历程中，“九人帮”可以说是一个传奇，在澳大利亚和中国都曾引起过轰动。请您对从事澳研的年轻人谈谈相关的情况。

胡文仲（以下简称胡）：说是传奇，有些过分。但这个团队确实有其不一般之处。1978年上半年，国家通过考试选拔了一批中年教师派出国进修。我们9个人（按年龄排序：胡壮麟、杨潮光、胡文仲、黄源深、钱佼汝、王国富、侯维瑞、杜瑞清和龙日金）来自北京、上海、南京、苏州、西安和重庆的9所大学，在北京集训后被派往澳大利亚悉尼大学学习。刚开始，澳方为我们单独安排一些课程，主要目的是提高我们的英语水平。我们要求在悉尼大学正式读硕士学位，经过反复交涉，最后他们终于同意。6个人进入了英语系，3个人进入了语言学系。英语系主任是著名澳大利亚文学教授Leonie Kramer，语言学系主任是著名语言学家M.A.K. Halliday（韩礼德）教授。虽然我们分了系，但实际上，在英语系注册的也到语言学系听课，在语言学系注册的也到英语系读澳大利亚文学。我们那时的想法很单纯，就是多选课，多学些东西，回国后多开课。我们选的课比澳大利亚学生平均多二分之一甚至多一倍，学习负担非常重，但是，大家的学习热情很高，废寝忘食，都希望把“文革”中丢失的时间夺回来。

头半年，我们住在悉尼大学对面的留学生大楼（International House）。在那里我们是最有人缘的一批外国留学生。每到周末，许多澳大利亚朋友开车到我们的住处接我们去度周末，这包括侨青社、澳中友协和中国教育学会各友好团体的朋友们，其他国家的留学生十分羡慕。后来，我们陆续迁出了留学生大楼，住到普通老百姓家里，以便更多地了解澳大利亚人民和他们的文化。我们除了在大学里学习，还参加各种活动，包括出席各种会议、座谈、到各地参观等等，与澳大利亚各阶层有了广泛的接触。我们在澳大利亚的影响逐渐扩大，引起了媒体的注意。他们注意到我们经常集体活动，关系十分紧密，可以说是很“抱团”，当时又是中国“文化大革命”结束不久，所以，

1 胡壮麟教授阅读了访谈初稿，并提出修改建议；黄源深、钱佼汝、王国富和杜瑞清教授曾提供有关材料，在此一并致谢。

他们戏称我们这一批人为“the Gang of Nine”。

两年后，这批人回到国内自己的学校，都成了教学的骨干，绝大多数被任命为系主任，其中三位还成为大学的校长或副校长。在全国外语教育领域，这批人也都做了比较多的工作，得到同行的认可，成为一批中坚力量，因而外语教育界有人把我们叫做“澳帮”。在澳大利亚研究方面，这批人中的大多数都在自己的学校发起成立了澳研中心，相继开设澳大利亚研究方面的课程。1988 年在各地澳研中心活动的基础上，北外澳研中心发起成立了中国澳大利亚研究学会。

“九人帮”回国后，每个人在自己的领域都取得了比较突出的成绩：在语言学研究方面，北大资深教授胡壮麟先生成就最大，成为系统功能语言学在我国的创始人之一，任学会会长，现为名誉会长，曾任中国英语教学研究会副会长（1987—2001）。出版了多部语言学专著，发表了 140 多篇学术论文。1992 年他主编的《语言学教程》获国家教委优秀教材一等奖。他是北京大学澳大利亚研究中心的创始人，至今仍然担任名誉中心主任。王国富教授在苏州大学创立了澳大利亚研究中心，他主持编译和翻译了几部澳大利亚辞典，包括《英汉澳大利亚语词典》、《麦夸里英汉双解词典》等，1998 年获得澳中理事会翻译奖，2008 年获澳中理事会奖章。侯维瑞教授 1984 年出任上海外国语学院副院长。在英国文学研究方面成就斐然，他发表学术论文 50 余篇，出版多部专著、译著，共计 200 多万字，其中《现代英国小说史》深受学界好评。杜瑞清教授担任西安外国语学院副院长、院长长达 13 年，80 年代末在西外创办了澳研中心，在词典编纂和跨文化交际研究方面取得了卓越成就。钱佼汝教授在南京大学外文系任教，在本科和研究生层次开设了文学、文体学、文论等课程，1992 年入选国务院学位委员会第三届学科评议组成员，曾获第七届和第八届台湾梁实秋文学翻译奖，是江苏省第六、七、八届政协委员，南京市第九、十届人民代表，1993—2003 年被派到联合国教科文组织中文科，担任高级译审。杨潮光教授在对外经济贸易大学任教，出版了两部专著《语用学教程》和《语言学导论》，曾任校党委委员和北京市人大代表，退休后先后在北京科技大学、北京大学文理学院和国际关系学院授课。龙日金教授曾任西南师范大学外语系系主任、高等学校英语专业教材编审委员会委员、重庆市外文学会副会长、重庆市政协委员。主编教材 4 部，发表学术论文 10 余篇，并出版专著《现代汉语及物性研究》（与彭宣维合著）。黄源深教授在外语教育和澳大利亚文学研究和翻译方面做出了很大贡献，下面专门介绍，这里从略。

2009 年——也就是“九人帮”赴澳 30 周年——我们再次全体聚会在北京，与悉尼大学原校长 Leonie Kramer 和副校长会面，并回忆了我们走过的这一段不平凡的路程。我注意到会上有人发言把“the Gang of Nine”改成了“the Group of Nine”。其实怎么称呼都无所谓，这 9 个人确实是一个团结奋进的集体。令人惋惜的是这时已经有两位成员（侯维瑞教授和龙日金教授）英年早逝，过早地离开了我们。

李：您能否谈谈“九人帮”的近况？近年来，您们还有联系吗？

胡：上面已经谈到赴澳 30 周年的聚会。实际上，这些年来我们这九个人（之后是七个人）一直保持着联系。大家不仅在全国的学术会议上见面，平时也经常有书信往来，在学术方面切磋，生活上互相关心。这次访谈就是不久前黄源深教授给我打电话，要我接受的。我对他说，一般情况下，我对于这类访谈都是谢绝的，但这个要求来之于你，我无法推却。有时我对于自已撰写的有关外语教育的论文中的一些提法没有把握，在发表前将论文发给胡壮麟教授，请他提意见，他从不拒绝，总是及时给我提出意见和建议。“九人帮”有过两次大的聚会，一次是 1999 年，杜瑞清教授邀请“九人帮”到西安聚会，并组织学术活动，纪念我们赴澳 20 周年。第二次就是我前面所说的 2009 年北京的聚会，纪念我们赴澳 30 周年。

李：我多次读到有关许多国内澳大利亚研究中心创办过程的艰辛，例如学校领导不支持等。请您谈谈北外澳研中心的创办情况。创办过程顺利吗？

胡：就北外来说，“学校领导不支持”这个说法不够准确。澳大利亚研究在当年还是一片 terra incognita, 我们回国后提出在系里开设澳大利亚研究方面的课程，但系领导心中没有底，不知道是否学生会选修这些课程，开了课究竟有多少学生会选，所以态度不是很积极，但最终还是同意我们开课。当时在北外，只有吴祯福、余志远和我三个教师分别开设澳大利亚历史、政治、文学等课程。实际上，学生对澳大利亚研究兴趣很大，选课人数大大超过系领导和我们的预期，学生听课以后，对于课程的反应很好。澳大利亚研究课程在英语系的课程体系中从此得到确认。除了在本科设课外，在研究生层次也陆续开了课。澳大利亚也派来一些教师协助，澳大利亚研究从此成为一个专业方向。我们陆续培养了一批又一批澳大利亚研究方面的硕士，还培养了澳大利亚文学博士，这样就确立了澳大利亚研究在北外英语系的地位。之后，一批中年教师陆续参加澳研，使北外澳研中心不断壮大，所开课程也越来越丰富，招收的硕士生的规模也比当年大了许多。这几年有更年轻的教师参加了澳研教学，队伍更加壮大了。在华东师大开设澳大利亚文学课程初期也经历了一段艰辛的过程，黄源深教授在一篇文章中曾经谈及。作为一个新的学科，经过这样一个过程可能有好处，它能够锻炼教师，激励人们更加奋进。

李：第一届全国澳大利亚研究研讨会 1988 年在北外召开，这次会议应该是具有历史意义的会议，会上成立了中国澳大利亚研究学会。请您谈谈这次会议以及中国澳大利亚研究学会的创办情况。

胡：从 80 年代初期到 1988 年，国内陆续成立了一些澳大利亚研究中心，如北京外国语学院、华东师范大学、苏州大学、安徽大学、厦门大学、西安外国语学院等，社科院本来就有大洋洲研究。有了这些澳研中心为基础，我们认为成立全国学会的时机已经成熟。大家经过交换意见，达成一致，决定1988年在北京外国语学院召开第一届澳大利亚研究国际研讨会。在筹办会议的过程中，我们得到时任澳大利亚文化参赞Nick Jose的大力支持，他帮助我们邀请了澳方的代表来参会。除了邀请国内澳研中心的代表外，我们还邀请了文化界的一些知名人物，包括吴祖光先生等。澳方的代表有诗人、作家、评论家、教授等，包括Geoff Page, Shirley Walker, Brian Kiernan, Carrillo Gantner等。教育部原副部长黄辛白出席了成立大会，北外的王福祥院长、王佐良教授也都出席并致词。会议大部分论文都是文学和文化方面的，涉及政治、经济、贸易、外交的比较少，但此后的澳研会议的内容越来越丰富，研讨的范围逐步深入到经贸、历史、政治、中澳关系等领域。在第一届澳研国际研讨会期间，我被选为全国澳大利亚研究学会会长，第二届会长是黄源深教授。我们从1988年起每两年召开一次全国的研讨会，推动国内的澳大利亚研究。我在澳研和中澳文化交流方面所做的工作得到澳大利亚方面的肯定。1990年悉尼大学授予我名誉文学博士学位，1996年获得澳中理事会翻译奖，1999年获得澳中理事会杰出贡献奖，表彰我在推动中澳关系方面所做的贡献。

李： 国内早年的澳大利亚研究主要以澳大利亚文学和文化为主，您的研究领域主要是文学。您能谈谈您的澳大利亚文学研究情况吗？

胡： 澳大利亚文学研究在我国开始比较晚，与英美文学研究的历史完全不同。最早应该是安徽大学的大洋洲文学研究所的工作，领头人是马祖毅教授。他们翻译了一些澳大利亚和新西兰的文学作品，但数量不大。我们这批进修教师从澳大利亚回来以后，陆续在自己的学校开设澳大利亚文学课程，受到学生的欢迎，在学术期刊和报纸上发表文章，介绍澳洲文学，同时，翻译了一批作家的作品。澳大利亚文学的影响日益扩大。在这方面，黄源深教授作出了突出的贡献，他撰写了几部有关澳大利亚文学和文化的专著，包括《澳大利亚文学史》、《澳大利亚文学论》、《澳大利亚文化简论》、《当代澳大利亚社会》等，翻译了多部小说，培养了一批澳大利亚文学硕士和博士。他的代表作《澳大利亚文学史》不仅篇幅长，涵盖面广，而且紧紧跟踪澳大利亚近年的发展。时至今日，国内还没有一部类似的著作可以比拟。2002年11月中澳建交三十周年，黄源深教授与其间中国驻澳大利亚的七位大使一起，获澳大利亚外交部长授予的澳大利亚政府勋章。此外，他曾任上海市翻译家协会副会长，在文学翻译方面成绩卓著，获得过澳中理事会翻译奖和其他多个奖项。我和李尧合作翻译了帕特里克·怀特的《人树》，与刘寿康合译了《探险家沃斯》，另外，我还翻译了怀特的中篇小说以及几部戏剧。其间，澳大利亚文化参赞甘德瑞邀请我将Jack Hibberd的*The Stretch of the Imagination*译为中文。在《想入非非》译成后，上海人民艺术剧院在上海和北京将此剧上演，受到观众的欢迎。在澳大利亚文学翻译方面，还应该提到李尧老师，他三十年来一直从事澳大利亚文学翻译，他翻译的澳洲文学的数量在国内首屈一指，总字数可能有一二百万。他多次获得澳中理事会翻译奖。不久前，他被悉尼大学授予名誉文学博士学位，表彰他在澳大利亚文学翻译方面的成就。澳大利亚文学翻译这二十几年来有了长足的进步，许多学者和译者都做出了自己的贡献，这里限于篇幅不能详细列举，澳大利亚文学在中国的影响日益扩大。

李：在国内，怀特研究一直受到重视。您和怀特本人有很好的私人关系，您能谈谈和他的交往情况吗？

胡：我在澳大利亚文学研究方面主要集中于怀特和澳大利亚戏剧。关于我与怀特的往来在我撰写的文章和论文中多有涉及，这里只简单谈谈。1980 年，我在悉尼大学读澳大利亚文学课程，对于怀特的作品很感兴趣，把他的小说几乎全部读完。有一天，悉尼大学东亚语系主任 Arthur Davies 教授问我是否有兴趣与怀特见面，我喜出望外，立即表示同意。后来，由 Davies 教授安排在怀特的家里见了面。我妻子吴祯福与我同行。从澳大利亚的报刊上看，怀特似乎是个性情古怪甚至刻薄的人，因此，我们去访问他时，心情十分紧张。实际上，一见面就发现怀特是个很和善友好的人。日后的交往更证实了这一点。我们多次会晤，在一起吃过几次饭，书信往来延续十多年，我们成了朋友。怀特是一位现代派作家，写作风格与传统的澳大利亚现实主义作家很不相同，他在作品中不断探索和创新，他一生中创作了 12 部长篇小说和 3 部短篇小说集、7 个剧本和一个电影剧本以及一部自传和一部演说集，为澳大利亚文学打开了一片新天地，在 1973 年终于获得诺贝尔文学奖。他的获奖提高了澳洲文学的地位，使得澳洲文学与世界文学进一步接轨。怀特是一位有高度社会责任感的作家，支持澳大利亚的年轻作家和画家，关心世界和平和人类命运这些重大问题。在他晚年，他反对在澳大利亚开采铀矿，参与成立核裁军党，甚至上街游行，表达澳大利亚人民的意愿。有人说，怀特是澳大利亚人的良心。怀特去世后，人们很怀念他，我也是一样。我把怀特写给我的十几封信件全部捐给了澳大利亚国家图书馆，因为我认为这笔文化遗产应该属于澳大利亚，而不是我个人。

李：2000 年后，您的研究兴趣主要在跨文化研究和英语教育方面，这对国内的澳研发展是一个很大的损失。您能谈谈当时的研究转移是出于什么考虑吗？

胡：回国以后，除了澳大利亚研究，我一直身处外语教育第一线，参与了全国外语专业教学大纲制定、教材编选、外语教育咨询等各种学术活动。2000 年起，我不再担任国家教委高校外语专业教学指导委员会主任。这时国家教委要我将中国英语教学研究会的工作恢复起来，因为原会长许国璋教授辞世后，研究会已经停止活动多年。所以，从那时起，我的主要精力集中到英语教学研究会上，被选为会长后，主持召开了几次大型的国际研讨会，加入了国际应用语言学学会（AILA），之后又开始申办在北京召开国际应用语言学大会。1995 年，我被选为中国跨文化交际研究会会长，在跨文化交际研究方面也投入了相当的时间和精力。无论是外语教育或是跨文化交际，要真正做好都需要毕生的精力。跟踪澳大利亚文学的研究也同样需要很多时间，需要阅读大量作品，与澳大利亚作家保持密切联系。我这时年事已高，精力有限，只好忍痛割爱，把澳大利亚文学研究暂时搁置。参与澳研方面的活动逐渐减少，后来就基本上不再参加。之所以产生这些变化不是我个人有什么考虑，而是工作的需要，任务的调整。

李： 您近年很少参加澳研的活动了，但国内的澳研界一直关心着您。请您谈谈您的近况。

胡： 2014 年 3 月我正式退休。如果说以前是“淡出江湖”，这次是正式退出了，但是，学术上的事情还没有完全结束。今年我把过去发表的跨文化交际方面的论文和文章收集成册，交外研社出版，书名是《跨文化交际教学与研究》，年底前问世。其他零碎的学术活动我还参加一些，但总的来说已经不多。年龄和身体都是制约因素，许多活动我都婉言谢绝了。今年我进入耄耋之年，正在朝着“清静心”的境界努力。谢谢你的书面采访。从你的问题可以看出你为这次采访做了很好的准备。

李建军，北京外国语大学英语学院澳研中心主任、中国澳大利亚研究会秘书长。

► 1979 年“九人帮”进入悉尼大学学习时合影。

前排左起：龙日金、侯维瑞、黄源深

后排左起：钱佼汝、胡壮麟、杨潮光、胡文仲、王国富、杜瑞清

► 1981 年“九人帮”中七人获得文学硕士时留影。

► 1982 年在怀特家中，胡文仲（左）与怀特亲切交谈。

► 1986 年，澳大利亚总理 Bob Hawke 访华时在北京外国语学院发表演讲。

► 1988 年首届澳大利亚研究国际研讨会在北京外国语学院举行。

► 1990 年胡文仲（左四）被悉尼大学授予名誉文学博士学位，其左侧是澳中理事会主席惠特拉姆先生，右侧是悉尼大学副校长，其余为中国使馆文化处官员。

An Email Interview with Alex Miller for Australian Cultural Studies at SUIBE

Ouyang Yu

Ouyang: It's nearly 30 years since you first visited Shanghai in 1987 on your research tour for *The Ancestor Game*. Do you still remember those days?

[**Alex:** I've attached my essay 'Impressions of China', which you might like to use instead of the answer I've given after this at the end of this interview.]

A: I began to write *The Ancestor Game* in the hope of coming to terms with the suicide of a friend, Lang Tzu, the fictional name of the man on whom the main character in the book is based. Lang was a fourth-generation Australian Chinese. He was an artist who had failed to achieve recognition for his work. In his mid-fifties he gave up the struggle and shot himself. Along with one or two of my fellow Australians I believed Lang Tzu was a highly talented artist and that one of the factors in his failure to achieve recognition had been the inability of Australians at that time to view the work of an ethnic Chinese as representative of Australian culture, this despite the fact that Chinese had lived in Australia in large numbers since the middle of the last century. I may be wrong — I hope not; it's always difficult to quantify these things — but my feeling is that this perception no longer holds true in Australia.

I began the book as a memorial to Lang Tzu's life and to our friendship. As I worked my way deeper into the material of the novel, this simple aim became complicated for me by questions about the nature of belonging and the meaning of the idea of home. Gradually I was drawn into an exploration of the ambiguities of colonialism and displacement, conditions which have limited and inspired the human race for centuries. The earliest poems in Old English, the works that mark the origins of English literature — *Beowulf*, *The Ruin*, *Widsith* and *The Seafarer* — all deal with journeying in distant lands, or with the presence of foreignness in one's own land. It hasn't always been as fashionable as it is today to write about life in the suburbs. I am an immigrant myself and my meditation on Lang Tzu's life soon became a kind of concealed autobiography. I was deeply intrigued by the experience of exile, by its positive aspects just as much as its negative ones. Exile as opportunity, rather than as cultural deprivation, was what interested me. And of course we don't have to leave the country of our birth to experience the condition of exile. Drusilla Modjeska's *Exiles At Home: Australian Women*

Writers 1925–1945 is a fine study in this condition.

After I'd been working on the book for a year I realised I would have to go to China to experience at first-hand the people and the place of Lang's origins, to breathe the air of West Lake in Hangzhou on a winter evening and to smell the smells of life in Shanghai. I knew by then that much of the book was to be set in Shanghai and Hangzhou. I travelled to China over the Christmas / New Year period of 1987–1988. It was my first visit. Through Ruth Blatt in Melbourne, and with the help of Nicholas Jose, I'd made contact with Chinese people in Shanghai and was able to travel as a Chinese for the brief period of my visit, which lasted ten days.

It was in Hangzhou, while walking among the evening crowds on the shores of West Lake, that I began to feel for the first time a confidence in my ability to write of Lang's life and his Chinese family background. I didn't take photographs or make notes. It was to be my impressions that would be important to me. I knew that.

When I returned to Australia I discarded the draft of the book I'd been working on before I went to China and began again. I felt an assurance about writing of the Chinese that I could not have felt if I hadn't visited China. My visit had dispelled for me the myth of difference and given me the assurance that in writing about Chinese Australians, providing I got the facts of their history right, I would be no more limited than I would be in writing about any other Australians.

I didn't go to China expecting to become an expert on Chinese life and culture. I went to experience a little of China and the Chinese for myself, so that I would have private memories and impressions to draw on for my book. Whenever we visit a foreign country for the first time we enjoy for a brief period a kind of honeymoon, during which the depth of our ignorance seems to insulate us from danger and to imbue our surroundings with a kind of glow of infinite goodwill. It is a bit like being in love. If we stay too long, we soon begin to be worn down by the frustrations and difficulties of daily life that the locals are nearly overwhelmed by. After a few weeks or months the struggle to get a place on the overcrowded bus has ceased to be a challenge to our determination to behave just like a local and has become a daily burden. The inability of the authorities to provide adequate public transport is no longer part of the exotic spectacle but has become a source of anger and resentment and a cause for frustration and criticism. The unvarying menu in the Mongolian restaurant in Hangzhou, after we have eaten there every day for a month, has ceased to intrigue us and has begun to disgust us.

With increasing familiarity we soon lose our tolerance of difference. I don't mean fundamental difference, if there is such a thing, but petty differences. The sharpness of our curiosity has been blunted against the repeated minor frustrations of ordinary daily life. The longer we stay, the harder it is for us to experience anything outside our own immediate area of endeavour. We begin to manipulate the status quo so that arrangements will suit us better. We cease to be uncritical. We begin to limit ourselves. We define our little area of interest. We become a political being, a struggling member of the local community, a foreigner suffering all the frustrations of foreignness and determined to overcome them.

Some foreigners who stay on respond to the problem by insulating themselves from the foreignness of the place, drawing over themselves a protective carapace composed of the customs and beliefs they brought with them from the country of their origin. They live in a ghetto, whether of the mind or an actual physical community which, with the passing of time, comes less and less to reflect the cultural reality of their homeland. In some ways, of course, it's easier for migrants and long-term foreigners to live in ghettos and ethnic enclaves. In this way the problems are postponed and are bequeathed to the next generation. The ghetto people are a people lost to history, their lives are lived outside history, they are castaways on an island that has become disconnected from their own culture and from the dynamic of change and conflict within their host culture. I encountered a little ghetto of such European foreigners in Shanghai. The Chinese referred to them as Foreign Experts with just enough irony to make me immediately want to translate this as *Foreign Devils*. With the foreign experts I ate the worst Christmas dinner I've ever eaten anywhere. The ritual of Christmas with them was more funereal than celebratory, and I couldn't wait to make a polite excuse to escape from them back into the living world of China, on which they'd turned their backs. Another writer might have stayed and written a novel about them. There was certainly a fictional offer in the peculiar melancholy of their lives — a kind of communal *folie*, in which they had each agreed to keep silent about the death of reality. Would I notice that they were ghosts? This was their fear. They watched me closely. They knew they had ventured a long way into the labyrinth and had no hope of ever finding their way back. They could scarcely remember the brief days of the honeymoon. After a few glasses of wine their resentment at the way I was able to take my pleasure in the country they had grown to hate began to find its voice. The ghetto, wherever it is, breeds hatred. Despite legislation prohibiting their permanent residence in Australia, Lang Tzu and his forebears had never been ghetto Chinese. They had married with the Irish and the Scots and the English and had lived in the general Australian community since 1848. And so had thousands of other Australian Chinese.

It wasn't the hazardous business of staying on and becoming a long-term resident of China that interested me. What interested me was the honeymoon experience, the precious period of being insulated by my ignorance and my lack of accountability, a period during which I might hope to be a detached observer of life, a kind of carefree visiting parasite, collecting my impressions and enjoying the uncritical blindness of a lover, not the hard-boiled attitude of a spouse. It was a peculiar privilege, this period of disengagement within a culture that I knew would never require from me an atonement if I failed. And art always fails. I already knew that. We never succeed in making the sublime incandescent object of our imaginations that beguiles us into undertaking the journey in the first place. For the novelist, the next novel may even be, in a very private way, an attempt to atone for this kind of spiritual failure of the previous novel.

Also, it wasn't history but impressions that remained my source. When he read the book, Professor Huang Yuanshen, who was born in Hangzhou (Oy comment: in a village in Zhejiang Province, of which Hangzhou is the capital) and who heads the Australian Studies Centre at East China Normal University in Shanghai, asked me, 'How did you manage to get the smell of duck droppings in Hangzhou in 1937 exactly right? I was in Hangzhou as a child,' he said, 'and I can tell you, the smell of duck droppings was then exactly as it is in your novel.'

Impressions that hadn't seemed important at the time, and which I thought I'd forgotten, surfaced again once I was back at my desk writing the book. I wasn't proposing an historical argument. A novel, I believe, deals in the currency of the universality of human nature. Isn't that why we can still read novels about nineteenth-century Russians and French or eighteenth-century Chinese and feel able to identify our own destinies today with the destinies of the characters in those novels?

When I began writing *The Ancestor Game* I didn't start out with the idea of celebrating a rich Chinese contribution to our immigrant culture in Australia. I couldn't possibly have started out with that idea because when I began work on the book, like almost every other Australian I'd ever met, I didn't know there had been a rich and complex Chinese contribution to our immigrant culture as we know it today. Such a contribution had not been noted. It hadn't been celebrated in the literature. When I began the book I was writing about friendship. And in the end for me, whatever else it might be for others, I think *The Ancestor Game* will always be a book about my old friend

Lang Tzu and my new friend Ouyang Yu. A book about friendship and home, and how those two things go together.

My first visit to China in 1987 remains vivid in my memory. It marked an important turning point in my life as a writer. Of course you and I met and became friends during that visit. My wife, Stephanie and our son Ross were with me and the whole journey has taken on in this family something of the importance of a legend.

I came to China at that time in search of the remains of the landscape and community in which my friend the Australian/Chinese artist, Allan O'Hoy, had his origins. Allan died in tragic circumstances some years earlier and I missed him greatly. Stephanie suggested I write a book about him in order to deal with my persisting grief. Allan was an extraordinary man and people in Melbourne's artistic community still talk about him and his exacting standards and richly sensitive knowledge of Australian art. I came to Shanghai and Hangzhou to learn first-hand something of the world from which Allan had come.

The book I eventually wrote about him, *The Ancestor Game*, was set in 1976, the year when the Cultural Revolution came to an end and China began to open itself to the West. In 1976 Allan had said to me, 'Now I can go back.' His brother soon went back to China for a visit but Allan never did return. When Allan told me he wanted to return to China I was astonished. He had never before indicated any desire to see China. When he said this it struck me that I only knew really his Australian side, or at last that I did not know his Chinese side very well. Going to China was partly in the hope that I would come to understand something about what was 'Allan' about him and what was 'Chinese' about him. Were some of those qualities which I found particularly attractive and interesting really Chinese cultural aspects that belong to all Chinese or were they just him, the man himself? I asked myself, 'What does it mean to be Chinese as distinct from Australian?' And I had no answer.

In China, in fact in Hangzhou when we were standing on the shores of West Lake watching the sun go down, with hundreds of Chinese people also doing exactly the same thing, I realised that there were of course no real differences between being Chinese and being Australian but that were all just people and I at once felt a new confidence to write about Allan. Of course I had to get the details of our histories and cultural styles right in my book. These differences, a Chinese woman said to me, are the kind of differences nations go to war over. But that really there are no essential differences. Of course she was right. So I read widely in Chinese history and culture and took care to note down in my memory those aspects of Chinese social custom at that time which impressed me as not familiar to an Australian.

From my visit to China, and through my lasting friendship with you, I found the confidence to write *The Ancestor Game*. How can anyone who has once visited China not wish to return? That visit left with me a deep and abiding empathy with and interest in China as a country, and fondness for the Chinese friends and acquaintances I made then and on subsequent visits. I never found China to be strange and exotic, as I had anticipated, but from the first day felt myself to be in a country that was deeply poignant and strangely familiar. I felt at home there, as we do whenever we are welcomed in a foreign country by its people. The struggles and trials and joys of the people around me where those same struggles and joys we all experience.

China has since then honoured me with several invitations and a notable literary award. My wife, Stephanie, has visited China to teach there several times. From that first visit our attachment to China has developed and grown stronger over the years. The translations of my novels by Professor Li Yao have given me a sense that my writing is at home in China. A classical scroll painting by the artist Yeh Ching hangs on the wall of the hall outside my study and reminds me every day as I walk past it that I have an abiding connection with China that was made when you and I first met that day in Shanghai and made our plans to travel to Hangzhou together.

O: When did you publish your first novel and how was it received?

A: In my case this is not such a straight-forward question as it might seem at first glance. The first novel I wrote, *The Tivington Nott* (Robert Hale, UK 1989), wasn't published until after I'd written and published my second novel, *Watching the Climbers on the Mountain* (Pan Macmillan, Aust 1988). The reason for this was that at that time I was unable to find a publisher in Australia for a book set in England. *The Tivington Nott* was in fact finished in 1985 and was considered for over a year by the Australian publishers McPhee Gribble before being declined by them and returned to me. In her letter (19th June 1986) declining the book, the principle editor of McPhee Gribble, Hilary McPhee, said, '*The Tivington Nott* in the revised version is brilliantly sustained and engrossing.' She also included a glowing reader's report on the book, in which the reader described it as 'powerful, involving, and intensely interesting ... in short, absolutely first-class.' Despite these glowing accolades for the book it was turned down. I felt a kind of helplessness at this. What was I to do if publishers decided not to publish books that they themselves described in these terms? In a state of anger and frustration I wrote *Watching* *the Climbers on the Mountain* in six months in one draft and sent it to Pan Macmillan. They accepted the book with enthusiasm within days of receiving it and published it the following year. The first review, in *The Sydney Morning Herald*, written by a fussy old lady, described it as 'the trough of Australian literature' in a review titled, 'Peaks and Troughs of Australian Literature'. I was more amused than dismayed. I'd given the publishers what they wanted and had proved my point. The following year I found a publisher in the UK for *The Tivington Nott* and it was released by them to glowing reviews, the principle reviewer for *The Herald* newspaper, Peter Pierce, described it as 'one of the most original pieces of writing of the year,' and editor of the highbrow *Supplement*, *Age Literary*, Professor Paul Carter, described it as 'mythical and darkly violent.' *The Somerset County Gazette* reviewer said it was 'altogether brilliant', *The Melbourne Times*, 'an extraordinarily gripping novel' and the Melbourne *Age*'s principal reviewer, John Larkin, said, 'It is a rich study of place, both elegant and urgent.'

I realised after this experience that the publishing industry in Australia at that time was lacking in confidence without the endorsement of England. Thankfully today that situation no longer exists. At the time I wrote *The Tivington Nott*, Australian publishing was struggling to establish a home-grown industry. Nowadays my own publisher of many years, Allen and Unwin, is the first Australian publisher in the history of this country to have acquired an established London publisher, Atlantic. This has never happened before and is an indication of the enormous growth and strength of Australian publishing in the last thirty years.

The Tivington Nott wasn't published in Australia until 1993 (Penguin, Aust 1993). Nearly ten years after it was written.

O: After we met, you sent me some short stories and plays. Can you talk about your days as a playwright?

A: I'd never considered writing plays until a hippy friend of mine came to stay with me. He had just received a grant to write a play. He was a painter, not a writer, and I don't know how it was that he'd received a writing grant. Anyway, he asked me to write a play for him so that he could show he hadn't wasted the grant. He was a pretty mad sort of guy and so I sat down and wrote the kind of play I thought would appeal to him. The play I wrote was *Kitty Howard*. It was a satire about how men in authority never listen to women, especially their wives. Kitty's husband was the chief of police and was responsible for the security of the State Premier and the King and Queen of Moomba. After he goes out, leaving his gun behind on the sideboard in his anxiety to be at work,

Kitty puts down the tray she's carrying and picks his gun. Her son is watching the television and rolling a smoke of dope. She brandishes the gun at him behind his back and says, 'So who will I shoot?' The son, believing her to be joking, replies, 'Start at the top, Mum. Shoot the king.' In fact Kitty then sets about undermining her husband's security in order to assassinate the King of Moomba. She makes no secret of her plans but no one ever takes her seriously or even really listens to what she has to say. She is successful and in fact kills the King.

By the time I'd finished writing the play — which took me a couple of weeks — the hippy friend had left and gone to Iceland. I didn't know what to do with the play so I sent it to the Union Theatre Company, which was our State Theatre at the time. The Director of the theatre was Ray Lawler, who is famous for his play *The Summer of the Seventeenth Doll*, the most successful play ever at that time. He rang me on the Monday and told me they thought my play was wonderful and they would produce it at their city theatre in Russell Street. My play was produced and it ran to full houses and was reviewed kindly and Ray Lawler said, 'Now for your next one.'

Compared to my experiences with novels and publishers this was just too easy and I mistakenly imagined I must really be a playwright. A bad mistake, as it turned out! I decided not to give any more of my plays to Ray Lawler's company but to establish my own theatre so that I could write and direct the plays myself. This was a disastrous decision that resulted in me wasting about five years of my life writing nonsense and dealing with incompetent and unproductive people who were always too busy to spend any time thinking and so everything they did was of a very low grade. They were pretty typical of the performance industry in that they mistook being busy for being successful and never understood it was their very busyness that undermined the quality of what they produced. The theatre also didn't suit me because I like to get my best work done in the morning and I go to bed quite early. They didn't begin their day till the afternoon and didn't go to bed till the early hours of the morning.

I don't remember sending you short stories. I've never written many short stories and can't imagine which ones they were.

O: Did you write poetry as well in the early days because you've got a longish poem recently published in *The Australian*?

A: All writers write poetry, of course, but not all writers publish it. Poets who do publish often ask me, 'Do you also write poetry?' Which seems a bit silly of them. I've even heard a senior Australian poet claim that poetry is a higher calling, thereby placing himself by implication at the pinnacle of callings. Whereas of course there is no such thing as a higher calling, but only higher achievements. Unless, that is, one is a fascist with hierarchical ideas of culture and people and does not believe in cultural pluralism. I've always written poetry but have almost never wanted to publish it. It has been a private thing with me as it is with many writers. The reason I published the longish poem you refer to, *The Good Visa*, was that it came to me in a vivid dream that I couldn't get out of my head and it seemed to relate to something important that was going on around us at the time. Now I look back on it as a poem about the same thing that all poems are about, meaning. I also liked very much the statement by Bertolt Brecht, that the simplest words should be enough. It summed up neatly my own endeavour with my writings, which has been to achieve simplicity and clarity of expression. They seem to me the most difficult things to achieve. I greatly admire writing and thinking that has elaborated its subject, no matter how complex, in a simple coherent and clear way. This has seemed to me to be the point of communication. It is my opinion that if the beauty of prose and its poetics are to be served then metaphor must illuminate a dimension of the subject that would otherwise remain obscure. I often encounter metaphor that obscures and distracts and is there simply because the writer mistakenly feels he or she has a duty to invest his or her writing with similes and metaphors and that they will enrich his or her work. The opposite is the usual effect. To shine with clarity, metaphor must be used sparingly, or it is just another soggy potato chip among a bag of cold potato chips.

O: I know you wrote three novels that were not published. What is it that drove you on to write more?

A: What was it that drove me on to write THREE? Why does anyone wish to be a writer? These three were written in the mistaken belief that novels are about society's ills and are not about the intimate lives of 'us'. When this mistake was pointed out to me, I went on and wrote another eleven novels about the intimate lives of real people. That these people, my characters, were also embedded in the cultural and social movements and events of their own times, and that each of them carried about with them, as we all do, a sense of their own and their inherited histories, was inevitably part of the story in each case, but it wasn't THE story, as it was in those three unpublishable novels of ideas in which characters performed the function of puppets — my puppets — and possessed no autonomy. I wrote those books according to my own plans, as if I knew what I was doing, and was impervious to the prompts of my imagination. I stuck to my plans instead of abandoning them. Plans were no good to me. My mistake with those pre-novels was to think the writer was the master of the story. Whereas of course the story is the master. It is the story we must follow, not the story that must follow us. Unless of course we're serving the recipes of some genre which requires certain ingredients to be in certain places. The literary novel is sourced from the prompts of the writer's imagination, and those prompts come from the unconscious of the writer. I hadn't learnt to listen to those prompts and cheerfully ignored them and plunged on with my plans. And those three pre-novels were, consequently, still-born.

I went on because I believed my pre-novels were my apprenticeship. I'd never imagined I could become a master of my trade without serving an arduous apprenticeship. I'd never imagined it was going to be easy. After those three I knew I'd learnt something and wanted to apply my new knowledge, and so on I went. What I'd learnt was to write not about my ideas but about something I loved. Love of what I write about has since then given my work some semblance of warmth and it has gained me a modest but enthusiastic readership around the world, including China.

O: Even when *The Ancestor Game* won the Miles Franklin, there was a view in some quarters that it was a 'challenge' as it seemed to them quite experimental. Was that a reflection of your early experimental writing experience?

A: I've never self-consciously set out to be experimental with my work, if experimental means that the writer is attempting to 'break the mould' or to 'make it new' in the sense that the American expatriate poet Ezra Pound exhorted writers to do. Each book has presented me with its own peculiar challenge. *The Tivington Nott* clearly presented me with a very different challenge to *The Ancestor Game*, and each book since those books has been a problem to which I've been required to find a solution. How is this story to be told? Is the question that faces me each time I approach a story. The only real exception to this has been *Coal Creek*, which I thought of and wrote in ten weeks. The solution, uniquely for me, arrived with the idea for the story itself. From my first idea for a book about Allan O'Hoy to the finished version of *The Ancestor Game* was ten years. For *Coal Creek* it was ten weeks.

Writers, such as myself, who respond to a need within themselves to reflect on their material at a level below its surface appearance inevitably require from the reader a like-minded enjoyment of reflection. In doing this, the writer slows the action down, and prevents the reader from moving swiftly across the surface without encountering any impediments. Plot becomes secondary in such works. This is not more admirable or less admirable than work that follows the surface line of the story to its end without impeding the reader's progress by pausing for reflection, but it appeals to fewer people, and in consequence the novel that indulges in reflection has fewer readers usually than the novel that follows a more direct line.

Every time I begin to work on a new idea for a book I am experimenting, not with style, as Ezra Pound wanted me to, but with ways of best expressing this story; my search is for the right 'voice', the tone that will carry the meaning most clearly. The voice came with *Coal Creek*. *The Ancestor Game*, on the other hand, set me a conundrum it took me years to solve. I'm probably more efficient these days at finding my solutions. *Autumn Laing*, for example, my biggest novel, took me five months to write after a lifetime of more or less thinking about the subject. Again, it was the confidence and the strength of the 'voice' of the narrator that shaped the story.

Experimentation with style and structure is inevitable, and it seems to me it is worthwhile if it serves to simplify the material and to locate the solution for it to the reader in a readable form. I think Ezra Pound, and the Modernist push, was to make it new for its own sake. This has never interested me. Unlike the sciences, the arts don't progress. We don't write better novels today than we did in the past, we write them differently. Making it new and experimentalism for their own sakes doesn't interest me.

O: By 1999, when we had lunch, you seemed to have found that story is the core to novel writing. If so, why?

A: People have often spoken of the death of the novel. But no one ever speaks of the death of story. Story, usually our own story, is at the heart of everyone's sense of themselves and everyone wants to tell their story — whether it's gossiping over the back fence with a neighbour or chatting with a companion in a cafe about what we were doing last night. Story and the human are inseparable. One is not conceivable without the other. Story is at the heart of us. There is no one whose life is not worth telling. In this we are all equal. My father didn't see story writing as an advance over story telling. For him the teller enjoyed the response of the audience and could accommodate the mode of his telling to the mood of his audience. My dad thought writing a story alone in your room must be a rather forlorn business.

People, critics mostly and so-called experimental writers, have often dismissed story as too simple to be of interest. But what makes a story grow in us is a mystery. We don't have to 'tell a story' to tell a story. We don't have to have a beginning, a middle and an end. We can say: I watched the boat dock and the four men carry his coffin down the gangplank and already we have a story to tell ourselves.

O: Can you say something about your novel, *Prochownik's Dream*, not winning a prize?

A: Prizes are the province of the judges not the writers.

O: You won your first Victorian Premier's Literary Award in 2014 with *Coal Creek*. How did that make you feel?

A: I was very pleased. None of my books had previously been short-listed for this home-town award, so it had a nice edge of satisfaction to it — a job done. At last!

O: I remember you were saying after the publication of *Coal Creek* that you were turning to memoir writing, a genre you had not tried before. Why's that?

A: I wanted to write about a friend who had been a great influence on me in my youth, Max Blatt, but I didn't want to make a fiction of him and the obvious choice seemed to me to turn to memoir in order to write about him. Since then I've embarked on a book which I've titled, *A Novel of My Private Life*, which is a non-fiction novel in the sense that I've not made anything up but I have left lots of people and events out of the picture and have changed quite a few names, so in that sense it doesn't seem to me to quite fit the description of memoir. Anyway I found I didn't like writing memoir. The genre doesn't greatly appeal to me. Memoir writers are penned in by their egos and self-esteem and aren't really able to reveal the unpleasant truths about themselves. I found it altogether too limiting and I didn't want to twist it into a form that might have resembled Nabokov's *Speak, Memory* — a book I admire in parts and dislike in other parts. In his fictions Nabokov felt it was a failure of imagination to make something up and preferred to observe with accuracy and wit.

O: Has any of your novels been published in the UK?

A: All my novels have been published in the UK and all eleven of them are kept in print by my UK publisher. My work has been translated into fourteen languages, including of course as you well know, Chinese.

O: What novels of yours have been published in China or in the Greater China, including Chinese mainland, Taiwan, Hong Kong and Macau?

A: *The Ancestor Game* was the first novel of mine to be published in both Chinese mainland and Taiwan Province. You yourself made the Taiwan translation and Professor Li Yao made the Chinese mainland translation. Offhand I can't remember how many of my novels have since then been translated and published in China, but Li Yao has done quite a few, including *Journey to the Stone Country*, *Landscape of Farewell*, *Autumn Laing*.

Hachette published a translation of Lovesong and Li Yao is currently working on the translation of *Coal Creek*. I think Li Yao also translated *Conditions of Faith* and maybe *Prochownik's Dream*. China has more of my novels in translation than any other country.

O: Technically, how would you describe your own fiction apart from what the critics say?

A: My aim is always for clarity. To make clear what is complex seems to me the greatest challenge. But let me quote an eminent critic whose authority on this technical question is far greater than my own. This is Professor Robert Dixon in the Introduction to his monograph on my work, *The Ruin of Time* (SUP 2014) page xviii: 'While Miller's novels are immediately accessible to the general reading public, they are manifestly works of high literary seriousness — substantial, technically masterly and assured, intricately interconnected, and of great imaginative, intellectual and ethical weight.'

O: Who's your major influence on fiction writing?

A: Before I had much of an idea of the kind of novelist I might eventually become, the friend and mentor of my youth, Max Blatt, gave me to understand that he admired the novels of the German writer Thomas Mann. Early in our acquaintance he gave me a copy of Mann's novel *Doctor Faustus*, which is without doubt one of the most difficult and complex of European novels of all time. Although I had little understanding then of the wider social and historical significance of that great novel, every line of it glowed for me with Max's confidence. What this experience left me with was the idea that my responsibility as a novelist would be to create works of a comparable weight and complexity of texture to those of Mann. Behind this was the more influential desire to write the kind of book that Max Blatt would have admired. It is this aim that is still present to me as I write today, this and Max's deeper question; 'Why don't you write about something you love?' There has been no greater influence on my writing than Max Blatt.

O: Do you have any advice for creative writing students in China?

A: I can think of no better advice than to write about what you love. The unconscious will provide you then with an abundance of imaginative prompts. To have the courage to follow the prompts of our imagination is the greatest thing.

O: When will the collection of your shorter works, with the title *The Simplest Words* be coming out? Can you say something about it?

A: My wife, Stephanie, has spent the past eighteen months selecting and arranging this collection. I would never have spent that time on it myself. It will be published in

November this year.

O: How would you assess your own literary output as a whole, looking back from today's vantage point?

A: I always feel that the real challenge lies ahead of me, not behind me, so it seems to me that I am in the middle of a struggle to create my work and not at a vantage point. As my dear friend Frank Budby used to say whenever people lamented the cultural dispossession of his people, 'The story's not over yet.'

O: If you were to name 10 best contemporary must-read Australian novels, which ones would you recommend to the Chinese readers?

A: Ten is not enough. I could happily name a hundred. And I would recommend books rather than all novels, as the distinction between non-fiction and fiction in the best works seems to me unclear and not useful. In no order of preference but simply as they occur to me I would name the following ten or twelve books, which are all wonderful and which I greatly admire and have been moved by. There are dozens of books that I'm conscious of leaving out:

The Tree of Man by Patrick White
Poppy by Drusilla Modjeska
The Spare Room by Helen Garner
The English Class by Ouyang Yu
House of Exile by Evelyn Juers
Patrick White by David Marr
East of Time by Jacob Rosenberg
Romulus My Father by Raimond Gaita
A Green Light by Ray Mooney
Julia Paradise by Rod Jones
The White by Adrian Caesar
Reading by Moonlight by Brenda Walker

The following essay is to be included in *The Simplest Words* and might be of interest to you here. You're welcome to use it.

Apart from chasing my tale I don't know what I'm doing. And I mean this in a very general way indeed. I've never been at all clear about what I'm doing. I can't be highly articulate about my writing. Andrew Riemer, the Sydney academic and critic, who is also a personal friend, told me that as a result of the publication of *The Ancestor Game* I'm now considered to be a revisionist historian by certain of his colleagues at Sydney University. When I read history at Melbourne University in the sixties with Marion Gibbs I learned, or thought I learned then, from that very great teacher that all history is revision.

So I'm not sure what being a revisionist historian means, but I do know it doesn't follow from a conscious intention of mine. My life, though I've always tried to disguise this fact, has been rather aimless. I've clung to the suggestion of a thread of sense that writing sometimes seems to offer me, perhaps the way some people cling to a religion they have never really learned to trust. Beyond this uncertain thread of sense, I don't know why I write or why I do anything else. I have, I'm afraid, a very strong affiliation with futility. Even now I feel a bit ashamed of admitting this. I look at the books I've written and, instead of drawing a satisfying theoretical position out of them, I wonder how I ever came to write them.

When I do write, however, when I'm working on a book and have reached the stage where it has fully engaged me, I feel that I don't need to worry about the problem of meaning. I feel I've left that awkward social demand behind. The business of writing fictions seems to me to be setting up barriers to intelligibility in the external sense, in the sense in which present reality is conducted, that is, and in which empires are understood to crumble and peoples to become post- or neo-colonial or some other thing.

Who has not heard writers say — *who*, if they are honest, has not themselves said at some time such things as, 'We have written about the migrant experience. Now we have moved on from that. We have left that behind.' Or, 'The realist novel is dead. The Dickensian novel can no longer be written. The novel has become the playground of ideas.' And so on. Pronouncements about the future that are proven false the instant someone produces a book that does freshly again those very things that one has claimed have been done-with for ever. When this annulment of some portentous *pronunciamento* occurs, those of us who care about the novel rejoice that once again it proves its resilience as the means for telling any kind of story about humankind we care to tax it with in any kind of voice we care to tax it with. As novelists we celebrate our liberty. We celebrate the fact that the novel keeps on surviving in all its elaborated forms, Dickensian and realist as well as magic-realist and post-modern. Apuleius's *The Golden Ass*, which is the only Latin novel that has come down to us intact, is magic-realist. Which seems to some people a very modern thing. Apuleius's novel was written in the middle of the second century of the Christian era. Reading it we are reminded that *nothing* is new. We keep learning the same lesson over and over and forgetting it over and over: the lesson that we are a language species and that language will do and redo anything we ask of it. The lesson that language underwrites our realities. That language is the first step in the process of making the things of our imagination tangible. Nothing is finished with. Not the migrant novel or the realist novel. It has all been done before and it will all be done again, and again, so long as we go on. The human species is also a migrant species. We have always travelled. In our wanderings we are forever coming across our old tracks and speculating on the perplexing nature of the creature who must have made them. In the strange place we are stilled by the presentiment of familiarity and we know that we have been there before. Home, indeed, may be for many of us no more than this fleeting intuition. A singular truth (which we do not often acknowledge because to do so kindles in us feelings of overwhelming futility) is that there is no place left that has not been visited by us and that there is nothing to be done that has not already been done by us. Round and round the mulberry bush, that's where the novelist is going. Chasing his or her tale ... as ever.

In our essentials, in our natures, morally and spiritually, we are today no further advanced than we were when Apuleius wrote his novel. The illusion of present reality, however, is always to insist that we are going somewhere, that there is a destination and that the day that is to follow this day will be different from this day. It is for this reason, in order to sustain our confidence in the illusion of a present reality that is taking us somewhere, that we invest our energies so heavily in innovation and change.

But really it's always questions without answers. The deeper we go into our material the more complex and irresolvable the contradictions of our material appear to us; and the more complex and irresolvable they appear, the more beautiful and alluring the material becomes for us, the more it casts its charms over us. It is not to resolve these paradoxes by making their structures of meaning intelligible that one can work as a novelist, but only to contemplate them in their irreducible splendour.

I suppose I believe a novel is like a painting or a piece of music, at least in the sense that it cannot be explained but can only be experienced. And this is one of the ways in which the concept of a work of art still remains useful to us, by enabling us to avoid (at least on the immediate level of appreciation) categories such as revisionist history and post-colonialism, categories which appear to explain things that don't require explaining on the immediate level of appreciation. To reveal these enormous wells of ignorance in ourselves. When we've completed the logical structures of our theories we have camouflaged those wells of ignorance, we haven't dealt with our ignorance or explained it, or moved on from it to a new and more enlightened place. We have cast a net of theory over our ignorance. The function of theories and ideologies, which are necessarily predicated on the insistence that we are going somewhere, that we are proceeding to the fulfilment of movements and tendencies whose ends are discernible in our present condition, is to support the necessary illusion of present reality. The art of the novel, viewed as post-colonial literatures, for example, seems to be about discourses in which power is being transferred from one cultural context to another. Viewed in this light the novels themselves seem to be about this process that is going on and that will one day, presumably, result in a fully empowered novel that is no longer post-anything but is fully present to itself and to its cultural realities. On the immediate level of appreciation, where we transcend our own individual and separate lives, where we transcend present reality, the novel is not going anywhere. It is *here* that art deals with. With us, here now. Art doesn't predict. Art isn't going anywhere. There is nowhere for it to go.

We can talk about art or we can talk about theories and ideologies. Art deals with now, theories and ideologies deal with change and the process towards something other than and different from now. The art of a thousand years ago is still dealing with now. Now is timeless. We can use art to illustrate our theories and ideologies but art is not itself an illustration of these things. Logical constructs only make it seem as though it is. Logical rigour, on which theoretical projections about the future must rely for their coherence and shape, pushes the issue of futility and meaning into the future. It postpones the problem of meaning. I'm not a philosopher but I think we can probably construct a theory out of any thought or idea, or even out of an emotion, if we are rigorous enough in our application of logic to its elaboration. Language will stand the strain. There is no doubt about that. Even this affiliation with futility could be theorised as an aspect of our age's fascination with the so-called unstructuredness of much of natural phenomena, which is a view that our new technologies of looking have revealed to us. I had dinner with James Gleick in September — it was the occasion of the Victorian Premier's Literary Awards and he and I were guests of our publisher, Penguin, at the same table. And while I was sitting there talking and listening and eating the smoked salmon and drinking the slightly too-sweet chardonnay, I thought about James Gleick's books: *Chaos* and *Genius*. And I imagined him writing another book. I could see the finished book, the single word FUTILITY in gold lettering on a white cover. The book inscribed the end of futility. The end of the struggle for meaning. We no longer needed to wonder if there was a God or not. The grand unified theory of futility: meaninglessness and faith made intelligible. I do Mr Gleick a great disservice, of course, by naming him in my fantasy. He ate his dinner in complete ignorance of my terrible thoughts.

Thanks for this wonderful opportunity to talk with you about my work Ouyang. It has been a great pleasure to follow your questions.

O: Many thanks for your wonderful answers, Alex.

(Interview ended on Wednesday, April 29, 2015, in Shanghai, China)

References

[1] 'Impressions of China.' Paper delivered at the World Chinese Writers' Association Congress, Singapore, December 1995; 'Impressions of China.' *Meridian* 15.1(1996): 85–89.

[2] 'Chasing My Tale.' *Kunapipi* XV.3 (1993): 1–6.

Alex Miller is the author of eleven novels. He has won Australia's premier literary award, The Miles Franklin Award, twice and is an overall winner of the Commonwealth Writers Prize. In 2008 he was awarded the "Weishanhu Award for Best Foreign Novel" in the 21st Century from the People's Literature Publishing House in China for Landscape of Farewell. *His books are published internationally and widely in translation. He has twice won the Christina Stead Prize for Fiction in the NSW Premier's Literary Awards, and The Age Book of the Year Award in 2010 for his bestselling novel* Lovesong. *In the same year he was awarded the Manning Clark Medal for an Outstanding Contribution to Australian Cultural Life. Alex was elected a Fellow of the Australian Academy of the Humanities in 2011. Miller was awarded the prestigious Melbourne Prize for Literature in November 2012, for an outstanding contribution to Australian cultural life. His collection of stories and essays,* The Simplest Words, *was published in November 2015.*

Prior to his turning 60, Ouyang Yu has published 77 books in both English and Chinese in the field of fiction, non-fiction, poetry, translation and criticism. His record of publication is close to zero after turning 60.

重复、拼贴与省略
——伊丽莎白·乔利之多元叙事[1]

梁中贤

摘要：伊丽莎白·乔利（1923—2007）是澳大利亚著名的女作家，其怪诞文风堪比帕特里克·怀特。以今天的眼光看乔利，其文风只不过是后现代思潮在文学创作上的表现。但在20世纪八九十年代，澳大利亚文学界对后现代文风尚处于懵懂的时代，乔利的作品确实让评论界甚感困惑。乔利的出色之处在于其能够轻松驾驭意识流、黑色幽默、戏仿、重复、拼贴、省略、蒙太奇、超现实的魔幻主义等表现手段，却让读者陷入了迷宫之中。本文仅就"重复、拼贴和省略"三个策略进行分析，以略解乔利文风的"怪诞"之谜。

关键词：伊丽莎白·乔利；重复；拼贴；省略；怪诞

Repetition, Collage and Omission
— On the Three Strategies of Elizabeth Jolley's Narrative Art

Liang Zhongxian

Abstract: Elizabeth Jolley (1923–2007), one of the most famous woman writers in Australia, had her own grotesque writing style that could be compared to Patrick White. From today's perspective, Jolley's style is simply the reflection of the post-modernist thoughts. But in the 80s and 90s of the last century, when the Australian literary field had quite a vague understanding of postmodernism, Jolley's style really puzzled her readers a lot. In fact, Jolley was outstanding in her control of so many skills, like stream of consciousness, black humor, parody, repetition, collage, omission, montage and the magical realism, which trapped readers into maze. This paper will analyze the three writing strategies of "repetition, collage and omission" employed by Jolley in order to interpret her riddle of being grotesque in style.

Key words: Elizabeth Jolley; repetition; collage; omission; grotesque

作为后现代主义作家，澳大利亚女作家伊丽莎白·乔利（1923—2007）的叙事话语无疑反映了后现代思潮在文学领域的语言哲学思想，即高度关注语言的游戏和实验。虽然总的来说她的叙事是简洁而抒情的，但她的叙事技巧却在简洁之中体现出了怪诞。2007年4月11日，《纽约时报》刊登了伊丽莎白·乔利的讣告，其中这样评价她的创作风格："乔利女士的怪诞风格并不是所有评论家都喜欢"（*New York Times* 2007: 4）。

1 国家哲学社会科学规划项目"澳大利亚女作家伊丽莎白·乔利研究 13BWW401"阶段性成果。

有的评论者指出："乔利创作的是阴郁的实验小说"（Knight）。迪波尔认为她的"叙事似乎不着边际"（Dibble 29），依德玛认为她的叙事"怪诞离奇"（Idema 3）。在思维方式上，她表现了叙事就是话语的思想，反映了以语言为中心的创作方法；在价值信仰上，代表了后现代的文化批评精神，即背弃了现代的封闭价值系统，表现出与传统价值和话语的断裂；进而选择了一种包容一切的价值取向，用话语表达出不同的群体和社会的声音。她用后现代叙事话语，以读者感到怪异的语言，叙述了一个个看似互不相关，但彼此在深层次上却相互关联的系列事件，还原了真实世界的面貌。为此，她打破了现代主义在创作上确立的原则和准则禁忌，体现了后现代创作话语上的不确定性、叛逆性和非体系性，使她的作品呈现出多种可能性和非逻辑性，用语言制造了看似怪诞的世界。这种怪诞文风在叙事技巧上突出的表现是话语的重复、拼贴和省略或空白。

一、叙事话语重复置读者于恍惚之中

托妮·莫里森认为，"我们的历史有怪诞的重复。"[1]正因为历史有怪诞的重复，重复就如同四季交替一样是现实世界的一种本质，我们就有了创作中的重复叙事，这种重复成为了读者必不可少的审美经历，在乔利的作品里则成为怪诞文风的装饰。尽管"重复是一种比较简单的小说叙事方式"，它"以不断重复小说中人物的对白、情节、段落篇章、语句等来达到一种强调或淡化主题的目的，用这些外在形式的不断重复出现来表现作者真实的艺术观、世界观"（刘，余 87—88）。但是乔利对重复的运用已经超出了读者的想象，正常而言，"人们都可能使用'重复'的表现方法，同时也都存在着避免下意识、无必要、在形式和内容上都不具有'增值作用'的重复的问题"（金 2011）。读乔利的小说，读者似乎看不到作者对"下意识、无必要、在形式和内容上都不具有'增值作用'的重复"所作出的规避。在作品中，重复似乎是一种常态，人物的重复使用、记忆的重复回放、场景的重复再现、话语的重复呢喃、情节的反复利用以及技巧的重复运用，令读者的阅读体验就好像是在一种精神恍惚中进行的。某一个片段场景、某一段事件、某一个人物的经常再现，会使读者怀疑自己的记忆、生活的逻辑以及审美的价值发生了问题。正是这种令人生厌的重复话语，又一次彰显出其文学创作的怪诞品质，体现了后现代主义"小说诗学的重复概念是开放性的"（方，麦 172）特征。

朱立元教授在《小说与重复·中译本前言》中指出，小说总体上可说存在着三类重复：微观重复（词语、修辞格、情态描写等），中观重复（事件与场景等）和宏观重复（一部作品与其他作品，包括同一位作家的不同作品或不同作家的不同作品，在主

---

1 There is *repetition* of the *grotesque* in our history.

题、动机、人物、事件上的重复）。乔利叙事话语的重复几乎囊括了这三个方面：

运用微观重复强调某个观点。她善于“运用重复的技巧强调引人入胜或重要的意象，抑或是从不同的视角重申某些观点或情景”（Knight）。[1] 在“亚当的新娘”（“Adam's Bride”）中，法官阿姆斯特朗在强调自己的洁癖和怪癖时重复地说，他无法向自己的工作妥协，他也无法向自己的成长经历妥协，他更无法向自己的感觉妥协（Jolley 11）。这里的重复叙事强调叙事者急迫心情导致了语无伦次。类似漫画般的重复比喻手法达到了某种怪诞的戏仿效果。故事第一段就以重复开始：“I was sick — sick unto death with that long agony”（Jolley 2）。通过两次重复“sick”（生病）这个词，法官力图把自己糟糕的感觉传递给别人。当法庭传唤亚当入庭时，亚当在他三段的叙述中，用了四句“I want to tell you”来表达他想为妻子开脱罪责的心情。试图引导法官从他的角度去看待这个事件。在法庭上，家庭戏剧上演了，重要的创伤片段被反复地陈述，引导着读者不间断地回归床上的场景。因此，无论是从字面含义还是比喻含义来看，重复就是回忆冲动的激烈标志。

运用中观重复渲染事件发生的背景，如偏远的农场、医院、学校、法院等，以暗讽事件的怪诞。《我父亲的月亮》（1989）、《斯科比先生的谜语》（1983）、《可爱的婴儿》（1985）、“希尔达的婚礼”（“Hilda's Wedding”）等故事都发生在医院或养老院，每一个故事中都有与其背景性质相悖的反讽式怪诞。再看“亚当的新娘”，该故事以法庭为背景，却叙述了一连串与法庭性质相违和的事件：当堂审问变成了犯罪嫌疑人丈夫叙事的舞台；原本该是以事实为依据、以法律为准绳的审案程序被叙事者的故事所替代；本应是彰显法理公义的法庭，却演变成情感纠结的人生戏剧；最怪诞的是当法官阿姆斯特朗休庭下班时，刚刚发动汽车却重复了犯罪嫌疑人所犯下的罪行：无意中撞伤了一个小女孩。法官重复了刚刚在法庭所审讯的犯罪嫌疑人的犯罪情节，暗示了完全超越背景的现实与超现实主义因素的重合。

运用宏观重复反讽事件的离奇，指的是同样的事件在不同的作品里再次出现。这种重复出现使乔利的作品产生了不同寻常的艺术效果，使本来相同的事件具备了差异，并产生了新的不同意义。米勒说，“这些重复超越单个文本的界限，与文学史的广阔领域相衔接、交叉……许多文学作品的丰富意义，恰恰是来自诸种重复现象的结合。”《果园窃贼》（1995）就是超越单个文本界限的典型，借喻《圣经》伊甸园的故事，以变异的方式表现了禁果“同性恋”的主题。这个主题同样在《白鬃马》（1980）、《井》（1986）、《皮博迪小姐的遗产》（1983）以及《善解人意的配偶》（1999）中重复。而谋杀事件在《克莱蒙特街的报纸》（1981）、《牛奶与蜂蜜》（1984）、《井》中的重复，

---

1 Knight, M. E. “Elizabeth Jolley.”［EB/OL］. “Her technique of using repetition to emphasize striking or important images, or to reexamine ideas and situations from various perspectives, is said to have a musical quality.” 汉语为作者译。

使谋杀主题与生活实践领域相衔接。另外通奸事件在《代理母亲》(1988)、《我父亲的月亮》(1989)、《无辜的绅士》(2001)中的重复，也彰显了不同作品之间主题交叉所产生的意义差异，而这些超越道德与法律层面事件重复出现也暗含其反讽性质。对于读者而言，单个事件的出现意味着新奇和偶然，但是频繁出现的同一事件就意味着夸张和普遍，隐含着作者借文学的张力促进社会变革的意义。在诗学意义上，德勒兹认为重复可以生发出丰富多彩的“间性”或“互文性”(方，麦 176)。这种间性一方面表达了揭示道德与法律规范无力绝禁的问题，另一方面呼吁社会高度关注特殊环境和文化背景下人类情感与心理问题。因此，某种意义上，乔利运用重复手法创作的怪诞离奇故事激发了读者想象的空间和对人生迷离境遇的严肃思考。

由于“互文性理论强调文本的断裂性和不确定性，文本之间互涉互阐，新的文本对旧的文本不断地进行一种定位、重复、解构、重构(方，麦 176)”，乔利小说的互文性就是这样经历了广播剧的初构、短篇小说的重复和长篇小说的重构而展开的。她非常善于在几部不同的小说中重构她的艺术人物，如在几部短篇小说集中都有对摩根(Morgan)家庭的描写。如短篇故事“梨树舞”(A Pear Tree Dance)中，一名叫摩根的勤劳清洁工渴望拥有一片土地，同样的人物在她的第二部长篇小说《克莱蒙特街的报纸》(*The Newspaper of Claremont Street*)中得到重现。广播剧“值夜报告”中的人物复现在“惊奇！来自护士长的惊奇”，最后变成了乔利的小说《斯科比先生的谜语》的开篇，这种苦心再用的素材在乔利的作品中十分常见。通过故事与故事之间主题的重复、人物的重复以及情节的反复再现，乔利在她的小说之间编制了一张互相交织的网，虽然令读者眩晕，但却深度表现了相似文本之间的意义差异。

二、拼贴叙事令读者难解其义

罗斯诺认为，拼贴指的是“一种关于观念或意识的自由流动的、碎片组成的、互不相干的大杂烩似的拼凑物，它包含了诸如新与旧之类的对应环节，它否认整齐性、条理性或对称性；它以矛盾和混乱而沾沾自喜”(罗斯诺 4)。这种矛盾和沾沾自喜正是生活中不以个人意志为转移的凌乱性和任意性。正如万物生长各自有自己的规律，人们的话语表达的是不同个体的心声，每一个个体对世界的感悟杂糅着各自对世界不同层面、不同领域的认识。所以，巫汉祥指出：“剪贴拼画式则是打破不同种类的文本界限，其叙事在文学、广告、科学、新闻、图形、图表等文本之间行进，其目的既要表现叙事对象(人的生存及面对的世界)的虚幻性，也表现叙事主体对话语乃至语言的真实性功能的质疑与否定”(巫 80)。

拼贴正是乔利作品令人感到困惑难解的重要原因之一。读她的作品，读者的思绪很容易被一些零散插入的片段所扰乱，这些片段与所叙述之事毫无关联，令读者感到杂乱无章、摸不着头脑，无法一遍就读懂其意。她的叙事不是简单的线性叙事，也不是情节叙事，更不局限于我们所理解的意识流的跳跃式叙事，毕竟意识流叙事还可以通过所叙的前后内容找到故事发生的线索。她的拼贴叙事却常常表现出跨领域、跨文本、跨学科的叙事特征，相互之间的内容并没有什么关联性，因此无法通过这样的叙事理出前后的关系。加上她有意打乱时间、因果、递进等逻辑联系的理性叙述方式，无论读者还是评论家都会有一种感觉，就是“乔利太缺乏文学常识、太不懂创作了”，甚至会发出“什么乱七八糟的东西”等疑问。

最突出的特点是她的作品打破了传统叙事话语的统一性，小说充满着差异，没有确定的中心思想。比如在不足三千词的短篇故事“希尔达的婚礼”中，乔利开篇就说，“人人都说夜班护士比恩（Bean）是个女巫”（Jolley 39）。让读者以为这个小说就是关于比恩的故事。但就这个话题刚说三句话，就突然插入了“烟熏鲱鱼有什么害处？”接着又听到斯莫豪斯（Smallhouse）讨论监狱农场、政府、养牛场，紧接着尸体搬运工讨论养鸡场，故事发展过程中，乔利又引入停泊在海港的大船来比喻人生。而真正的故事是临时起意为怀孕护士希尔达小姐与尸体搬运工撮合婚礼，至于比恩为什么被人称作女巫，故事最后只是幻想等比恩真正有机会在大手术现场工作时才能看得出来。乔利正是利用了拼贴的手法表达了后现代社会迷宫式的生活和感觉，这种以拼贴构建的文学故事更像是一个“东拼西凑的大杂烩”（姜 215），令读者不知所云。这就说明拼贴叙事与现实的关系并不是简单的话语与事实的关系，叙事话语并不表达人们所期望的真实事件，它所表达的是话语主体的叙事对象，而不是作者或读者所期待的叙事对象。

这种拼贴所体现的正是后现代的多元关系，即个人在社会的众多关系中只是一个节点，每一个节点都有其独特的视角和关系。因其独特的视角和关系，每个人所关注和经历的事情就不一样。在同一个节点上，不同的人在做不同的事情，在思考不同的问题，因而所关注或感兴趣的内容就不一样。表现在叙事上，就一定是同一个场景不同的人在做不同的事情，在叙述不同的故事，在表达不一样的诉求。因此，特定的叙事主体表达的是特定的叙事对象，那么在一个故事中，有不同的叙事主体就有可能表达了不同的叙事对象。在这一点上，乔利只是再现了现实，因为现实远比文学复杂得多，即便是在现实里，错综复杂的万象也足以让人们迷失在多元关系的迷宫里。对于习惯了文学线性叙事的读者来说，面对这种对现实素材不加修剪的再现方式，就很容易迷失在不同叙事主体叙述不同的叙事对象的迷宫里。这种叙事话语是真实现实的再现，但并不是读者所期望的文学“真实”。乔利对拼贴叙事话语的运用，表达的就是后现代文学叙事话语对现代主义文学叙事话语的质疑与否定。

应该说，乔利对后现代主义的文学理论领会颇深，所以她能够自如地运用这些叙事话语进行创作。她实际上是那个“有意破除传统文学的有机整体性，突破结构、叙事等方面的限制”（黄 36）的作家。严格地说，拼贴叙事最适合表现当今多元复调的生活现实，因为在这个时代，人人都要通过发声证实自己的存在价值。在“希尔达的婚礼”中，乔利还原了人人都以自我为中心，人人都是他者边缘的生活原貌。现代意义上的整体、单个中心的神话已经被打破，取而代之的是碎片化、多元化的现实。但对于当时的澳大利亚读者而言，读她的作品堪称是一种折磨，因为如果要读懂她的作品，必须具有足够的耐心和基本的后现代文学常识。拼贴这种话语叙事，“在传统叙事话语那里似乎并不存在或不明显”，尽管“这便是后现代文学对人类艺术宝库的一个贡献”（巫 80），但对于普通读者而言，却是一个巨大的挑战。

三、叙事省略令读者陷入想象

“后现代主义小说打破了传统小说的结构模式——事件、人物之间的时间顺序和因果关系，使小说的结构呈现为一种情节缺损和零散化的并置。情节缺损使叙述线索出现断裂，从而造成叙事结构的缺失和空白。”（甘 2008：102）结构上的空白、缺失和线索及情节的断裂正是乔利创作风格怪诞的表现，这些省略实质上是话语的缄默与沉默。通过这种叙事风格乔利不仅做到了话语上的节约，规避了相关叙事的直白，同时也为读者提供了想象和解读的空间。在这些空白、缺失和断裂中，既有文学审美在叙事变化和转折上的需要，也有乔利所传递的隐形道德选择和掩盖现实谜团的需要。

结构的省略有宏观和微观上的空白。宏观上的空白体现为故事篇章之间的空白。就《果园窃贼》来说，这部小说从结构上看，有三个独立的叙事对象。第一部分叙述了祖母与大女儿的关系，讲述了祖母对老处女女儿的怜惜与疼爱。第二部分叙述了祖母与孙子孙女们的关系，讲述了祖母对于孙辈们偷吃果实的宽容与博爱，她认为任何人小时候都会犯点类似的小错，但不影响他们的成长成才。第三部分叙述了祖母与从伦敦回来生孩子的二女儿之间的关系。不仅每一部分结束时作者都留出了一整页的空白，而且每一部分开头时作者也留出了三分之一的空白页。这些空白恰到好处地标明一个故事的结束和另一个故事的开始。令读者读完一部分后可以放松一下身心，同时期待下一个部分的推陈出新。

微观上的空白体现为段落与段落之间的空白。在《果园窃贼》中，类似的空白有二十四处。而且这些空白的大小也不一样，有的空白只有一行，有的空白有两行，有的空白有三行。细看之下这些空白代表了不同的含义。小空白代表着情节的转折，叙事的视角没有改变。如第 11 页第一段和第二段之间有两行的空白，第一段讲述着祖母打算给大女儿过生日，而大女儿却说自己已经没有生日可过了；第二段展现的却是祖母的思绪飞回到学生时代的制服上了。大空白代表着叙事主体的改变。如第 39 页有一个三行的空白，上段叙述的是祖母内心渴望有一种长生不老药能够防止她忘记生日等类似的记忆衰退，下一个段落就变成了她的大女儿告诉侄子侄女们可以在她的房间玩半个小时。这种情节结构的转换和空白预示了小说叙事上的转折和逻辑断裂，因此比常规小说更显新意，但也迫使读者阅读时不得不用心以避免意义上的混乱。

乔利善于以空白代替缺失的情节，即指小说语言和情节结构的省略，乔利的小说几乎每一部都有这种省略。正如张清芳评论徐则臣那样，“每一篇小说的省略和空白的位置均不同，或在语言上以无代替有，或是人物身份背景不明，充满神秘色彩，抑或是省略掉某一重要的情节结构，当然也有的作品是混合了以上几种情况，而这些不同的省略和空白对小说叙事和情节发展产生的作用就相应地有差别”（张 32）。《斯科比先生的谜语》是这方面的典型代表。与《果园窃贼》不同的是，该作品没有明确的篇章序号标注，作者似乎主要以大篇幅的省略空白和下一页的顶格书写暗示另一章节的起始。作品随处可见省略性的空白，这样的空白虽然没有语言和文字，但常常给人以“此处无声胜有声”的意蕴。斯科比先生（Mr. Scobie）刚住进圣·克里斯托弗和圣·裘德养老院时，听到勃拉姆斯交响乐，他就忆起了当年教丽娜（Lina）姐妹学钢琴时发生的一个场景：丽娜小姐想找几张圣画让斯科比先生来解读，就带着他来到楼上母亲的卧室。丽娜在翻床垫找画时，保姆弗罗雷音·丽恰（Fraulein Recha）突然进来，她以无比惊骇的声音问他：“你在这里干什么？！”（Jolley 24）故事接下来是一连串的省略号和一片空白。这里的省略空白作为富有意义的叙述过程而凸显其重要性，一方面它表达了保姆的迷惑，另一方面也表达了斯科比先生无比尴尬的大脑空白。此处无言，但隐含了保姆的道德谴责。作为作家有意识的选择，空白和省略显示给读者的是无尽的道德内涵和黑色幽默，这正是海明威所提倡的“水下冰山”的效果。

当乔利以空白替代线索的省略时，这种省略常常掩盖着某种无法言说的噩梦或残酷的事实真相，掩盖了难以入目的悲惨，释放出一种悲天悯人的情怀。省略叙事就是无言，无言则体现为沉默。正如周春宇指出，“在一般的情况下，叙述总是以叙述主体的某种道德观念为导引，它贯穿叙述过程的始终而默默起着作用。但有时，事件的发展打破了这一沉默，使一种不为叙述主体所理解的道德内涵显露出来”（周春宇 62）。这体现了作家有意识的选择。凡有缄默之处必有不可言说之秘密。凡秘密之事必有与叙述主体的道德观念相悖之处。在《牛奶与蜂蜜》中，主人公海姆巴奇从不提起自己的妻子，似乎他就没有妻子。事实上，他的妻子因为精神病被送进了疯人院。作为高雅生活的追求者，海姆巴奇竭力对妻子保持缄默的目的是为了维护家庭的道德秩序，因为疯癫代表无序、无德和丑闻，与高雅的生活无缘。叙事中女主人公线索的断裂暗含了主人公对疯癫现象的价值判断。疯癫是海姆巴奇无法摆脱的噩梦，缄默就是对其存在意义的省略。“这样一来，省略就被用作一种达到除魔驱邪的神奇目的。”

乔利的省略还表现为情节的断裂。应该说，叙述什么，省略什么，是作者写作风格的体现，这种体现常常与作者的写作创新有关。情节的断裂表现在叙事上给读者的印象往往是事情的结果直接呈现给读者，而对带来结果的过程给予叙事上的省略。乔利的小说具有叙事平淡之风，这与她善用省略分不开。她用这技巧避免了惨剧在读者眼前发生。在《牛奶与蜂蜜》中，乔利对恶性事件的叙述省略事实上是避免挑战读者的心理极限和道德信念。因为人们因仇恨而产生的报复行为常常不受理性控制，极易导致杀戮。当雅克布在花园中绊倒在情妇麦洁身上时，他看到的麦洁衣服被撕烂，颈部被刺穿，脸色肿胀青紫，被胡乱裹在毯子里（Jolley 145）。麦洁是怎么死的？谁杀死了她？这一直是个谜。乔利巧妙地利用情节的断裂省去了对麦洁悲剧的描述。地上的假牙暗示了谋杀与疯癫的内弟有关，读者可以想象其残忍与恐怖。但乔利只字未提就保护了读者脆弱的心灵。这种情节的断裂使小说作品具有了更高度的真实性，表达了作者对生活认识的穿透力。同时，能够使小说文本的形式结构简练精巧，内涵主题更加内敛和丰富厚重，亦能够产生一种陌生化的效果，调动读者的想象力。

正如巴尔所指出，“被略去的部分——省略的内容，不见得是不重要的；相反，未置一词的实践可能是由于令人如此痛苦，以至于恰恰就为了这一原因而被略去了，或者事件是难以行于言表从而宁愿对它保持沉默”（巴尔 120）。由于省略，读者常常在断裂的虚实两端呆想，试图辨识乔利叙事中的因果关系、时间顺序和逻辑顺序，因而不自觉地陷入想象，这就使虚构的小说与读者真实的思想发生了联系，作品的意义得以延伸，作品的结论就呈现出无限的开放性：不同的读者将创造出不同的结论。这样，乔利的读者就不仅仅是一个简单的意义接受者，同时还成为了文本意义的阐释者和创造者。

四、结语

乔利的怪诞文风说起来不过是后现代文学叙事方式的表现罢了。但对于绝大多数不谙后现代理论的读者来说，她的重复恐怕就意味着梦呓、她的拼贴则意味着混乱、她的省略则意味着意义的断裂。但对于乔利来说，无论是重复、拼贴还是省略，都是话语，都是叙事，都具有特定的语言意义。这些策略最大可能地避免了读者仅凭字面意义去理解作品的单一意义，留给读者更多的机会和更大的空间去发挥自己的想象，因而不同的读者便会有不同的解读意义。这种多元化的意义延伸恰恰是社会生活原生态的特点。乔利期望读者具备创造性和想象力，因此读者在阅读乔利时就不可能是简单的被动的读者，而是一个能够积极介入作品创作过程、参与意义解读并具有想象力的读者。就这样，乔利以反澳洲文学民族之风的态势，带着“怪诞”的标签辟出了一条澳大利亚与国际趋势接轨的后现代文学道路，经历了评论界从不解到困惑、从困惑到质疑、从质疑到接受的历练过程，因此被称为“澳大利亚最大胆的作家之一”。弗莱曼陀艺术中心——乔利第一部短篇小说集的出版商芮·考菲（Ray Coffey）说，乔利“在最大程度上拓展了我们对澳大利亚文学创作的欣赏视野”（Moran 2007）。在这个意义上，乔利也已成为悖逆审美现代性或艺术现代性的怪诞文风符号。

参考文献

[1] Dibble, Brian. "Jolley Excellent." *Australian Book Review.* May 1982:29.

[2] Idema, James. "Tops Down under She Writes from a Far of Themes That Are Universal." *Chicago Tribute,* May 20, 1988.

[3] Jolley, Elizabeth. "Adam's Bride." *Woman in a Lampshade.* Melbourne: Penguin Books Australia Limited, 1983.

[4] Jolley, Elizabeth. *Milk and Honey.* Perth: Fremantle Arts Centre Press, 1984.

[5] Jolley, Elizabeth. *The Orchard Thieves.* New York: The Viking Books, 1995.

[6] Knight, M. E. "Elizabeth Jolley." [EB/OL]. http://www.enotes.com/topics/elizabeth-jolley/critical-essays/jolley-elizabeth

[7] Moran, Rod. "Writer Elizabeth Jolley Dead." *Sydney Morning Herald,* Feb. 20, 2007.

[8] "Ms. Jolley's off-kilter style was not to every critic's taste". *New York times,* 4 Apr. 2007.

[9] 波林・玛丽・罗斯诺．后现代主义与社会科学．上海：上海译文出版社，1998 年．

[10] 方颜玮、麦永雄．重复、戏仿与差异的力量——互文理论观照下的《洛丽塔》．江淮论坛 .2011(6).

[11] 甘正芳．美国后现代主义小说的叙事策略．江苏技术师范学院学报（职教通讯）.2008(6).

[12] 胡爱舫、杨泽雯．澳大利亚二十年来的乔莉小说研究．外国文学研究 .2001(3).

[13] 黄鸣奋．碎片美学在"超现代"的呈现．学术月刊 .2013(6).

[14] 姜华．大众文化理论的后现代转向．北京：人民出版社，2006 年．

[15] 金志勇．关于诗词写作中避免重复问题的探讨．诗词世界 .2011(5).

[16] 刘琼、余华．小说创作中重复艺术的价值．重庆邮电大学学报 .2010(3): 87–88.

[17] 米克・巴尔．谭君强译．叙述学．北京：中国社会科学出版社，2003 年．

[18] 米勒・希利斯．王宏图译．小说与重复——七部英国小说．天津：天津人民出版社，2007 年．

[19] 巫汉祥．后现代叙事话语．厦门大学学报（哲学社会科学版），1999(1).

[20] 薛志娇．后现代话语权中语言所赋予的寓意 .[EB/OL]. http://blog.sina.com.cn/s/blog_5077496f0100c089.html.

[21] 张清芳．省略和空白的叙事美学——论徐则臣小说的叙事特点．当代文坛 .2007(6): 32–34.

[22] 周春宇．空白，文学叙事策略的重要手段．朔方 .1994(5): 62.

梁中贤，女，牡丹江师范学院教授，东北师范大学兼职博士生导师。

成为“完整的人”
——《特莱庞的爱情》中后现代身份问题

刘金龙

摘要：本文分析了澳大利亚作家帕特里克·怀特的小说《特莱庞的爱情》中主人公埃迪·特莱庞的身份问题。埃迪通过改变自己的性别以不同的身份生活，试图寻找属于自己的理想身份，从而成为既能爱自己又能爱别人的“完整的人”。埃迪最终成功找到了自己的理想身份，展示了应对碎片式身份的方法。怀特通过刻画埃迪的三次性别转换经历，解构了传统的男女二元对立身份结构，揭示了人类身份的流动性、不稳定性。怀特通过小说向读者传递了一种超脱人文主义，更为后现代视角下处理身份问题的方法：“拼装”。区别于追求介于男性身份与女性身份中间状态的“雌雄同体”，“拼装”不追求性别上的所谓平衡，而是以更为灵活的方式处理身份问题，即在不同关系中以不同身份出现。

关键词：帕特里克·怀特；《特莱庞的爱情》；身份；“拼装”

Becoming a “Complete Man”:
Issues of Postmodern Identity in *The Twyborn Affair*

Liu Jinlong

Abstract: This article is an attempt to discuss the protagonist Eddie Twyborn’s identity issue in Patrick White’s *The Twyborn Affair*. By changing gender to live in different identities, Eddie tries to pursue the ideal identity and become a “complete man” who can love both himself and others. Eddie finally gains the ideal identity and presents the strategy to deal with fragmented identity. White deconstructs the binary opposition of male/female via depicting Eddie’s three gender changes, and reveals the fluidity and instability of identity. White shows readers a beyond humanistic, postmodern solution to identity problem in *Twyborn*: “bricolage”. Different from “androgyny” which focuses on mediation between male and female identity, “bricolage” doesn’t aim for equilibrium of gender but manages identity problem in a more flexible way, which is applying different identities in different relations.

Key words: Patrick White; *The Twyborn Affair*; identity; “bricolage”

米兰·昆德拉（Milan Kundera）曾定义小说为“一种散文的伟大形式，在其中，作者通过实验性的自我（人物），彻底地探究关于存在的重大主题”（Kundera 94）。怀特的小说很好地诠释了昆德拉笔下的定义，因为他的小说常常关乎人生中的一些重要主题，例如“上帝的存在与否，生命的意义，在物质世界中追求人性的崇高，以及对身份的探索等等”（黄 127）。英格玛·伯约克斯坦（Ingmar Björkstén）将怀特作品的主题概括为人类对自身存在的意义与价值的探索（Björkstén 117），而对自身的探索与追求这一主题，在他的《特莱庞的爱情》中体现得尤为明显，相较怀特其他同类作品，《特莱庞的爱情》中这一主题的呈现也更为复杂，所以也成为怀特眼中自己写得最好的三部小说之一（White, *Flaws* 145）。

对自我的探索一直以来都是人类活动的重要组成部分，其中一个探索方向就是对"完整的人"（Complete Man）的渴望。"完整的人"这一概念并没有明确的定义，但一直在西方思想中占有重要地位，许多思想家都是从这一概念出发，建立起自己的思想体系（曹 172）。"完整的人"在不同的思想体系里或是唯物的，或是唯心的，具体所指也不尽相同，但相同的是"完整的人"始终是人类追求的终极目标，是一种最理想、最自由的状态。诚如卢梭（Jean-Jacques Rousseau）所言，"人生而自由，却又无往不在枷锁之中"（Rousseau 45）。在《特莱庞的爱情》中，怀特笔下的主人公埃迪·特莱庞（Eddie Twyborn）也同样被无形的枷锁所桎梏，为自己的身份，特别是性别身份所困扰。简单来讲，小说讲述了主人公通过三段迥异的生活不断寻找自己的故事；主人公试图通过性别及身份的变换，从原本难以接受、碎片式的自我中找到最被接受、最完整的自我。

埃迪所一直追求的"完整的人"就是既能爱自己又能爱他人的理想状态。爱在埃迪这里是一个复杂的问题，其中包含对自己的爱，也包含对他人的爱，有与性相关的爱，也有与性无关的爱，不同类型的爱占据埃迪生命的不同部分，同时又相互纠葛。能否处理好这些不同性质的爱，便是他能否找到"完整的埃迪"的关键所在。

一

在小说的第一部分，埃迪化身少女尤特夏（Eudoxia），与年迈的希腊丈夫安吉洛斯（Angelos）共同生活在法国。从格尔森（Golson）太太与尤特夏初次相遇可以看出，主人公原本的男儿身被隐藏了起来，对格尔森太太而言，出现在她面前的是一位"年轻女士"，有着"修长纤细的胳膊"、"完美的下颚线"、"优美的身姿"，活生生一位"尤物"（White, *Twyborn* 14）。埃迪一直以来无法爱自己的根本原因就是他无法接受自己的身份，以尤特夏的身份出现并与安吉洛斯结婚，一方面是试图确定一个完整的女性身份，接受自己；另一方面也渴望在安吉洛斯身上学会爱他人。现在，埃迪似乎建立起了一个完整的女性身份，尤特夏无论是行为举止还是装扮仪容，在旁人看来都是一名真正的女性。

埃迪能成功地建立起尤特夏这一女性身份，得益于他成功地"操演"（perform）了他的性别。在分析埃迪是如何进行操演之前，有必要理清三个概念，即性属（sex）、性别（gender）和性相（sexuality）[1]。简单来讲，性属指生理性别，侧重人体的生理构造；性别指社会性别，侧重以性征为体现的社会属性；性相是个综合性概念，这里可以简单理解为性取向（杨 3）。埃迪并没有改变自己的性属，生理上他依然是男儿身，他让众人误以为是女性是因为他在性别上动了手脚。朱迪斯·巴特勒（Judith Butler）认为，“性别是可以操演的（performative），即构建出声称的身份”（Butler 33）。埃迪通过操演自己的性别，构建出了他声称的身份——女性尤特夏。最能体现操演（performativity）的一类行为就是“扮装”（drag），“通过对性别的模仿，扮装暗示出性别结构自身的模仿性，以及偶然性”（Butler 175）。所谓扮装，简单来讲就是穿着异性的服装，画上异性的妆容等行为。尤特夏这一女性身份的建立主要就是归功于扮装，尤特夏就曾对安吉洛斯说“你永远记不住我穿什么，但对我来说，他们意义重大”（White, *Twyborn* 124）。

但尤特夏并不是埃迪一直追求的完整的自己，扮装不能使他变成一个真正的女人，他也无法爱这样的自己。因为埃迪苦心经营看似扮装成功的尤特夏，其实并非无懈可击。当尤特夏扭伤了脚踝，被格尔森太太扶到房间休息时，格尔森太太提议让她脱掉鞋子处理扭伤，但尤特夏坚持不脱。这一举动让格尔森太太注意到，尽管尤特夏的脚踝形状优美，但“这少妇的脚和手都显得有些大”（White, *Twyborn* 52）。当格尔森夫妇受邀拜访尤特夏时，她的大脚又一次出卖了她，格尔森太太看到“那光着的双脚，她第一次意识到，看起来是那么大……”（White, *Twyborn* 101）。埃迪可以靠扮装使自己无限接近女性，但一旦离开扮装他就会暴露自己，那双不符合女性身份的大脚随时会让人起疑心。

埃迪内心深处依然恨着自己，无法原谅他是这样的自己。“我很可笑吗？或许是吧。当人们盯着我看时，我必须接受”（White, *Twyborn* 27）。埃迪希望面对真实的自己，但他此时还不知道什么才是最真实最完整的自己，他还在探索当中。“我的一切都非我所有，甚至是被给予居住的这副身体，和为这身体而选的伪装……真正的埃迪还没有被发现，或许永远也无法发现”（White, *Twyborn* 79）。

以尤特夏的身份生活，埃迪不仅无法爱自己，也无法爱他人。她从未真正爱过安吉洛斯，“我被禁锢在这可怕干瘪的混蛋身边，全因被命运和高潮所缚，从不是因为爱的缘故”（White, *Twyborn* 36）。安吉洛斯对于埃迪 / 尤特夏来说，只是埃迪的父亲爱德华（Edward）的替代品。埃迪有着强烈的恋父情结，这份爱不单纯是儿子对父亲的亲情之爱，更带有与性相关的爱。当梦中父亲亲吻埃迪的嘴唇时，“我就像纺纱机般用线将他缠绕，使他这尝试性的突然举动无法收回，让这爱一直捆绑着我”（White, *Twyborn* 35）。弗洛伊德（Freud）关于梦的解析指出：“（1）梦的内容是愿望的一种实现，（2）梦的动机来自幼年时期受压抑的愿望。”（Blass 55）埃迪从小就对父亲有一种

1 关于 sex、gender 和 sexuality 该如何翻译，有着不同的说法，笔者在考量后采用杨洁在《酷儿理论与批评实践》一书中的译法。

迷恋，渴望与父亲发生乱伦关系的愿望在现实中受到压抑，埃迪只能借由梦境来实现。为了满足自己的愿望，埃迪用安吉洛斯代替了父亲的角色（吴 84），与安吉洛斯发生性行为实则是借此满足自己与父亲发生关系的愿望。

由于害怕格尔森太太发现自己的身份，埃迪 / 尤特夏与安吉洛斯匆忙离开原来的住所，没多久安吉洛斯就因心脏病发去世。"'他死了，' 她说，声音听起来不仅仅是伤心，同时更像是如梦初醒。"（White, *Twyborn* 126）埃迪想以女性身份生活的梦破碎了，他无法真正爱上尤特夏这个身份，也无法真正爱着安吉洛斯，更没能找到完整的自己。

二

在小说的第二部分，埃迪恢复了自己的本名回到了故乡澳大利亚。随着埃迪的回家，他与父母之间的问题也渐渐浮出水面。埃迪无法找到完整自己的原因，很大一部分归咎于他不知道该如何爱自己的父母。他的母亲伊迪（Eadie）与格尔森太太有着女同性恋关系，性格强势并有着强烈的控制欲，这一切都令埃迪感到不知所措。这样的伊迪对埃迪的身份确立具有破坏性，"他害怕被异性恋社会所不容，而她正是这份恐惧的中心所在；她在家庭关系中占据领导地位；在性角色上，她是有争议的被排斥的人，同时也是恋母情结危机的来源"（Trejo 192）。

尽管埃迪对母亲有所害怕，但他潜意识里仍然希望与母亲保持亲密，甚至是与母亲融为一体。埃迪认为"伊迪 = 埃迪……伊迪就是自己假装而成"（White, *Twyborn* 150）。也就是说，在埃迪心里自己与母亲应该是一体的。有学者就认为他的"一生都在追寻着自己的母亲……变成与之相同"（Blamires 79）。拉康（Lacan）将人的发展分成三个阶段：实在域（the Real），想象域（the Imaginary）和符号域（the Symbolic）（克拉吉斯 76）。"实在域是一种精神领域，那里有着原始的统一。"（克拉吉斯 77）埃迪就是渴望一直处于实在域中，这样他就可以像婴儿一样与母亲不分你我而是一个整体。拉康指出，正常的成长过程需依次经历实在域、想象域和符号域从而形成自我（'I' dentity），而这一过程必须以丢失"原始的统一"为代价。也就是说，只有放弃与母亲融为一体才能够确立自己的身份。客观上，埃迪已经是成年人早已结束了实在域阶段，但他在心理上却一直希望重返实在域。埃迪梦到一个"熟悉"的女人给"让人嫉妒"的婴儿洗澡，埃迪想参与其中，但被拒绝了（White, *Twyborn* 352）。这段梦里"熟悉"的女人就是母亲，"让人嫉妒"的婴儿就是小时候的埃迪，那时埃迪还处于实在域阶段与母亲是一个整体，现在的埃迪看到当时的自己不免心生妒忌，他想参与洗澡表现了埃迪想再次进入实在域的愿望，他被拒绝则暗示了埃迪的愿望无法实现。埃迪陷入了进退维谷的境地，一方面，实在域一去不复返，另一方面，对实在域的留恋或者说强烈的恋母情结，又影响了埃迪顺利找到完整的自己。

埃迪不仅无法处理好与母亲之间的爱，也不知道该如何与父亲相处。埃迪喜欢自己的父亲，父亲对他来说有性吸引力。当埃迪回到家中，想唤起父亲与自己的过往经历，“您还记得吗，父亲……您带着我一起……我们睡在一张大铁床上，上面有蜂窝纹布的床单”（White, *Twyborn* 158），但父亲坚称不记得，并说这一切都是埃迪编的故事。埃迪怀念“蜂窝纹布床单下与法官父亲的完全接触”（White, *Twyborn* 392），但父亲却想逃避这段回忆，“我们非要这么病态吗？”（White, *Twyborn* 159）

无法用自己的方式去爱父母，埃迪感到自己在这个家中是陌生人般的存在，他选择去乡下工作，逃离这一切。在父亲的介绍下，埃迪来到了父亲的好友克莱格（Greg）先生的农场。但新的环境并没有让埃迪摆脱一直困扰他的身份问题，一方面他很高兴这里的工作“使他自我感觉更为阳刚”（White, *Twyborn* 186），另一方面尤特夏的影子又时不时出现在他身上：当埃迪不小心从马背上摔下来后普劳斯（Prowse）救了他，“尤特夏……想谢谢，或者以什么方式回报这大汗淋漓的粗暴之人……她甚至允许他强奸她，给她持久又痛苦的高潮”（White, *Twyborn* 203）。

不久，埃迪与克莱格的妻子玛西亚（Marcia）有了奸情。不过两人之间只有性没有爱，埃迪与玛西亚通奸另有目的，他想借玛西亚“试图建立起自己阳刚的身份”（White, *Twyborn* 223）。“荣格（Jung）将男性身上的‘女性’原型称作女性意向（anima），将女性身上的‘男性’原型称作男性意向（animus）”（Salman 65）。与周遭强烈的男性气息相比，埃迪身上的阿尼玛就显得格外明显：刚一到农场泰瑞尔（Tyrrell）夫人就感觉到他的与众不同，“这里需要女孩，从不缺男孩。并不是说你不是男孩……但是跟一般的男孩不一样”（White, *Twyborn* 185）。通奸使得埃迪像正常男性一样与女性发生性行为，使他感到自己的阳刚之气增强，阿尼玛不再那么明显。

玛西亚除了被埃迪用来增强自己的男性气息外，也被用来维系他与克莱格间的关系。这种关系被称为“男性同性社会性欲望”（male homosocial desire），即男性间的亲密关系，其中既包括一般社会性纽带，也包括男同性恋关系（Sedgwick 1–2）。“情欲三角”（erotic triangle）最能说明这种关系，典型的情欲三角涉及两名互为敌手的男性以及一名被他们争夺的女性，“在情欲三角中，敌手间的纽带更为强烈，对行动和选择更具有决定性，强于其中任何一个求爱者与被求爱者间的纽带”（Sedgwick 21）。所谓敌手间的纽带，就是两名男性间的同性社会性欲望，这种关系要强于其中任何一名男性与被争夺女性间的关系，因为“男性将女性用作‘关系通道’，这种关系中，他真正的伴侣是另一个男人”（Sedgwick 26）。“戴绿帽子”就是一种典型的情欲三角关系，“‘戴绿帽子’从定义上讲是一种由一个男人施加给另一个男人的性行为……男人通过这种行为试图与其他男人建立满意的关系”（Sedgwick 49–50）。埃迪与玛西亚通奸就是给克莱格戴绿帽子，他想通过这种行为与克莱格建立更亲密的关系，玛西亚不过是其中的媒介，埃迪真正的伴侣是克莱格。“如果他给克莱格·勒欣顿戴了绿帽子，他对这体面男人的喜爱和尊敬就完整了”（White, *Twyborn* 245）。埃迪有着强烈的恋父情结，他渴望与父亲亲近但被父亲拒绝，现在克莱格扮演了他父亲的角色，所以埃迪渴望从克莱格身上体验与父亲亲近的感觉，给克莱格戴绿帽子就实现了他的这一愿望。

不过，埃迪并没能就此最终找到自己满意的身份。当埃迪赤身在河中游泳时被普劳斯看见了，“小心点，埃迪。你要是那样晃屁股的话，小心有人会跳进去鸡奸了你”（White, *Twyborn* 250–251）。普劳斯发觉到了埃迪的与众不同，“我想我认出你了，埃迪……我想我认出你他妈的是个同性恋了”（White, *Twyborn* 284），于是普劳斯鸡奸了埃迪。事后埃迪哭了，“但并不是为了他所受的侮辱，而是因为他最终接受了”（White, *Twyborn* 284）。埃迪痛苦的并不在于他被普劳斯侵犯这件事本身，而是他自己不加反抗地接受了普劳斯的侵犯。埃迪此时的目的是想建立一个阳刚的男性身份，但他选择接受与普劳斯发生性行为，就意味着他在摧毁一直构建的男性身份。因为性行为与性相之间被社会赋予了强烈联系，这种联系体现在“如果你与同性发生了性行为，那么你不仅是发生了同性性行为，也代表你就是同性恋”（克拉吉斯 115–116），而“同性恋被归类在‘女性化’行为里”（Tyson 88）。所以埃迪接受与普劳斯发生同性性行为，就会被归类为同性恋，进而被贴上女性化的标签，这与埃迪试图塑造的男性身份相违背。埃迪悔恨的正是自己前功尽弃使自己女性化，没能成功建立起令自己满意的男性身份。

埃迪的身份更加混乱了，他成了“假—男人—精液—隐秘—女人”（White, *Twyborn* 298）这样一种存在。又一次没能实现既爱自己又爱别人的愿望，埃迪选择再次离开继续去寻找属于自己的完整身份。

三

这一次，埃迪化身伊迪丝（Eadith）夫人，在伦敦做起了妓院老鸨。伊迪丝虽然经营妓院，自己却不充当妓女，“她非常厌恶自己以及人类，不想再涉猎性，更不用说涉猎大矛盾——爱”（White, *Twyborn* 311），因此伊迪丝刻意与其他人保持距离。唯一与伊迪丝关系较为密切的男性是她妓院的赞助人格雷文纳（Gravenor），但即便是对格雷文纳，伊迪丝也有所顾忌，这位“有希望在一起，但又被她拒绝的情人，可能会跨过底线而摧毁了她的生活”（White, *Twyborn* 322），所以她一直没有答应格雷文纳的追求。

封闭自己，与他人保持距离的确可以让埃迪成功地经营伊迪丝的身份。“在孤独里，他是自由的，是完整的，但只是暂时的”（White, *Twyborn* 251），因为这样的生活与埃迪的初衷是违背的，用压抑自己换来的平静生活并没能让埃迪喜欢伊迪丝的身份。回顾一直以来的尝试，“她不得不承认，她在这几种生活里都不是确确实实的存在……不管她以什么方式出现，不管暂时陶醉在什么样的幻觉中，对于真实的爱，也就是真实这东西的核心所在，她始终都不知为何物，可能永远也都弄不明白”（White, *Twyborn* 336）。

梦又一次揭示了埃迪/伊迪丝的真实内心，伊迪丝梦见自己身处一个没有窗户的房间，里面有许多孩童哭闹不止想从房间里出去，而这囚笼般房间的始作俑者就是她，她认为这里安全便阻止他们，但孩童们不惜伤害她也要逃出去。梦里的房间象征着伊迪丝这个身份，埃迪活在这样的身份下感到安全，那些孩童代表了埃迪的其他身份，他们被强行束缚在伊迪丝这个身份下。这就是所谓的碎片式身份（fragmented identity），“解构主义认为人的身份是流动的、碎片式的、一种许多可能‘自我’的动态集合”（Tyson 335）。埃迪的身份也是如此，一直以来都是碎片式的，房间里的每一个孩童代表他的一个碎片式自我。就像爱默生（Emerson）讲的，“因为灵魂是不断发展着的，所以它不会自我重复，而是在每一次行动中试图创造新的更加完美的整体”（Emerson 295），所以埃迪不断变换自己的身份，无论是作为尤特夏、埃迪还是伊迪丝，都是放大自己的某一个碎片以期创造一个新的更加完美的自我。伊迪丝就是被放大的一个碎片，埃迪建造了伊迪丝这个密不透风的房间，将其他碎片都关在房间里，期望以伊迪丝来代表全部，但其他碎片想要冲破伊迪丝的桎梏，因为伊迪丝并不能真的代表全部。因为“碎片式的身体……总在梦中显现自己……”（Lacan 4），所以埃迪/伊迪丝通过梦意识到了自己的碎片式身体，意识到单凭伊迪丝的身份不能使自己变成理想中完整的人。

“在特定情况下，欲望能化为顿悟”（White, *Twyborn* 417），埃迪/伊迪丝的内心越发地明白，他/她知道“在这满是碎片与绝望的世界，即使是罪恶的反常也能带来某种重生”（White, *Twyborn* 420）。当埃迪/伊迪丝再次与母亲相遇，他们之间多了几分和谐与淡定，“你是我的儿子埃迪吗？”“不，但我是你的女儿伊迪丝。”“我好高兴，我一直希望有个女儿”（White, *Twyborn* 422–423），母女相认的过程简单而平静，如同伊迪丝这个名字一样（Eadith 与 Eadie’s 发音接近），她终于被母亲接受了，“他们之间的和谐完美了”（White, *Twyborn* 423）。埃迪找到了爱母亲的方式，即以伊迪丝的身份做母亲的女儿，“她渴望去抚摸她的母亲，”（White, *Twyborn* 423），母亲也回应伊迪丝的爱，让她与自己一起回家：“……我们可以一起生活，我可以预见我们洗着头发，一起坐在花园里将头发弄干”（White, *Twyborn* 425）。

解决了与母亲间的问题，但埃迪/伊迪丝仍然不知道该如何回应格雷文纳的爱，最后是格雷文纳的一封信给了他/她勇气。格雷文纳在信中写道：“如果我们找到勇气的话，我们是可以彻底地、像普通人一样地爱着对方的。男人和女人并非人类体系中仅有的组成部分，你我都可以在其中找到归属……我可以接受任何形式的你……”（White, *Twyborn* 426），格雷文纳表明了自己对埃迪/伊迪丝的爱无关他/她是以什么方式存在，无论他/她是男人还是女人。于是埃迪换上了男性的装扮，决定以男性的身份去找他爱的格雷文纳，但却被炸死在了路上。

四

小说的故事情节就如同其中人物的身份一样破碎，不过这样的设计也完全符合怀特的风格，怀特曾说过："人物比情节更吸引我，我不认为我的书里有你们所谓的故事情节"（White, *Speaks* 21），但怀特的这种风格使得从整体上把握他的作品十分困难。小说中充满了值得推敲的细节，可"怀特故意阻止我们做出任何确凿的解读……埃迪最终明白了什么……全凭读者的推测，从一堆杂乱而冲突的线索中寻找答案"（Bliss 181）。对于其中最为关键的问题，即埃迪最终是否找到了他想要的身份，胡怡君认为怀特在小说中要体现一种从"我"到"非我"的过程，埃迪重生的梦想没能实现（Hu 102）；徐凯认为埃迪身上一直存在着含混性，尽管最终他自己、母亲和格雷文纳认可了这种含混性，但象征着现代文明的战争夺走了埃迪的生命，说明埃迪的身份仍为现代文明所不容（徐 73–74）；吴宝康认为，埃迪体现的是一出生存悲剧，他希望重生但战争终结了他的梦想，他死时身着男性服装化着女性妆容，象征他的身份仍未确定（吴 86）。

以上三位学者认为埃迪寻找身份的结果是失败的，但笔者认为埃迪是成功的，因为他的目的达到了。埃迪的目的是要找到完整的自己，可以让他爱自己也爱别人的身份，从这一点来看的话，埃迪最后找到了这样的身份。因为埃迪最终在乎的两个人是母亲和格雷文纳，处理好与他们的关系也就解决了他的身份难题。以伊迪丝的身份做母亲的女儿，以埃迪的身份做格雷文纳的情人，这样的做法让埃迪分别成功解决了自己与母亲、格雷文纳的关系。以不同的身份面对不同的人让埃迪在两种情况下都可以既爱自己又爱别人，所以说埃迪已经找到了他想要的完整身份，他寻找身份的结果是成功的。

这样的完整身份与一般概念的身份相冲突。最被广泛认可的身份概念仍然是人文主义视角下的统一的、滞定不变的身份，而埃迪的完整身份却是分裂的、流动变化的身份。怀特借由埃迪传达的身份概念已经超脱了人文主义，更倾向于后现代视角。

怀特曾说："我在我所有书中都持同一个想法：努力接近现实的核心，现实的结构，而不是仅仅停留在表面……小说应该升华生活，应该给人以启发……"（White, *Speaks* 21）。在《特莱庞的爱情》中，怀特对现实的关注集中在了人的身份层面，他所要发现的是身份的结构与核心，向读者传递关于身份的新观点。结构主义认为，人类总是以截然二分的方式来认识世界，其中也包括如何看待身份，在这种二元对立视角下，人的性别身份被局限为男性和女性两种，"没有中间项……你或者是男性或者是女性，如果你不是其中一个或另一个，那你一定就是有问题的"（Tyson 110）。怀特显然不是站在这一观点上，通过刻画埃迪在男性身份与女性身份间来回转换，怀特解构了看似稳定的二元对立身份结构，他透过《特莱庞的爱情》要给读者的启发就是如何应对身份结构的不稳定。徐凯和陈弘都认为怀特借小说要传达的是"雌雄同体"

(androgyny)的观点:“对于怀特来讲,雌雄同体是作为一个普通人和作家的最理想状态”(Xu 57);“雌雄同体的埃迪·特莱庞……代表了人类性相一种新的完整的形式,雌雄同体象征了男性和女性间新发展出的平衡”(Chen 139)。

雌雄同体这一概念自古有之,现在常常被解读为性别上的中间平衡状态,被认为是消解了传统男女二元对立的最好证明。但实际上,“在古代,雌雄同体并不是指男性和女性的平均融合”(Conway 79–80),而是将弱的女性一方归入强的男性一方,将女性男性化。从这一点看,雌雄同体并不代表男性和女性间的平衡,而是让男性和女性都变成重新整合后的男性(Thatcher 150),所以在性别身份问题上,雌雄同体不仅没有解决男女二元对立,反而更说明了这个问题(Glover and Kaplan 48)。

怀特在《特莱庞的爱情》中传达的观念并非是以雌雄同体来应对碎片式的身份。首先,如上所述雌雄同体这一概念本质上并不是强调性别上的平衡,反而是强调男性一方;其次,即便时代赋予了雌雄同体新的含义,从埃迪对自己最后一刻的装扮的态度可以看出,怀特所要追求的也绝不是介于男性和女性中间的所谓平衡状态:最后埃迪决定以男性身份去找格雷文纳,他特意换回男性的服装,但在路上“他看到自己忘了卸掉伊迪丝的妆而感到恶心”(White, *Twyborn* 428)。如果他追求的是男性与女性在自己身上的平衡,那么男性的衣服配上女性的妆容不正好体现了这种“雌雄同体”的状态吗?可他看到自己的这副装扮感到的不是达成了“雌雄同体”的喜悦,而是充满了厌恶,因为他此刻所要做的是一名纯粹的男性,女性的妆容只会让他的男性身份变得不伦不类。

怀特借埃迪之身要向读者传递的是更为后现代的看待身份问题的方法:“拼装”(bricolage)。列维–斯特劳斯(Lévi-Strauss)率先将拼装一词用来形容“神话思维”(mythical thought),不管应对什么样的问题,都可以用同一套有限的手段来处理(Lévi-Strauss 16–17);德里达(Derrida)进一步引申了拼装的含义,将其推广至任何学科,其中也包括了文学批评(Derrida 360);德勒兹(Deleuze)和伽塔利(Guattari)认为精神分裂式的生成方式就是拼装,其特点就是能够以全新的方式来处理碎片(Deleuze and Guattari 7–8)。简单概括起来,拼装并不在乎面面俱到,而是处理好眼前的部分,意义在“拼装者”(bricoleur)眼里并不是永恒不变的,而是临时的、流动的。怀特笔下的埃迪就是一种精神分裂式的存在,埃迪最后对于碎片式身份的选择,不是在男性和女性间找到某种平衡来一劳永逸地解决所有问题,而是拼装式地处理。埃迪作为拼装者,要处理的问题简单来讲就是做女人(伊迪丝)还是做男人(埃迪),他意识到无法只靠一个身份将自己与母亲和格雷文纳的关系都处理好,于是他放弃全面式地处理问题,转而将问题分开来处理,在母亲面前埃迪选择做母亲的女儿,而在格雷文纳面前选择做他的男情人。埃迪最后找到的完整身份就是这样一种拼装式的身份,面对不同的人以不同的身份出现,他/她的身份不是永恒不变的,而是临时的、流动的,这也就是怀特透过《特莱庞的爱情》所要传递的后现代视角下处理身份问题的方法。

参考文献

[1] Björkstén, Ingmar. *Patrick White: A General Introduction.* Trans. Stanley Gerson. Queensland: University of Queensland Press, 1976.

[2] Blamires, David. "Patrick White: The Twyborn Affair." Critical Quarterly 22.1 (1981):79.

[3] Blass, Rachel B. *The Meaning of the Dream in Psychoanalysis.* New York: State University of New York Press, 2002.

[4] Bliss, Carolyn. *Patrick White's Fiction: The Paradox of Fortunate Failure.* London: Macmillan, 1986.

[5] Butler, Judith. *Gender Trouble.* New York: Routledge, 1999.

[6] Chen, Hong. "Sexuality in Patrick White's Fictions." Diss. East China Normal University, 2006.

[7] Conway, Colleen M. *Behold the Man: Jesus and Greco-Roman Masculinity.* New York: Oxford University Press, 2008.

[8] Deleuze, Gilles, and Felix Guattari. *Anti-Oedipus: Capitalism and Schizophrenia.* Trans. Robert Hurley, Mark Seem, and Helen R. Lane. Minneapolis: University of Minnesota Press, 2000.

[9] Derrida, Jacques. *Writing and Difference.* Trans. Alan Bass. London and New York: Routledge, 2005.

[10] Emerson, Ralph Waldo. *The Essential Writings of Ralph Waldo Emerson.* Ed. Brooks Atkinson. New York: The Modern Library, 2000.

[11] Glover, David, and Cora Kaplan. *Genders.* London and New York: Routledge, 2005.

[12] Hu, Yijun. "The Death of Man — the Collapse of Subjectivism in *The Twyborn Affair*." Diss. Shanghai University of International Business and Economics, 2007.

[13] Kundera, Milan. *The Art of Novel.* Trans. Linda Asher. New York: Grove Press, 1988.

[14] Lacan, Jacques. *Ecrits: A Selection.* Trans. Alan Sheridan. London and New York: Routledge, 2005.

[15] Lévi-Strauss, Claude. *The Savage Mind.* Trans. George Weidenfield and Nicholson Ltd. Letchworth: The Garden City Press, 1966.

[16] Rousseau, Jean-Jacques. *The Social Contract.* Trans. Christopher Betts. New York: Oxford University Press, 1994.

[17] Salman, Sherry. "The creative psyche: Jung's major contributions." *The Cambridge Companion to Jung.* Ed. Polly Young-Eisendrat and Terence Dawson. New York: Cambridge University Press, 2008.

[18] Sedgwick, Eve Kosofsky. *Between Men: English Literature and Male Homosocial Desire.* New York: Columbia University Press, 1985.

[19] Thatcher, Adrian. *God, Sex, and Gender: An Introduction.* Chichester: Wiley-Blackwell, 2011.

[20] Trejo, Mary. "The Importance of the Destructive Maternal Figure in Seven Novels by Patrick White." Diss. The University of Tulsa, 1983.

[21] Tyson, Lois. *Critical Theory Today: A User-Friendly Guide.* London & New York: Routledge, 2006.

[22] White, Patrick. *Flaws in the Glass.* London: Jonathan Cape, 1981.

[23] White, Patrick. *Patrick White Speaks.* Leichhardt: Primavera Press, 1989.

[24] White, Patrick. *The Twyborn Affair.* London: Jonathan Cape, 1979.

[25] Xu, Kai. "Strangers in A Solitary Land: Contextualizing Eccentricity in Patrick White's Fiction." Diss. East China Normal University, 2005.

[26] 曹卫东．从"全能的神"到"完整的人"．文学评论，2003(6): 172.

[27] 黄源深．视角·感悟．上海：上海外语教育出版社，2010 年．

[28] 克拉吉斯．文学理论．上海：上海外语教育出版社，2009 年．

[29] 吴宝康．死亡与重生——浅析《特莱庞的爱情》中的生存悲剧．王光林．澳大利亚文化研究．第一辑．上海：上海外语教育出版社，2014 年．

[30] 徐凯．作为隐喻的性别含混——论帕特里克·怀特的《特莱庞的爱情》．当代外国文学，2005(2)：73–74.

[31] 杨洁．酷儿理论与批评实践．北京：中国社会科学出版社，2011 年．

刘金龙，上海对外经贸大学国际商务外语学院英语语言文学方向研究生。

Hero and Tragedy:
An Analysis of Sybylla Melvyn in *My Brilliant Career*

Li Fangtao

Abstract: *My Brilliant Career*, published in 1901, is the first and also the most influential work of Australian writer Miles Franklin (1879–1954). It depicts a "new woman image" which represents an ambitious, imaginative, rebellious bush girl and genuinely reflects the late 19th century Australia. She rebels and fights but fails to get out of the colonial women's miserable life without any patriarchal persecution. She is reproached and excluded by public. She is left lonely and helpless and is nearly on her breakdown. She is a brave warrior of feminism, but still another tragic character of patriarchy.

Key words: Miles Franklin; *My Brilliant Career*; patriarchy; characteristics; feminism

摘要：《我的光辉生涯》(*My Brilliant Career*) 于1901年出版，是澳大利亚著名女作家迈尔斯·弗兰克林（Miles Franklin, 1879—1954）的成名之作，小说塑造了一个雄心勃勃、充满幻想、追求独立人格并富有反叛精神的"新"女性形象。这一形象是新一代的澳洲丛林女性形象，真实地反映了澳大利亚19世纪末期的社会风貌。她叛逆、斗争，却始终未能摆脱她所一直逃离的女人的悲惨命运。她离经叛道，遭受社会和传统的孤立，备受孤独的煎熬，始终挣扎在崩溃的边缘。西比拉是女权主义无畏的战士，却也是父权制时代下的另一个悲剧角色。

关键词： 迈尔斯·弗兰克林；《我的光辉生涯》；父权制；性格；女性意识

1. Introduction

My Brilliant Career successfully depicts a bush girl Sybylla Melvyn with unique characteristics growing from an unbridled tomboy to an ambitious woman. She is brave and independent. She strives only to be herself. Though the same spirit can be found in previous notable English novels such as *Jane Eyre* or *Pride and Prejudice*, *My Brilliant Career* still holds its unique pioneering state in the literary history of Australia with the construction of female image neither as a prostitute nor a housewife. Marriage has always been considered as the ultimate fulfillment and integration of a woman into the so-called conventional family. However, the characterization of Sybylla in this novel does not end with a marriage as Elizabeth Bennet or Jane Eyre who all settle for marriage. What makes the novel of great significance not only lies in the novel itself but also in the fact that it has greatly accelerated to the development of women's movement.

Throughout history, Australian women writers have made their great efforts for the claim of women's right and status through more and more participation in various affairs of social, economic, cultural and political fields. The late nineteenth century and early twentieth century have witnessed the first wave of women's movement in Australia. Meanwhile, feminist literature starts to emerge. Those women writers struggled and stumbled but never hesitate in their efforts to cultivate and explore new space for the improvement of women's literary condition. They have been persisting in their strenuous and arduous endeavors to tell about women's experiences. It is with the brave female writers' unremitting efforts that more and more works have come into being dealing with the profound interpretation of women's status in the system and women's issues in their professional area or personal lives. The works have been the century-long accumulation of life experiences of women and reflect the real situations in which women survive.

Miles Franklin, one of Australia's pioneering female writers, made her presence on the literary stage with her highly acclaimed maiden work *My Brilliant Career* which emphasizes the pains and afflictions women have suffered in life as well as in mind.

Since *My Brilliant Career* was first published in 1901, it has drawn great attentions from a number of readers as well as critics home and abroad. In the preface of the novel, Henry Lawson writes: "the description of bush life and scenery came startlingly, painfully real to me, and I know that, as far as they are concerned, the book is true to Australia — the truest I ever read." (Franklin 8) The famous Australian literary critic A. G. Stephenson comments the novel as "the first Australian novel" (Ken 54). For a time, this novel was lauded for its portrait of Australia while the feminism and socialism were ignored or omitted. Now, the novel is more intended to be interpreted from the perspective of feminism. For example, *My Brilliant Career and Feminism* by Susan Magarey provides a feministic perspective to the career background of Miles Franklin and to the role of the protagonist in the work. Jill Roe commented that "the full story of women's writing in Australia has yet to be told, but when it is, Franklin will be pivotal, touching four generations. She was perhaps the first to draw attention to the tradition of women's writing" (Roe 9). What's more, some foreign scholars also pay much attention to Franklin's this great work from sociological and historical perspectives.

Studies of Miles Franklin in China are still in the early stage and have not been so fruitful comparatively. But it is encouraging to see that there have been an increasing number of papers and researches on Franklin each year. It is well worth mentioning that the notable achievements gained by Huang Yuanshen have been pushing ahead Franklin studies in China. Since his translation of *My Brilliant Career* published in 2007, quite a few influential papers and researches have been conducted at home. And there are also some articles being found with various topics such as rebellious spirit, distorted character and autobiographical elements and so on.

From above, we can see that there has not been much study on Miles Franklin's *My Brilliant Career* in China. Moreover, the few papers are mainly done in a praising tone to the protagonist's victorious rebellion and free spirit. This article, with given historical and cultural background, intends to uncover the roots of Sybylla Melvyn's tragic endings. The findings of the study may have certain limitations to some extent, yet, it pays off if it can offer a kind of implication or enlightenment, little as it is, for any scholar to make further studies or from other perspectives.

2. Formation of Sybylla's Unique Characteristics

In *My Brilliant Career*, Sybylla is ambitious, imaginative, rebellious and full of self-consciousness. To pursue her spiritual dream and artistic longing, she rebels, challenges and fights at all hazards against all the obstacles and barriers on her way to a brilliant future.

From the very beginning, we are attracted by the description of Australia's bush environment. "I can remember the majestic gum-trees surrounding us, the sun glinting on their straight white trunks, and falling on the gurgling fern-banked stream, which disappeared beneath a steep scrubby hill on our left" (Franklin 1). "The bold and unstrained bush environment not only gives her spacious independent time and spiritual support, but also has a great influence on the development of her characteristics." (杜 37)

Sybylla's father Richard Melvyn takes possession of Bruggabrong, Bin Bin East and Bin Bin West, in which Sybylla has lived a happy life. It is exactly in this place where Sybylla forms her boyish characteristics. When she is still a small kid, her father would take her everywhere, which results in her being a "native bushman" and daddy's "little companion" (Franklin 1). Sybylla was brave and courageous. "Fear I knew not. Did a drunken tramp happen to kick up a row, I was always the fist to confront him, and from my majestic and roly-poly height of two feet six inches, demand what he wanted." (Franklin 3) Meanwhile, Sybylla has the chance to meet with people from all kinds of occupations because her father is a "swell in those days" (Franklin 2) — doctors, lawyers, squatters, commercial travelers, bankers, journalists, tourists, and men of all kind. These people unconsciously broaden Sybylla's horizons and cultivate her artistic talents. She also notices the unusual phenomenon that none of these people are women, which buries the seed of gender awareness in her innocent heart.

However, the happy pastoral life of Bruggabrong, Bin Bin East and Bin Bin West does not last long. Sybylla's father conceives the idea that he is wasting his talents by keeping his family rolled up in the small napkin of an out-of-the-way place like Bruggabrong and Bin Bin stations. Therefore, he determines to take up his residence in a locality where he would have more scope for his ability. Thus they move to Possum Gully where he thought he would have made a fortune by raising cows and "dealing in stock" (Franklin 12). Sybylla lives a stagnant life there and her father has soon reduced to a man addicted to alcohol. Before long, they become penniless. "Summer is fiendish, and life is a curse." (Franklin 21) Sybylla has never been so longing for arts in her life.

At Possum Gully, like the other Australian bush woman, Sybylla has to "do everything. They do all the milking and pig-feeding, and poultry rearing" (Franklin 11). Sybylla becomes more and more dissatisfied with the monotonous lifestyle and grows more interested in poems and music.

> *There was a third part in me which cried out to be fed. I longed for the arts. Music was a passion with me. I borrowed every book in the neighborhood and stole hours from rest to read them. In it I lived a dream-life with writers, artists, and musicians. (Franklin 17)*

Through extensive reading, Sybylla has learned every celebrity in the fields of literature, arts, music and theatre. The more she reads, the more dissatisfied she is with the stagnant living states of Possum Gully and more wants to enter the world of arts. Unfortunately, her dreams of arts are too far away from reality. During the long years of drought, she has to save the dying cows with her family, which leads to her endless weariness. In the chapter of "A DROUGHT IDYLL", Sybylla uses "weariness" eighteen times to express her exhaustions from the labor. The "weariness" is a desperate cry from the depths of a fifteen-year-old bush girl's heart. It is indeed a horrible scene: The sky is full of dust and hot wind. The ruthless sun burned the soil and rocks. To a young girl, it is hell.

The tiredness from the heavy farm work and all-day laboring constantly makes her depressed. The unbearable life makes her feel suffocated and nearly in the state of hysteria and frustration. She could not reconcile herself to a life full of hardship and poverty, for she has a dream of being a brilliant writer. In the severe natural environment, to lead a materially rich and safe life is nothing more than a life-long hope and considered as great blessing for most common bush people. Yet, Sybylla is the exception. She strives for her brilliant dream — to be a writer. Therefore, the unchangeable reality and living condition may serve as the external reason for Sybylla's rebellion.

Living in a patriarchal society, women are inferior to men. Men tend to consider themselves as the undoubting power and women as the unpaid servants doing household chores. In their domain, men are manipulative and engulfing narcissists, who hate retorts and demands uttermost respect and submission from their women. Females, as a result, suffer in an atmosphere of sexual repression and male tyranny. "In Australian cultures, women have no position in social relation" (Schaffer 149). "If there was a budding Madame Curie, or a female Pasteur or Einstein, or a Charlotte Bronte, in Australia, she'd still be compelled to be a charwoman; it's the supreme preoccupation of my country women" (Modjeska 177). Therefore, the concerns of the patriarchal oppression can be illustrated with unusual clarity. A woman is being the submissive role of the society where the male dictates.

As for Sybylla, her father served as the decision maker of the family. Father is always the director and the pillar. When Sybylla is still a kid, she would ride among the musterers as gamely as any of the big sunburnt bushmen. Her mother strongly opposes to this kind of behavior for fear of her growing into a "great unwomanly tomboy" (Franklin 3) while her father ignores the idea and tells his wife Lucy to "Let her alone, let her alone." (Franklin 3) Later, the whole family has to move to Possum Gully for his father decides to seek livelihood there. Other family members have no say in this family; her father makes all the decisions for the whole family. Even when they are in debt, her father, though lack of capability, stands for patriarchy in a household that possesses the dictator's voice unconditionally. Sybylla knows that life would never get changed and things never be different from the past without resistance and challenges. Therefore, rebelling comes to be a way to defend and search other possibilities.

Nothing changed, nothing gained. Sybylla's experience shows that the traditional old admonition and stale infusion could be questioned and must be questioned if we are to find a way for selfhood. To overcome the ordeal, to fulfill the odyssey, the heroine has to stay strong and toughen up facing various kinds of challenges.

For Sybylla, family seems to be the key factor in forming the characteristics of her, especially in the value of marriage she holds on to. Two people, her father — Richard Melvyn and her mother — Lucy Bossier, have a great influence on her.

Sybylla's father, Richard Melvyn, is used to be a swell in those days of Bruggabrong, Bin Bin East and Bin Bin West. Sybylla's early memories of his father are full of affection. "Richard Melvyn, you were a fine fellow in those days! A kind and indulgent parent, a chivalrous husband, a capital host, a man full of ambition and gentlemanliness." (Franklin 4) However, it is exactly this man who in the end breaks the unity and destroys the whole family. Sybylla's father is heavily addicted to alcohol which leads the whole family into deterioration and degradation owing lots of debts and surviving on the breadline. Her father is not the adored daddy any more who had been once with great consciousness and sense of responsibility. He is now dulled and diluted in the poisonous alcohol. He accepts the breakdown and poverty with cowardliness even without any struggling or little regret. Sybylla blames her father for the degradation of the home and says that her father "was a despicable, selfish, weak creature, and as such I despised him with the relentlessness of fifteen, which makes no allowance for human frailty and weakness" (Franklin 15). In order to find a way out, she had to be independent and self reliant.

Sybylla's mother, Lucy Bossier, used to be an elegant, sweet, charming and happy woman. But due to a series of poor business decisions by her husband, the whole family is reduced to subsistence level, losing all the property and prestige they have ever enjoyed. Even worse, with her frustrated husband drinking excessively, the family gets into heavy debt. Living in the rural outback of Australia and struggling with the drought and monetary problems, mother Lucy was forced to take over the responsibility of being the bread owner and sustain the whole family. She is struggling with tough life and trying every day to make ends meet. Washing, sewing, poverty, ignorance of her husband and the overburden on her gentle weak shoulder have deprived of all her gracefulness and dignity. She became increasingly strict to Sybylla, mainly because of Sybylla's failure to fulfill the traditional duty of a woman. She has difficulty in understanding Sybylla's untraditional behaviors and often ends up with fights with Sybylla. She claimed Sybylla as a "perfect she-devil" and "mad" (Franklin 27). Once, after a big fight with her mother, there are three things in her head — "a pain of swollen eyes, a heavy pain, and a fixed determination to write a book" (Franklin 29). In a sense, the conflicts between Sybylla and her mother also serves as some kind of catalyst of Sybylla's writing.

3. Feminism in Sybylla

All the natural, social, and family elements form Sybylla's unique characteristics, which result in her revolting against the traditional conventions and pursuing her own dreams in spite of the pressures she receives from her family members and social peers. She is the perfect epitome of feminism.

Sybylla Melvyn is an imaginative, headstrong young woman, dreaming to become a well-known writer. She is thirsty for writing and craves for literature and creation. She spends a great deal of time reading, tasting and producing those literary works, feasting her eyes on the words and feeling the deepest pleasure in the world. She could find a sense of power and privacy in her writing and allow her imagination to express herself who would not comply with the values of male-dominated system. Writing benefits her with the strong force to resist social traditions and seductions.

For Sybylla, literature is a means to tell the truth about her thoughts and passion. She expects, in this form, to get her world existed and recognized by both men and women. Her behavior implies that mankind has the internal thirst to construct and create. Her pursue of writing is both the symbol and the illustration of her liberated subjectivity. More to the point, it is a construction of herself as a liberated agent.

At that time, writing is conducted exclusively by men. A woman is not supposed to pursue writing or she will be punished as a violator. In order to be a writer, Sybylla writes at the cost of her sleeping time. She "sneaked out of bed every night at one or two o'clock to write a prodigious novel in point of length and detail" (Franklin 29). She sends her book to the leading Sydney publisher, but what she receives is a polite memo to the effect that "the story showed great ability, but the writer's inexperience was too much in evidence for publication" (Franklin 29). However, instead of discouraging her, this experience motivates her to write another book.

Sybylla differs much from other traditional women in that she holds different attitude and perception towards the conventional marriage. Three tragic marriages — her own mother's, her aunt's and Mrs M'Swat's, have enforced her decision of opposing to marriage. Sybylla has seen enough the sorrows of women and perceives well the constriction and affliction life imposes on women. She tries to escape the destiny of traditional women who are miserably dependent on men for emotion and finance. Sybylla comes to examine her relationship with men in her communication and develops her own perception of love, marriage, liberty and individualism through the accumulation of social knowledge and life experience.

First of all, because of the marriage, mother Lucy "was roughened and temper-soured by endless care and an unavailing struggle against poverty" (Franklin 45). She is now bony, sad and angry. Mother loses youth, freedom, and energy and sacrifices all valuable things as a woman. "Marriage has turned an angel into a miserable woman" (陈 2). Sybylla is afraid that "mother's world is the daughter's future world in the future" (Eichenbaum and Orbach 86) and fears to repeat her mother's destiny. She resolves to give up marriage and resists being another domestic servant.

Aunt Helen is "one of the most beautiful and lovable girls in Australia" (Franklin 49). Although she doesn't need to work as hard as her sister Lucy, Helen bears a worse marriage. She adores and falls in love with Colonel Bell who had come to her town on a visit and married him in some part of America. But tragedy occurs to her no more than one year when she is still immersed in her ideal husband. The Colonel is "tired of his lovely bride, and becoming enamored of another woman; he therefore deserted her and openly lived with the other woman as his mistress" (Franklin 49). She was forced to return home. "Her life was wrecked. She had been humiliated and outraged in the cruelest way by the man whom she loved and trusted. He had turned her adrift, neither a wife, widow, nor maid" (Franklin 49). Lucy goes through spiritual affliction and humiliation because of marriage. Realizing what Aunt Helen has suffered and afraid of being another sorrow Aunt, Sybylla makes her firm resolution not to marry.

Another representative victim of marriage is Mrs M'Swat, who is the hostess and also the renter when Sybylla serves in Barney Mountain as a tutor to pay for her family debt. The first impression Mrs M'Swat gives Sybylla is that she is "a great, fat, ignorant, pleasant-looking woman, shockingly dirty and untidy" (Franklin 170). However, "most peasant mothers with a family of nine have no time for idleness, but Mrs M'Swat managed things so that she spent most of the day rolling on her frowsy bed playing with her dirty infant" (Franklin 179). It seems that she is quite satisfied with her life. However, because of her ignorance and self-contentedness, she is unable to realize she is nothing more than a man's slave as a productive tool. Married women's situation was just comparable to the cow, usually bearing ten to twelve children in their life.

Traditional marriage is like "a gold chain that has fettered women and turned them into the appendage of men" (黄 186). Having witnessed the miserable marriages around her and the bitter cost women have paid for their marriages, Sybylla is more and more aware of the misery marriage brings to a woman, so she became pessimistic about marriage.

In Sybylla's life, three men, Frank Hawden, Everard Grey and Harold Beecham are the three options for her to marry. However, marrying to anyone of the three men means the deprivation of freedom and selfhood. To win freedom and to gain independence, she is never to marry any men.

The shepherd Frank Hawden is one of Sybylla's adherers with little character but with essence of patriarchal social values in personality and behavior. Being a great admirer of beauty, he is ready all the time for condescending towards any young girls. That is why he is the easiest to decline. When he proposes to Sybylla, he says "when I am twenty-four, I will come into my property in England. It is considerable, and at the end of that time I want to marry you and take you home" (Franklin 70). He views his property as the most lure for Sybylla, which inevitably shows his superiority over her. However, his property, to Sybylla, is nothing. She scorns at his showing off and considers his speech really childish and annoying. The very thought of marrying him makes her disgusting and even shameful. In her view, he is just a playboy who falls in love with any girl, on an average, about twice a week. Although he is going to inherit a big fortune to be a millionaire, Sybylla doesn't care. While money is always the pillar of traditional marriage, Sybylla insists that true love should not be established on money. She has her own faith for love: "If a man was a lord or millionaire I would not have him if I loved him not, but I would marry a poor cripple if I loved him." (Franklin 154) She refuses him without regard to her Grandma's lots of persuasion, declaring "I would not marry him or any one like him though he were King of England. The idea of marriage even with the best man in the world seems to me a lowering thing" (Franklin 72).

The second man making a proposal to Sybylla is Everard Grey from Sydney. In Sybylla's eyes, he is not only handsome and charming but also a gentle man who is good at art, music and literature. He is full of wisdom and artistic sense. His humor could bring her a great joy and she really likes talking and making friends with such kind of man. More importantly, he much values Sybylla's art talent and intends to take her to Sydney for further development. However, a conversation Sybylla overhears between Aunt Helen and Grey changes her attitude and feeling towards Grey. In the conversation, he reveals his intention to marry Sybylla, which is believed to be a best way to establish her reputation on literary stage and also can remove any scandals of a single girl along with a man. This causes Sybylla feel extremely uncomfortable and a sense of being dominated. She is averse to be despised and even to be conquered by anyone. She could not bear this kind of inequality in the soul of love even if she likes him.

In *My Brilliant Career*, Sybylla's relationship with Beecham seems to be the most intriguing part, reflecting, in a sense, the general pattern of gender relationship in the Australian colonial society. Disgusted by Frank Hawden and unsatisfied with Everard Grey, Sybylla has a different and nearly obsessive feeling toward Beecham who attracts her much in quite a few aspects.

On her first sight, Sybylla is held captive by the appearance of Beecham.

> *He was a young man — a very young man, a bushman — tremendously tall and big and sunburn, with an open pleasant face and chestnut moustache — not at all an awe — inspiring fellow, in spite of his unusual, though well-proportioned and carried, height. (Franklin 76)*

And more favorable description on the appearance of Beecham can be found as following.

> *He had washed, combed his stiff black hair, and diverted himself of his hat, spurs, and whip — his leggings has perforce to remain, as his nether garment was a pair of closely fitting grey cloth riding breeches, which clearly defined the shapely contour of his lower limbs. (Franklin 76)*

Besides his attractive handsome appearance, Sybylla is also fascinated by Beecham's distinctive characteristics. He is intelligent, capable and courageous. Manly but gentle, in Sybylla's mind, he is almost an ideal and perfect lover. In comparison with other suitors, Beecham can be said to be the only eligible man to win the heroine's heart and the only one to be seriously considered for marriage. However, what really makes Sybylla hesitates and withdraws when coming to marriage is her trip to Beecham's home Five-Bob Town. In his own domain, she recognizes that the gentle and polite Beecham is in virtue as manipulative and dictatorial as other colonel men. He could not be the exceptional one. "He has a roaring deny on disobedience. Everyone has to obey him like winkie or they can take their beds up and trot off quick and lively." (Franklin 118) That is a man, underlying all those charming personality with strong notion of male privileges and conventional doctrines which perceive women to be used and be served. He can be generous enough to concede to Sybylla some male tolerance, nevertheless not the kind of liberty Sybylla really desires for.

When she eventually and resolutely terminates her ambiguous attitudes towards marriage, Sybylla does not merely disengage her from the unproductive spiritual tangle, but also successfully walk out of the fantasy she has been enchanted in. In this sense, the fact that Sybylla gives up marriage stands for a significant phase of her personal development. Her every encounter, trivial as it is, tends to re-enhance Sybylla's view of herself and encourage her to search her own inner-world. Virtually, her renunciation to marriage means that she has been able to go beyond her old self and face her future with faith, courage, optimism and witticism.

4. Miserable Ending of Sybylla

In the harsh environment of male-dominated country, colonial women are ignored, submerged and subjected both at family and in society. It follows that careers are never impossible to have a full integration into the part of Sybylla's lives. Women always play a kind of assistant role in work which is nothing more than a means for survival.

At last, Sybbyla goes back to Possum Gully where she probably spends the rest of her life. Possum Gully is as poor as before and life is as hard as usual. Millions of grasshoppers "had devoured many of the trees by eating the bark, and now they were stripping the briers of foliage" (Franklin 219). Sybylla has to live as a peasant laboring day and night, with no books and newspapers. She lives as a peasant but refuse to be benighted as a peasant. She never stops her pursuit of the life she has always been dreaming of. However, her turning down of Beechem's proposal breaks her last chance to have all those things she has been pursuing. Finally reality has gradually wiped out all her passions. She has to face up her own decisions and live a painful life.

This sorrow ending illustrates that how powerless and incapable a female is in the ruthless patriarchal milieu. Although she may be proud and arrogant with great ambition, she is destined to be submitted to the male dominated ideology.

In most people's eyes she does not fulfill the task a traditional woman should do. All her friends and acquaintances are appalled and repelled by her such determination. She is destined to be isolated from public acceptance and to lead a lonely spiritual life forever. Loneliness is a terrible price to pay for independence, as every step in the way to self actualization will have a painful price to pay. That is the unavoidable punishment from patriarchal system and the payment for being refractory. Since to be both a woman and free man in her environment is simply out of the question, she has to make a choice.

Hard as it be, she is quite firm about her determination compared to those sufferings all the married women stand.

Sybylla's career is never to be brilliant. She eventually understands that freedom she has been striving for can only be temporary or transient. She knows well what being a girl entails. Sybylla sees well enough that even time is biased against women, which is viewed to be fair to everybody. Sybylla writes in *My Brilliant Career* to comment on women's circumstances: "Time rules us all. And life, indeed, is not the thing we planned it out, ere hope was dead; And then, we women cannot choose our lot." (Franklin 230)

5. Conclusion

My Brilliant Career ends with Sybylla choosing to stay single and eventually turning to writing as her career. The resolution is all for earning freedom and control of life which she values and relishes beyond anything else. While the novel upholds some aspects of the heroine's individuality and freedom, it apparently indicates how Sybylla is tormented due to patriarchy persecution. She tried to construct her own worlds in hostile circumstances through reforming her own realities and dreams. "Sybylla does not recover, however, the point is that because of the deeply engrained patriarchy of her nationalistic society, she can never be successful Australian artist, or, by extension, a happy person, but remains isolated, a creature without a sphere" (Hamelin 140). Because of the clashes between the ambitious girl's desired world and patriarchal norms, her assertion and positioning of herself in the landscape is miserably followed by great punishment and pain, both physically and mentally. She is torn between conforming to society's expectations and rejecting them as unfair.

None of women in *My Brilliant Career* can "escape the limitations of their gender" (Bird 176). Lucy is a victim of a hard life; Helen is a silent wife towards betrayal; Mrs M'Swat is a productive tool of man; Sybylla is a lonely rebel in frustration. All of them are isolated, perplexed, trapped within an institution or a society which seems a temporary residence or imprisonment, but from which there is no escape. They are the representatives of the fringe dwellers who attempt to register and possibly to reconcile a perplexing dilemma.

Through the analysis of the novel, the predicaments of women are clearly revealed. Miles Franklin is appealing to the society that more attention should be paid to the situation of women and more efforts should be done to realize the equality between man and woman and among different social classes.

References

[1] Bird, Delys. "Review of *Tirra Lirra by the River* by Jessica Anderson". *Westerly*, 4(1980): 78–80.

[2] Eichenbaum, Luise, and Susie Orbach. *Understanding Women.* Middleesex: Penguin, 1983.

[3] Franklin, Miles. *My Brilliant Career.* London: Virago Press, 1980.

[4] Hamelin, Christine. *Gender Mapping Genre Studies in Female Kunstlerromane from Canada, Australia and New Zealand.* PhD Diss. Queen's University, 1994.

[5] Ken, Goodwin. *A History of Australian Literature.* New York: St. Martin's Press, 1986.

[6] Modjeska, Drusilla. *Exiles at Home: Australian Women Writers, 1925–1945.* Sydney: Harper Collins Publishers Australia, 2001.

[7] Roe, Jill. "For Australians Only." *London Review of Books*, 10(1988): 9.

[8] Schaffer, Kay. *Women and the Bush: Forces of Desire in the Australian Culture Tradition.* London: Cambridge University Press, 1988.

[9] 陈茂庆．反抗婚姻的丛林少女．西华大学学报．2007(2): 1–6.

[10] 社学增．澳大利亚语言与文化．北京：外语教学与研究出版社，2000 年．

[11] 黄源深．澳大利亚文学史．上海：上海外语教育出版社，2002 年．

[12] 迈尔斯·弗兰克林．我的光辉生涯．黄源深译．上海：上海译文出版社，2007 年．

李方涛，华东师范大学澳大利亚研究中心 2014 级研究生。

诗是否可译?
——以《窗口：当代澳大利亚诗歌——中英双语选集》[1]为例

陶乃侃

摘要： 本文旨在廓清诗歌可译性之问题。正如德莱顿、珀兹，不少著名的诗人兼翻译家都怀疑并倾向否认诗歌翻译，而诗歌从古至今一直被翻译，为此诗能否译实为一悖论。然而，问题的症结并不在于诗歌能否翻译，而在于诗歌翻译中的散失。德莱顿视译者为"仆人"，而巴斯奈特则强调翻译中的"创造"精神，并针对翻译讨论中惯于过分强调翻译的"散失"的倾向指出翻译亦有所"获取"。本文进而探讨诗歌翻译的得失这一关键问题。在指出由一源语文本转译为宿语文本中，原文的押韵，音律节奏等声音特质有所散失，同时也展示翻译的某些重要语言、文化的获取。诗歌翻译的得失皆以我翻译当代澳大利亚诗歌选集的某些实例论证。

关键词： 诗歌的可译性，直译与意译，苏姗·巴斯奈特的理论，当代澳大利亚诗歌

Is Poetry Translatable?
— Translating *Open Window: Contemporary Australian Poetry*
—*A Chinese-English Bilingual Anthology*

Tao Naikan

Abstract: This paper attempts to clarify the issue of the translatability of poetry. However, the question whether poetry is translatable is a paradox because while quite a few renowned poet-translators like Dryden and Paz tend to deny the translation of poetry, poetry has been translated from ancient to present. The key point of the issue is not whether poetry is translatable, but what gets lost in the translation of poetry. Dryden sees the translator as servile, yet Bassnett emphasizes the "creative" spirit in translation, and points out "gain" in the translation against the persistent tendency to overemphasize on "loss" in translation in discussions of translation. This paper hence focuses on the key issue of "loss and gain" in the translation of poetry. As it proceeds to reveal the loss of sound qualities of the original in transferring a SL text to a TL text, it also displays some significant gains in the translation. All this is demonstrated and justified with concrete cases in my translation of an anthology of contemporary Australian poerty.

Key words: the translatability of poetry, direct translation and free translation, Susan Bassnett's theory, contemporary Australian poetry

1 该书即将由上海三联出版社出版。

当我们面对诗歌可译性这一问题时，我们似乎在面对一个似非而是的现象。正像贞·韦伯与保罗·赫瑟林顿在《序言》中谈及那样，不少像约翰·德莱顿、奥克塔维欧·帕兹那样的名人都十分怀疑诗歌翻译，并倾向否认诗歌翻译的可能性。这不由得让我们想到罗伯特·弗洛斯特那句有名的话："诗是翻译中丧失的东西。"弗洛斯特由此而否定了诗歌的可译性。然而事实却是从古到今诗歌一直被翻译。我相信人们从孩提时代起就涉及两种文学：本国文学与世界文学，前者是汉语写的作品，后者是译成汉语的世界名著。因此多数人从年青时就开始阅读由多种文字翻译而成的作品，例如荷马、萨福、奥维德、卡图卢斯、维吉尔、但丁、莎士比亚、歌德、波德莱尔、马拉美、聂鲁德等。此外还有现代汉语翻译的《诗经》、《罗摩衍那》和《贝奥武夫》等。在我习得足以阅读原文的英语之前，正是通过阅读汉语的翻译作品我才认识了乔叟、弥尔顿、彭斯、雪莱、布朗宁、济慈、柯勒律治、华兹华斯、叶芝等最著名的英国诗人；以及最著名的美国诗人，例如惠特曼、狄金森、弗洛斯特、金斯伯格、艾略特和庞德等。每个时代都有人在翻译诗歌，每个时代都有人在阅读翻译的诗歌并受其影响。人们从翻译名著所汲取的并不少于从本民族文学所汲取的，这恐怕是难以否认的事实。

那么问题的关键并不是诗能否翻译，而是诗在翻译过程中会丧失什么。这才是真正令诗人兼翻译家的德莱顿和帕兹烦恼的症结所在。当他们强调诗歌的隐晦和非确定性时，他们忽视了诗歌较为本质的方面：叙事性以及对历史与神话的记录（如《荷马史诗》），或反映社会和民风习俗的诗歌的社会功能（如《诗经》）。《诗经》是中国最早的民歌民谣及匿名文人诗作的结集，相传为孔子编辑，其实是春秋时代君王令乐府乐官于公元前 7—11 世纪收集而成的，因为春秋诸侯（及汉武帝）均认为民歌民谣记录了反映对王权统治的民众舆论（吴 7-8）。诸如此类的诗，又如《圣经》中的赞美诗，一般而言，主要传达一种信息，即一个事件、一个念头、一种思想或情绪。如果这种信息可以翻译，那么诗大体上是能翻译的。

德莱顿如此强调翻译的忠实以致在他对"直译"（metaphrase）的定义中，如韦伯与赫瑟林顿在《序言》中指出，将译者的角色贬为"仆人式的"（2）。以此而论，译者便被看作只为一个主人工作的仆人，即原文的作者。但是德莱顿忽略了这一事实：译者同时也为另一位主人工作，译文的读者。因此，与其说是仆人，不如将译者视为一个中间人，既为作者也为读者工作，并且是在源语（the source language）与宿语（the target language）之间工作。假如你采取了一个"仆人式"的译者角色，你必然相当被动地工作，缺少创造精神。而这种"精神"正是为苏珊·巴斯奈特这样的学者所强调的，她认为翻译是"一个创造过程"（15），并也阐述了"译者对宿语读者的职责"（32），这是自贺拉斯和西塞罗提出他们对译者角色的看法以来一直在争论的问题（50）。在巴斯奈特看来，译者"既是接受者又是发送者”（45），即先是某一源语文本信息的接受者，然后是通过翻译发送这个信息的人。以此而论，译者便是制造出“一个基于不以字对字而以意对意的原则翻译的宿语版本”（52）的人。就我而言，我宁愿将翻译理解为一个基于被译源语文本的再创造过程；而将译者理解为作者的平行者，或者说作者的对手，为在宿语中寻找同样好的词汇、短语、句型、语调、风格等以表达作者用源语所表达的内容而与作者搏斗。

由于源语与宿语之间的差异，字对字的硬译几乎是不可操作的。因此译者常见于两种方法之间运作，一种一般称作直译（direct translation），即翻译紧紧遵循原文的句法结构，并试图制作出一个尽可能接近原文的宿语文本。另一种是所谓的“自由译”（free translation）。对我而言，“自由”仅限于遣词用字，但是严格地受制于原文的意思及其他主要方面，是一种类似意对意的传统译法，或者德莱顿称之为“意译”（paraphrase）的方法。我认为大多数译者都偏爱直译，因为可以确保对原文的忠实而又不必去冒改变或者曲改原文之险，而且也有允许直译的机遇。我们来看一看保罗·芒登的诗《傻瓜照相机》中的两个诗节实例，并用庞德用来翻译《华夏集》的费那罗萨式的文字图解译法来说明我的翻译方法：

in the rearview mirror	后视镜 hòu shì jìng (*adj.*+ *n.* rearview mirror)		里 lǐ (post. in/inside)	
a snaking black crack	一道 yī dào (one + m.w)	蜿蜒的 wān yán de (*adj.* zigzag)	黑裂缝 hēi liè fèng (*adj.*+ *n.* black crack)	
across the snaking road	横跨 héng kuà (*v.* cross/crossing)	那条 nà tiáo (indicator + m.w. that)	蜿蜒的 wān yán de (*adj.* zigzag)	路 lù (*n.* road)

既然汉语没有冠词这类词，第一行中的定冠词就自然而然省略了，而前置词 in 被作为后置词后移到符合汉语语法的惯用位置。第二行中，每个词都互相吻合，不过英语的名词性词组在翻译时按汉语语法的要求添加了一个量词“道”。第三行也与英语原文基本相吻合，只有一个词性改变，由前置词（across）变为动词分词。但是汉语的形容词“蜿蜒”二字都带有表示昆虫或爬行动物的部首“虫”，巧妙地传达了原文的意象，甚至增添了其视觉效果。然而，译者不会总是这么幸运，总有如此巧合的机遇。每一种语言都有自己的一套法则，都必须遵循其语法规则。这就往往否定了直译法，正如另一诗节的翻译所示：

for the eagle-eyed	一棵	栖息的	树	上
	yī kē	qī xī de	shù	shàng
	(one + m.w. for tree)	(*v.* particle, nested)	(*n.* tree)	(post. on/upon)

a pile of sticks	有	一堆	干枝
	yǒu	yī duī	gàn zhī
	(*v.* there be)	(one pile)	(*adj.+n.* dry twigs)

in a nested tree	等着	那	目光犀利的	飞鹰
	děng zhe	nà	mù guāng xī lì de	fēi yīng
	(*v.* waiting for)	(indic. that)	(*adj.* eagle-eyed)	(*v.* + *n.* flying eagles)

第一行的介词 for 有很多意思，而当这样置于句首，其意似乎留待读者诠释。我因此把它理解为"(wait) for"，同时也把这一行由介词短语转换为动词分词短语。此后我们必须知道什么在等待什么。于是第二行就变成汉语语法要求的主语，而原文的第三行是一介词短语，修饰第二行。在英语中，修饰短语总是置于被修饰成分的后面，但在汉语中，修饰短语必须置于被修饰成分之前。这样一来，整个诗节的顺序就恰好颠倒（即原文的第三行变成译文第一行而原文第一行变成译文第三行）。尽管如此，这一诗节的意思和意象均被保留在汉语文本中。原文的关键词组"the eagle-eyed"蕴含了一个鹰的形象，而这一词组在译作汉语时，鹰的形象可能消失。因此我加上了"飞鹰"以保留这个词组所暗示的鹰的形象。除据汉语语法的要求对这一诗节的行序做重置处理，我在此处仅应用了减词和增词——两种翻译中最常用的方法，只要译者知道何处当增，何处当减。那么这一诗节在翻译中丧失了什么呢？似乎只是首置词 for 对读者诠释的开放被关闭了，因为我在翻译中解释抑或具体化了这个词。但在同时这一诗节也获得一些东西：汉字固有的抑扬声调，以及象形文字的汉语同等词语更为生动的形象。

就我而言，翻译并不是从解码开始，而是从阅读开始：一种新批评式的细读源语文本，即只专注于文本本身而置其社会语境和作者背景不顾；对原文进行逐字逐行的阅读以期既见树木又见森林。因为只有对原文有了细致、准确、全面的理解才能着手翻译，否则，无论辞藻有多美，无论见解有多深，只会误入歧途。假如一首诗超出我的理解，我宁愿放弃而不愿在"翻译"中曲解它。

然而，正如诗被视为"一个有机结构"（Bassnett 85），诗的翻译亦然。对翻译某一方面的过度强调只会造成另一方面的丧失。对译者而言，除了抓住原文的意思外，把握诸如内在精神、风格、韵律、基调等方面亦十分重要。我们再来看几个例子吧。选入本集的诗人中，朱迪·艾尔彼思敦惯于关注自我的内心世界，并由此而观望外部世界。而她的话语常为一种普拉斯式的独白所主导，或者说为女性独白主导，这种独白其实可追溯至宋代著名女诗人李清照，而且也是当代女诗人翟永明所喜爱的手法。另一方面，艾尔彼思敦诗歌中的言说者常以笛卡儿式的自我面目出现，总是在怀疑在探询，有时还自相矛盾，因此有时在与自己争辩，有时在讯问读者。而在音律上，她的诗往往节奏轻快，像摇滚乐或者轻音乐一般，大体上呈现一种紧循英语口语自然声律节奏的非规律诗步。例如：

it is cold　she walks to the corner　vers-	天气寒冷　她走到街角　反面
o recto left right left　turns the corner	正面　左页右页左页　转过街角
thinks about karma　wonders exactly	思考因果报应　认真思忖
which stars are extinct　she steps　stops　forgets	哪几颗星已灭迹　她走　停　忘记
remembers the whole world is dead as a	想起整个世界死寂如一颗门钉
door-nail　shot while it blinked someone said	而被击中　它眨眼的瞬间有人如是说

比较这两个文本可以看出，由于英汉语言的差异，要用同等数量的音节来传达原文的十音节诗行是不可能实现的，要保留原文所有的声音品质亦同样行不通。例如英文的头韵和谐音重叠：“she steps / stops / forgets”（vs. tazou / ting / wangji）；同样难以实现的还有原文的韵脚以及押韵，如首二行所示：“the corner / vers- // o recto / left right left /”（vs. jiejiao / fanmian // zhengmian / zuoyeyouyezuoye / ）.

在这个例子中，原文的意思主导翻译而以牺牲原文声音品质为代价，诗歌翻译中大多实例皆亦然。在这种情况下，译者不能强求声音的等同，而是将其留给自然而然的巧合，正如以上第二例所示，汉语词组自然形成自己的韵脚因而或多或少保留了原文的押韵效果，而不是去刻意追求声音特质并以破坏译文的自然声律和通顺为代价。我在翻译这首诗时，只是去模仿原作的声律节奏，因为我认为声律节奏对它极其重要。就现代诗而言，声律节奏也是至关重要的，因为诗歌已经由韵律决定的古典诗转移到由日常用语的自然声律节奏决定的自由诗。这一点中外亦然。为此，无意中也运用了德莱尔的“模仿”说。

与艾尔彼思敦相反，朱迪斯·贝弗里奇惯于关注外部世界，并将自己的思绪融入周围的自然景物。她的诗因而一方面与澳大利亚的“自然诗”传统（McAuley 6）相关联，另一方面与源于魏晋时期（公元220—589）的山水诗相似。她的诗，有的读来像美妙的抒情曲，并显现出着意追求韵律与语言的音乐效果，如《湖泊》一诗：

At dusk she walks to the lake. On shore	黄昏她走到湖边。湖滩上
a few egrets are pinpointing themselves	有几只白鹭把自己钉
in the mud. Swallows gather the insect lint	在泥沼里。燕子在采集昆虫飞绒

off the velvet reed-heads and fly up through	从毛茸茸的芦苇头上飞起穿过
the drapery of willows. It is still hot.	那些杨柳帷帐的飞绒。天气仍热。
Those clouds look like drawn-out lengths	那些云彩看上去像一段段用夹子……

这首诗每节由三行组成，但每个诗节并不是诗人的思绪单元，而是她的形式框架单元，用以实现诸如押韵、谐音、声律、节奏等声音特值。同时她的思路总是从一个诗节连通到另一个诗节，犹如她一边沿湖畔散步一边在作这首诗，将思想感情融入自然景物之中。这样通过自然景物形象巧妙地与人文艺术、音乐术语的结合而突出诗歌的视觉和听觉效果，例如："几只蝉仍在敲击它们的响板"。一般而言，贝弗里奇的诗作，像中国的山水诗一样，表现了对自然的挚爱，对天人合一的渴求，由此而追求一种宁静美："她的脑里 / 充满宁静的振幅——也许是济慈的宁静"。

翻译贝弗里奇的诗并非易事，要保留她所有的声音特质亦无可能。我只能尽力而为，在翻译中尽量重现她的内在精神和风格，保留她诗节独有的主题线延续和形式框架的特色，用汉语习语和音乐术语使译文贴近她动人的意象和声音特色，用中国古典诗中的词语来提示她独特的古典美。

此外，贝弗里奇的诗作还显现出道德价值：对弱势群体的人道关怀，如《在德里城外火车站台洗身的男子》和《采藏红花的女工》（这两首诗都是用更为个人化的词语和口语风格写成的）以及对社区公益的关怀与参与，如《鲸鱼》一诗。在这首诗中，她并没有炫耀，把处理鲸尸说成是什么大事，而是用平淡而幽默的口吻把它作为一件社区日常生活中的平凡小事来讲述。这样就把这件义务工作表现得真实而符合千万澳大利亚男女共享的国民道德行为。

黛安娜·费荷则采取居于上述两种之间的一种风格。她惯于同时关注内心世界和外在世界，正如《花园肖像》一诗中所言："看着朦胧的光也看着内心——/ 犹如看进群山合抱的一小湖 / 深处：眸子对着苍鹰、浮云、璀璨的星爆"；同时诗人的思想感情强烈地溶化于她从外在世界捕捉的意象，无论是"苍鹰"还是"星爆"，无论是"风"、"海洋"还是"蟑螂"，每个意象都因此独特而富于蕴意。费荷的诗因而往往具有悖论性和隐喻形象性；行文轻快简洁，运韵巧妙而节奏明快，如《海洋》一诗英文所示：

Life rolls towards you, giving and breaking. You hear:
生活朝你滚滚涌来，给予又打碎。你听见：
grief-cries, hunger's anger, despair's numb crash.
悲哀的恸哭，饥饿的愤怒，绝望的麻木撞击。
A torn whisper conjures the ghosts of chance.
破碎的低语化出机遇的幽灵。

> Longing flowers inside its lapse, white
> 渴望之花盛开在自己的过失里，白色的
> foliage rustles ... Sighs from a cloud throat —
> 树叶飒飒响……发自一朵浮云深喉的叹息——

翻译时，我并没有尝试所谓的“音译”，去刻意再现诗人押韵的词语，而是专注于她的悖论性和隐喻形象性这两个诗歌特色，并十分在意她的声律节奏。由于她的诗歌主旨与渗透众多中国诗歌以及道家和儒家思想的“天人合一”的哲学观念相似，我在翻译她的诗时能够感到一种亲切与自信，尤其是翻译这样的诗行“the first sound and the last, both conjoined; / a sound curved as the Tao”（太初和终极的声音，二者相合为一；/一个隆起如道的声音）。一定意义上，我无非是把“道”这个词译回到它的源头，同时在用“太初”（宇宙之初）和“终极”（宇宙之终）这两个词时也为这一行增添了一些文化蕴意。

至此我们可以来审视一下翻译过程中的失与得这一关键问题。对此，巴斯奈特这样评道：“这个问题再次表明翻译的地位如此之低以致这么多的时间需要花来讨论在把一个文本从源语转译到宿语的过程中丧失什么而同时忽略也可能获得些什么这个问题，因为译者往往通过翻译而丰富或者明确那个源语文本。”（36）的确也有这种情况在翻译过程中会失掉一些东西，特别是诸如韵律、谐音、节奏等源语的声音特质。既然一首诗可以是一个文字游戏，或声音游戏，或音和字的游戏，翻译往往顾此失彼，不可能保留原文所有的文字与谐音的特质。例如贝弗里奇的《鲸鱼》一诗中几行：“as big as the Hindenburg blimp. We move out, bumping // over the breakers”。尽管我能看出英文的“blimp”和“bumping”这两个词运用了头韵和谐音，但是要刻意追求汉语的相似声音效果就有可能破坏译文的流畅，甚至改变原文的意思。因此我只是遵循汉语词组的自然节奏律。另外一个例子是双关的运用，如韦伯的诗《四个城市》的诗行所示：

> the earth has been closing over you
> for days. Earth? or its fault lines,

韦伯借用“earth”一词多义中的“土壤”和“地球”二义在此运用了一个双关。然而汉语似乎没有这样一个可以同指此二物的等同词。因此我只有专注于该词的词义而牺牲它的双关蕴意，最终选择用“尘土”译第一行而用“大地”译第二行。不过在处理该诗另一难点时情况有所好转：

> oh and here come the ants.

Take heart, sweetheart, something

与英语习语“take heart”等同的汉语应是“鼓足勇气”，但这个习语跟后面的词“sweetheart”毫无关系。假如我使用它，此二者之间的巧妙游戏及其隐含的幽默感皆丧失殆尽。我因此改用另一习语“鼓起信心”以致能与随后的词“甜蜜的心”关联，通过“心”一词而相互作用而保留原文的谐音效果以及幽默感。但是，这种机遇可遇不可求，由于两种语言的差异，任何刻意追求只会导致某个方面的丧失。

以上英语引文也显示了语调在诗歌中的作用。如“啊，蚂蚁来了”，暗示一种喜悦的惊讶。不同的语调能传达不同的情绪，甚至不同的意思，例如“我恨你”以一种特别的语调说出时意味是“我爱你”，反之亦然。再者从广义来说，正如绘画和作曲，基调建构了一件作品的情感基础。因此语调的蕴意在翻译中应该给与足够的注意。韦伯对基调在诗歌中的作用十分自觉，因而四种不同的基调明显出现在她的诗《四个城市》里：“在布莱顿海滩”一节的基调显现的是一种无忧无虑、欢天喜地的情绪；“在乔治大街”一节的基调显现的是一种懊恼而忏悔的心情；“在克里斯特彻奇”一节的基调显现的是自我振作的情绪以及寄希望于未来；而“秋天，柯林斯街”一节的基调显现的是一种急促感，以及为现代城市生活困惑的心情。正是围绕这四种基调，韦伯呈现了她的意象以及在这四个背景中的个人经历。翻译时，我试图使用蕴意和色彩与她基调相吻合的词语。

毋庸置疑，译者必须是主动的创造性的而非被动的“仆人式”，尤其是在处理含有一般认为“不可译的”成分的情况，诸如本土植物和动物的专用名词。试以朱迪·约翰逊的《在卡瑞卡勒德岛》中的一节为例：

Here, seabirds with the names of bi-planes:
Gillemot, Kittiwake,
twist and turn

我查遍我的词典和网络，却找不到任何有关“gillemot”的汉字，因为中国及其邻近都没有这种鸟。在谷歌查到的“kittiwake”汉语是“三趾鸥”。但考虑到诗人在此强调的是这种鸟的名字的声音，而且英语的鸟名定义也有“大声鸣叫，其声与其名相像”，我因此决定用音译加意译来处理，于是造了“吉乐莫鸟”和“唧啼三趾鸥”二词以传达原文的意思与声音。幸运的是“吉乐”二字不仅传达这个鸟名的声音而且传达鸟的特有形象。同样的方法也用来处理芒登的诗行：“where the wallaby’s head/was lopped by a quoll”。因为查不到任何有关“quoll”的汉字，我只得根据英文的定义自造“白斑野猫”一词来译这个专名。

创造性翻译对处理象声词亦是必须的。我们再来看一个芒登诗的实例：

hello possum!	负鼠，你好！
that hullaballoo on the roof	房顶上那胡拉吧噜的响声
has to be you	一准是你

在此例中，他用的呼语及语调十分重要，传达了一种友谊：把负鼠作为一老朋友来问候。此外，牛津辞典给象声词“hullaballoo”的定义是“a commotion”，而汉语的等同词是“骚动”。与“hullaballoo”相较，这两个词都显得既羸弱又毫无色彩。无论该词的词源是什么，诗人在此着重的是它的声音效果。于是我决定用音译“胡拉吧噜”来模仿该词的声音。出自同样的目的，我也保留了安东尼亚·庞特诗中的象声词：

da-thum da-thum da	哒-吵、哒-吵、哒（da-sha, da-sha, da）
they crack like pods	像豆荚一般爆裂

简言之，我主要用音译加意译的方法来试图保留选集中所有象声词以及诗人企及的声音色彩。

语言与文化的关系如此紧密以致彼得·福朗斯评道：“除非语言渗透于文化的语境，否则不存在语言；除非文化在其中心建构了自然语言的结构，否则不存在文化”（Bassnett 22）。换言之，语言就是文化的载体。当译者选择等同词语——并非完全相同的词语因为“即使在同一文本的两个宿语版本都不存在完全相同的词语，更不用说在源语文本与宿语文本之间”（Bassnett 36）——译者在选择词语把一个源语文本传译到宿语文本时，就有可能将该宿语固有的文化蕴意带进那个宿语文本。于是，选择正确的词，或是福楼拜主张的用词精确（*le mot juste*），其意义对译者而言与对作者一般重要。例如，在处理约翰逊的诗的标题“Wods, after an absence”（词，一段空缺/空白/空闲之后）时，我找到了三个跟“absence”等同的词，因为英语名词倾向于抽象而汉语名词倾向于具体。这三个词属于同义词，但又不尽相同。认真斟酌一番后，我决定选用“空白”，是因为这个词在汉语中诗味较浓，也切合这首诗的语境。以下是同一首诗的另一实例：

Tend the graves of photographs,	祭奠照片的坟墓，
love letters, dried daisies.	回顾情书，以及干枯的雏菊。

英语动词“tend”可用来搭配句中的三个宾语：“graves”，“love letters”和“died daisies”，而放在汉语中就不那么合适，需要用不同的动词搭配不同的宾语。我因此选用“祭奠”搭配坟墓——中国人上坟时一般要供奉祭品，焚香，烧纸钱——而用“回顾”搭配“情书”和“雏菊”。由于语言所载的文化因素，译文自然而然为原文获得一些文化价值。由译文自然获取文化价值同见于对标题“Instanatic”的翻译：“傻瓜照相机”。汉语强调的是这种照相机如此简单连傻瓜都会用，但是这首诗展现的是敏锐的观察以及美妙的视觉和听觉意象，因此译文的标题自然为这首诗获取了一种反讽的意味。此外再举两例，对马斯格雷夫的诗《具体的星期二》中的习语处理：

On such a day as this I wish I was following someone
在如此这般的一天我但愿我在追随某人，

纯属巧合，汉语习语“如此这般”完全吻合英语习语“such ... as this”，所以这是一个译文既无遗失也无获取的例子。但是下一个例子就完全不同：

a set of special horizons in which we zoom about,
一套特别的视界我们在其间蝇营狗苟，

对应英文习语“zoom about”的汉语等同词应是“蝇营”，但这只是汉语习语的一半，另一半是“狗苟”。若用一半，总觉不适。另一半便自然加上译文，同时也加上了汉语迭声独有的音乐效果：蝇营狗苟。更为有趣的一个例子是对贝弗里奇的《黄昏的苍鹭》中一短语的处理：

And look! how they stand — at last — stilled to perfection.
快看！苍鹭站住了——终于——止于至善。

虽然我不能肯定这是不是作者的意图，但这个短语“stilled to perfection”让我想到儒家经典《大学》第一句中的话，“大学之道在明明德，在亲民，在止于至善”。而下一句是“知止而后有定，定而后能静，静而后能安，安而后能虑，虑而后能得。物有本末，事有终始，知所先后，则近道矣”（朱 1）。因此，作为儒家核心思想之一，“止于至善”这一观念是孔子为君子至道而规定的起点与终点。考虑到贝弗里奇表面描写自然和动物，其实是在描写人，我决意用这句话从而为这首诗的译文添加了一个儒家伦理的意味。

致使诗可译的其他重要因素还包括澳大利亚诗人与亚洲作家共享的审美共场。

除贝弗里奇和费荷外，选集中很多其他诗人也都显现出对东方哲学和诗学颇感兴趣。我们于是看到一种对诗画交融的当代追求，例如凯文·布罗菲的《海洋 / 钓鱼》和斯蒂芬·埃德加的《迷失在风景里》，这两首诗精神上都与“诗中有画，画中有诗”的中国传统相似，由唐代诗人兼绘画大师王维（701—761）建立的传统。

此外，埃德加的《迷失在风景里》和布罗菲的另一首诗《橡树·松树·柳树》都显现出对禅诗精神的追求。虽然二人都涉及融我于物来表现自我，但在景物表现上又不尽相同。埃德加显现出一种西方的逻辑思维，在融我于物中仍意识到自我的存在。起先自我迷失于风景（“风攫住树摇撼，/ 而树似乎如此自足 / 而不摇”），但后来自我又被召唤回来（“呼唤他退回去让自己做 / 这幅风景的主人”）。这首诗创造的情境在中国诗学中被称为“有我之境”。布罗菲却显现出类似庄子的物我齐一的观点，因而把自我表现得同房间里的物完全一样以致不见（“房间显得冷漠 / 那些花儿受到损害 / 依然美丽，惊愕得 / 无声无息”）。由于这种移情于物的手法，这首诗创造的情境便是“无我之境”。

除此以外，其他个性化的禅诗尝试还见于艾尔彼思敦的试验诗作，其内容和形式皆显而易见：

— empty sentence — kōan — heavy	——空洞句子——禅家公案——重似
as nothing — words flown the coop	空无——词语潜流出鸟笼
— cicada prison fits precisely what is gone	——蝉狱精确地囚住那飞走之物

以及芒登的意象式诗《偶尔的响声》，尤其是以下一节：

the tell-tale taps	一把榔头倾诉
of a hammer are building	的轻敲正在修建
an identical quiet.	一个同样的宁静。

在此二例中，最本质的诗艺是悖论的效应。艾尔彼思敦的诗似乎在强调诗歌创作中自由与限制，形式与变形的悖论而形式是俳句。芒登的诗让人想起声音使景物更显清静的悖论，此类诗常见于中国古典诗，如《入若耶溪》：“蝉噪林愈静，鸟鸣山更幽”（吴 80）。而芒登的诗妙就妙在仅用“一把榔头”如此平凡的意象就营造了相似的气氛，并且运用了他的西方逻辑思维（“修建一个同样的宁静”）。二者相较，中国诗注重感觉，英文诗注重理性。翻译中，当不以东方感性代替西方理性为宜。

除了曾一度风行中国和日本的禅诗传统外，我们还可以在入选诗人的作品中读到其他东方文化的因素，例如，克里斯平的《情歌》中的藏传佛教教义，贝弗里奇的《在德里城外火车站台洗身的男子》中的印度教教义和观念，布洛克对俳句诗的尝试（未选入），哈斯克尔在《最后一个皇帝》一诗中对当代中国的敏锐观察和尖锐讽刺以及他对李白的兴趣与引用（未选入）。同时，西方文化与传统也渗透了他们的作品，例如，韦伯作品中对希腊神话的隐喻，克里斯、赫瑟林顿、约翰逊等作品中的基督教因素；此外，各种西方诗歌传统的痕迹在入选诗人的作品中也比比皆是。

诚如韦伯和赫瑟林顿指出那样，“选集中每位诗人都有表达自己趣味盎然的方法”（1）。既然内容和形式一定意义上是一个不可分离的有机体，关注一下这些诗人所关心的事物有助于看出他们不同的风格。他们有的志在探索某些永恒主题，如爱情与死亡（两个渗透选集中大多数诗人作品的主导主题），例如克里斯平、马斯格雷夫、韦伯、赫瑟林顿等的作品；有的宁愿探讨当前科技对我们生活的意义，从太空探险（如艾尔彼思敦）到数码技术（如芒登）；有的宁愿探讨目前的社会问题，从环保问题（如拉德）到移民问题（如《外籍人》，《侨民》）；有的选择关注日常生活，专注于自己周围发生的日常事件，从生活流中汲取一个个生活片断，并融入自己的思情，以致揭示一种真实，一种对日常生活的认知及其对我们的意义（如道根和庞特）；甚至创造出日常生活的新世界。

丽莎·戈顿的诗尤其如是。戈顿是个讲故事的好手，并在叙述日常事件中擅长发挥她丰富的想象力。无论是叙述她参观展览的个人经历，还是回忆她童年的一个玩具小偶，还是描述记忆深处的一所房子，她的想象，往往以梦或白日梦为伪装，使日常生活陌生化，并由此创造出新世界和新视角。因此她的诗歌风格独特：叙事与意象相交织，诗意的想象融入对“现实”的描述，真实与超现实相融合，同时以抒情曲的悠扬和音乐的快感娓娓讲述她的故事。

与贝弗里奇的作品一样，塞缪尔·瓦甘·沃森的作品也显现出一种道德价值观，而且一方面回应着津狄沃罗巴克派发现“独具澳大利亚特色的”澳洲现代诗歌传统（Webb and Hetherington 2），另一方面则强调诗歌的教喻功能，约翰·德莱顿所倡导的一个近代英文诗歌传统，在西方可以追溯到古罗马的贺拉斯的诗学，而在东方可追溯到孔子的诗观之一：“诗言教”。一般而言，沃森的诗特色有三：其一，对土著人民和故土的挚爱，其二，视人与其他生物平等（“这个黎明我自己是一生物，并不想去捕猎而是被猎走”），其三，采取他自己的土著文化和土著人民的视角进行创造，如《忏悔》一诗。这些特点使他的作品成为本集中一个不同的心声并为本集增添了土著文化特色。

令我惊喜而难忘的是看到选集中的一些诗人采取简朴而亲切口吻来表述自己的生活际遇。这不由得让我想起中国古代诗人的一大优良传统，如魏晋的阮籍（210—

263）、嵇康（224—263）、陶潜（376—427），唐代的杜甫（712—770）、白居易（772—846）、孟浩然（691—740）等。对这些诗人而言，诗并非什么宏大叙事或者崇高的写作藉以沽名钓誉，而主要是一种日常生活的记录，所谓的“悲欢离合”的诗式笔记。在选集的诗中，也可以读到相似的诗式笔记。例如，布洛克用诗来赞美母亲，道根用诗来记录一次家庭争执，而马斯格雷夫、韦伯、赫瑟林顿、约翰逊等用诗来复活他们对已故亲人的记忆。还有的诗人用诗来减轻对患病亲人的忧虑（如《珈玛》、《化疗之后》、《涨潮：父亲的痴呆症》等），或发泄一种委屈并对挫折进行哲理反思（如《失败的面试》），或从成人的角度反思童年的天真并为唤醒童年回忆的欣喜融入一种智慧，如赫瑟林顿的《爬树》：

> 我们固执的欲望之树，枝叶茂盛，
> 我们欲望有多高就爬多高，
> 心里隐藏些念头响如教堂的晨钟——
> 但唯有我们才听得见欲望刺痛的声音。

简而言之，诗人题旨各异，各有偏爱，形成自己的风格，特色众多故难以概括，也难以在此一一评说，只有留待读者自辨。

就英语文学而言，美国和英国的翻译作品主导着中国读者阅读的文学翻译出版物，而澳大利亚文学的翻译作品在中国仅处于边缘。翻译毕竟是一种跨越语言和文化障碍而有助于扩大深化作者与读者之间交流的手段。假如通过翻译，澳大利亚诗人在境内外的华人社群中得以被接受，我将深感欣慰。翻译一定意义上被视为一种“艺术”，其可能性是无限的。而我对这些诗的翻译是有限的，还有可能出现由我无意识的误读造成的错误。我愿接受读者方家对这类错误的指正，并期待有机会更正。正如一个作家创作的作品就像他的孩子，作为一个译者，一首诗的翻译也就像我的孩子——一个我必须给与特别关照的继养的孩子。至于诗能否翻译，我愿把这一问题留给读者去回答。

参考文献

[1] Bassnett, Susan. *Translation Studies*, London and New York: Routledge, 2002.

[2] McAuley, James. *A Map of Australian Verse*. Melbourne: Oxford University Press, 1975.

[3] Webb, Jen and Paul Hetherington. “Fingering the Devotions”,《窗口：当代澳大利亚诗歌——中英双语选集》序言，Shanghai: SDX Joint Publishing Company, 2014 (forthcoming).

[4] 吴开晋、耿建华编 . 三千年诗话 . 南昌：江西高等教育出版社，1998 年 .
[5] 朱熹编 . 大学、中庸、论语 . 上海：上海古籍出版社，1993 年 .

陶乃侃，澳大利亚学者，研究兴趣为比较文学、诗歌和翻译。

The Politics of Memory: Autobiographical Narratives of Indigenous Child Separation

Xu Daozhi

Abstract: This paper is interested in autobiographical narratives that document and represent experiences of Indigenous child separation from their families. Reconstructing the memories of the Stolen Generations in the form of autobiography is inevitably subject to mechanisms of selection, verification, and commodification within the dominant discourse. However, it is necessary to recognise the agency of Aboriginal people who tactically unsettle the racial ideology and bring into consciousness what has been forgotten by Australian historiography. By examining how memories of child removal have been shaped in public discourse, and exploring Aboriginal authorial agency in recollecting an archive of separation stories, the paper argues that the multi-faceted memories of the stolen children open up a critical space to expose racial injustices and to articulate Indigenous visions of history, plights and rights.

Key words: the Stolen Generations, politics of memory, autobiography, Aboriginal child removal

摘要：本文探讨“被偷走的一代”土著作家的自传体叙述对历史记忆的建构及策略性呈现。土著个体与群体记忆不可避免地受到社会主流话语的影响，包括对主题的选择性接受、叙事真实性的质疑以及商品化的问题。但值得关注的是土著作家如何策略性地颠覆种族意识形态，再现被权威历史刻意遗忘和抹杀的记忆。通过审视“被偷走的一代”记忆的重构过程，本文认为多样性的土著自传体叙述挑战权力话语的束缚，揭露了澳洲社会的种族矛盾与歧视，展现了土著群体的历史观以及争取自身权利的不懈斗争。

关键词：被偷的一代；记忆的政治；自传；强抢土著儿童

In 1995 the Human Rights and Equal Opportunity Commission (HREOC) initiated the National Inquiry into the separation of Aboriginal and Torres Strait Islander children from their families. In May 1997, the *Bringing Them Home* report (hereafter referred to as “the report”) was tabled in Parliament. Unprecedentedly, the issue of the Stolen Generations provoked intense debates around reparation and reconciliation. Much anguish and sorrow, together with guilt and shame, in the public discourse gave rise to a proliferation of Aboriginal autobiographies in remembrance of child removal experiences.

Nevertheless, the Stolen Generations narratives are not a recent phenomenon. Nor is the privileging of autobiography coincidental. According to Bain Attwood, Aboriginal experiences of being separated and institutionalized were documented before the 1980s, when Peter Read first used the term "the Stolen Generations" for Aboriginal children of mixed descent who were forcefully taken away by the authorities; since then the issue of child removal has been brought to light (Attwood 184–185). Aboriginal autobiographical narratives can strike a chord among a general readership, as these first-person, semi-documentary accounts reveal the traumatic tragedy of forcible removal from parents, wrongful treatment by the adoption agencies, physical and sexual abuses, and their difficulties to live on the brink of white settler society. For Indigenous people, the storytelling is "the most fundamental mnemonic act," which makes the pain of forcible removal not only "interpretable" but also psychologically "bearable" (Attwood and Magowan xii).To heal the "historical wound" involves both a remembrance of the past tragedy and a cure of the present pain (Chakarabarty 77). As a matter of fact, Indigenous children of today are still threatened by high rates of domestic violence, sexual abuse, juvenile delinquency and suicide; they continue to be taken away from their families through welfare and juvenile justice systems. These problems are a continued impact of the systematic removal of Aboriginal children from as early as the mid-19th century to the 1970s.[1]The revelation of forcible removal and its devastating impacts unsettles the racial dominance and brings into consciousness what has been neglected by Australian historiography.

Indigenous living memory of child removal experiences is resonant through representation and reinterpretation. To reconcile with the past, nevertheless, is a disturbing process. Edward Said remarks that reflecting on an unsettling history involves "not only of what is remembered but how and in what form. It is an issue about the very fraught nature of representation, not just about content" (176). In this view, this paper is interested in autobiographical accounts of Aboriginal child removal from their families. As I will elaborate shortly, retelling the memories of the Stolen Generations is inevitably subject to mechanisms of selection, verification, and commodification within the dominant discourse, which may counteract or neutralize the resistant power revealed by Aboriginal autobiographical narratives. However, it is equally important to recognise the agency of Indigenous people who may mobilize the liberating moments of enunciation to make their stories heard by Australian public readership. By tracing

---

1 See "Apology to Stolen Generations: Questions and Answers" in Stolen Generations: The Way Forward. Ed. Justin Healey. p.9.

briefly how autobiographical narratives construct and constrain Aboriginal memories of child removal in the public domain, and exploring Aboriginal authorial agency in documenting an archive of separation stories, the paper intends to argue that the tactical retelling of Aboriginal living memory of separation and displacement initiates a transformative process that exposes racial injustices and furthers Indigenous interests in the project of reconciliation.

"Narrative Accrual"

The Stolen Generations narratives are not merely stories of the oppressed against the oppressors, or ones that promulgate a hidden truth (Attwood 183; Muecke 409–410). Rather, they constitute what Jerome Bruner terms "narrative accrual" — a set of stories that have been transmuted through memorising, sharing, circulating and re-interpreting (18). Before the 1970s, the stories of child removal seldom occupied a central position in Indigenous oral or written narratives, and few non-Indigenous Australians were informed of the facts that Aboriginal children were forcibly removed and institutionalized.[1] Aboriginal memories of removal experiences were probably neither solicited nor disseminated beyond the affected families.

From the early 1970s Aboriginal writers began to reminisce about their childhood experiences at the Children's Homes, whose memories revealed much poignancy and frustration, but also included some happy and memorable moments they spent with caring sisters or adoptive families (see Attwood 199). Much encouraged by the recognition of Aboriginal citizenship in the 1967 referendum and the landmark *Aboriginal Land Rights (Northern Territory) Act 1976*, Aboriginal narratives of child removal gradually shifted the focus from the personal to the political and embraced Aboriginal or part-Aboriginal identity which had long been negated or suppressed (see Attwood 191–192; Read, "Review" 22). From the mid-1970s to the 1980s, critical reflections on the practices of child removal could be found in the autobiographies written by Jimmie Barker and Margaret Tucker (Read, "Review" 22). Tucker's accounts of her experience at Cootamundra Domestic Training Home appeared in her autobiography *If Everyone Cared* (1977), the television series *Women of the Sun* (1982) and

1 According to the historians, the experiences of stolen children were scarcely mentioned within Aboriginal communities before the 1970s, though there must be some sketchy accounts in various documents. It contrasts greatly to the outpouring of separation stories from the 1980s onwards. See Read, "Return" 8; Attwood 185.

a documentary film Lousy Little Sixpence (1983). The publicity shaped Tucker's stories into a thematic exemplar of disrupted childhood and miserable adolescence as a young apprentice (see Attwood 193–195). Since then, the stories of child removal have shown a departure from reminiscences which included caring and loving moments (though occasional) at the Children's Homes to an emphasis on the heart-wrenching suffering of removed children (see Attwood 199–200).

From the mid-1980s to the 1990s, the narratives of the stolen children increasingly became a central part of Aboriginal collective memory, in which the loss of Aboriginal children echoed the dispossession of their land following the European invasion (see Attwood 195). Led by Sally Morgan's widely read *My Place* (1987), there emerged a number of Aboriginal autobiographies that centred on the Aboriginal origin of the writer and his/her later separation. These included Glenys Ward's *Wandering Girl* (1987), Alice Nannup's *When the Pelican Laughed* (1992) and Doris Pilkington's *Follow the Rabbit-Proof Fence* (1996). As Attwood notes, compared to the earlier narratives, the narratives of the early 90s gradually addressed the removal experiences from a specific locale to a regional or even national scale, and foregrounded the events' symbolic meaning and emotional evocation (200).

The most significant event in the construction of the Stolen Generations narratives was the release of the *Bringing Them Home* report in 1997, following the two-year National Inquiry which collected oral and written submissions of testimonies from 535 Indigenous people across Australia. The report documents the devastating impact of government policies, laws, and institutions in severing the familial bonds between Indigenous children of mixed descent and their parents through means of "compulsion, duress or undue influence" (HREOC 5). The most astonishing fact elicited by the Inquiry was that the practices of child removal primarily aimed to eliminate Aboriginality, or to "breed out the colour" in a systematic manner. According to the child removal policy, the government agencies, churches and welfare institutions were responsible for taking away "half-caste" or "part-Aboriginal" children, placing them in Children's Homes, dormitories, orphanages, or with foster families before sending them to serve as domestic helpers or stockmen. In doing so, these young Aborigines were supposed to be assimilated into the mainstream settler society, allegedly in their best interests. Although most people involved in child removal were well intentioned,the report shows that many removed children experienced physical, sexual, and psychological abuse and their original families were shattered and damaged. The report concludes that the racially motivated removal of mixed-descent Aboriginal children was tantamount to genocide and in serious breach of the Convention on the Prevention and Punishment of the Crime of Genocide ratified by Australia in 1949.

The report provoked unprecedented attention to the project of reconciliation by revealing Indigenous separation memories for the first time on such a large scale. It stimulated the publication of more Aboriginal accounts of their removal experiences, which then widely circulated in the public arena to articulate the suffering endured by Indigenous people. Fuelled by the continued public debates of the late 1990s and 2000s, the Stolen Generations narratives became instrumental in the formation of Aboriginal identity and historical consciousness. These stories not only recollected individual and personal memories, but also served as a moral force calling for the national engagement in a reckoning of the past and taking responsibility for the wrongs.

The Genre of Autobiography as an Agency and a Constraint

Autobiographical narratives have historically become an inseparable part of Indigenous life writing, documenting their struggles under colonial control and making their voices heard in settler society. Nevertheless, the genre of autobiography is ambivalent for being both objective in narration and subjective in nature, and to some extent both speaking of personal experiences and representative of collective voices. In the discussion of the Stolen Generations, the malleable capacity of autobiographies have promoted Indigenous narratives to shift the focus from individual and personal events in a specific area to a collective memory that bears significance in the national history. In this discursive expansion, on the one hand, Aboriginal autobiographical narratives enable at least a symbolic moral redress for past wrongs. On the other hand, the retelling of Indigenous memories through the genre of autobiography is accused of being symbolic instead of historic, as well as inconsistent and fallible, for "memory can be notoriously malleable and so unreliable" (Attwood 209). The problem of veracity does not so much concern the difference between truth and lie; rather,it has to do with the representative limits of the genre itself (see Gilmore 5). Due to the absence of much documented evidence to support the retelling of memories, the ambivalent nature of autobiography inevitably undermines the credibility of Aboriginal accounts of forcible removal and constrains the transformative effect that these counter narratives intend to achieve.

In stories of forcible removal, Aboriginal traumatic memories were often considered to be a revelation of the deepest and truest feelings, hence an increasing number of Aboriginal autobiographies were readily marketed as "the psychological outcome of social oppression" (Muecke 416). Stephen Muecke summed this up as a repressive/expressive paradigm. In his analysis of Morgan's *My Place* and Ward's *Wandering Girl*, he challenged the "repressive hypothesis" by pointing out that actually there had been a "readiness, even eagerness, to publish works by Aboriginal writers" (413). At this point, it is necessary to address the reception of Aboriginal autobiography by a white readership. The redemptive impetus within white society sustains the desire to liberate the suppressed and in a sense precipitates the demand for Aboriginal trauma stories in the market. The commodification of separation stories could then be turned into "a politics of guilt and reparation that risks co-opting Aboriginal writing to the white-literal Australian cause" (Huggan 160). In addition, the traumatic descriptions of sadistic flogging, sexual harassment and abuse, the twists of fate tend to stimulate the voyeuristic curiosity among the readers. As a symptom of consuming other than experiencing trauma, voyeurism boosts the book sales, but poses a potential danger to the privacy of Aboriginal witnesses. The feelings of remorse and guilt in a public white readership are to an extent satisfied by the signifiers of trauma in Aboriginal autobiographies; alternatively, thenarratives that do not conform to the hypothesis of repression might not receive wide acceptance in the book market. From these perspectives, the market apparatuses of selection, commodification and consumption underline the contextual conditions which channel and constrain the autobiographies of the stolen children.

Examining the representative nature of autobiography in the process of narrative accrual, however, Muecke reminds us that Aboriginal separation stories are written in "a site of multiple constraints pertaining both to forms and contextual relations" which are not necessarily "negative, [for] they tend to make sure that a text will have a specific application in renegotiating meanings" (417). In this regard, Aboriginal autobiographies as the voices of the weak can possibly function as a tactical resistance in Michel de Certeau's sense, which "plays on and within a terrain imposed on it and organized by the law of a foreign power" (37). A tactical action claims no space other than that of the enemy; the operation of a tactic is thus contingent upon the agency of the weak and the right timing to launch the attack (Certeau 37). From this vantage point, while it is necessary to keep in mind the generic constraints and marketing apparatuses, it is important to recognise Aboriginal authorial agency that enables the recollection of memories tactically within this constrained territory.

An Archive of Living Memories

Here I will consider three Aboriginal autobiographies: Lowitja O'Donoghue's *Lowitja* (2003) Doris Kartinyeri's *Kick the Tin* (2000) and Nancy Barnes' *Munyi's Daughter: a Spirited Brumby* (2000). Each of the writers spent some of their early life at the Colebrook Home for Children in South Australia, which was initially established at Quorn in 1927 and later moved to Eden Hills in 1944. Until its closure in 1981, over 350 Aboriginal children had lived at Colebrook (see HREOC 30). While examining O'Donoghue's inconsistent memories of her childhood days, and considering Kartinyeri's and Barnes' different, if not entirely contradictory, perspectives of remembering their removal experiences, I intend to suggest that the evocation of different versions of memories in the form of autobiography cannot be simply reduced to an attempt at political expediency or personal gain. The multi-faceted autobiographical accounts open up a critical space to reflect upon the politics of memory operating within the dominant discourse and to explore the authorial agency of articulating Indigenous visions of history, plights and rights.

Lowitja O'Donoghue is a well-known Aboriginal public administrator, Australian of the Year in 1984 and the founding chairperson of the Aboriginal and Torres Strait Islander Commission in 1990. The biggest controversy of O'Donoghue's stories involves the way in which she had been separated from her Aboriginal family. In her autobiography, O'Donoghue recalls her childhood experience of being taken away at the age of two and brought up in the Colebrook Home. She never saw her Irish father again and she only met her mother when she was in her thirties. O'Donoghue's brother and three of her four sisters were also removed from home. In the episode entitled "Taken Away," O'Donoghue writes, "We are called the stolen children" (2). She uses "taken away" and "stolen" alternatively in this autobiography published in 2003. Two years earlier in an interview with Andrew Bolt, however, O'Donoghue revealed that her removal was probably at her white father's request and she would see herself "as a removed child and not necessarily stolen" (Bolt 1). At that time her concession was sensational amidst the already intense debate on the issues of Stolen Generations. Criticism from both sides — for and against the national reconciliation project — came "in a rare moment of unity" (Neill 13). Some Aboriginal activists were furious that O'Donoghue's remarks contradicted her public persona as a high-profile member of the Stolen Generations and that it might jeopardize the Aboriginal community's demand for a formal apology and reparation from the government.[1] At the same time, political conservatives criticised inconsistencies in her stories and took her case as evidence that the Stolen Generations did not exist.

The controversy does not so much deal with the factual circumstances of her removal, but ties in with the political and moral implications for the reconciliation project. Keith Windschuttle comments on the nuanced differences between taken away/removed and stolen: children who are "taken away" from their parents and "removed" to institutions deserve compassion and sympathy towards their plight, but not necessarily the moral judgment of the act of removal itself; whereas being "stolen" means something different, which immediately directs the public attention to the perpetrator for moral and legal judgment (330). *The Weekend Australian* has an editorial entitled "Sad Semantics Betray the Stolen Children" (qtd. in Windschuttle 324). Facing the debate of semantics underlining the politics of memory, O'Donoghue delivered a speech at the 2001 Stolen Generations Conference in Adelaide, under the title of "Stolen, Taken or Removed, We Suffered all the Same," in which she pleaded with the public to recognise different forms of separation and called for an understanding of Indigenous pain over the years.[2]

According to Windschuttle, the inconsistencies in O'Donoghue's childhood memories can also be found in her contradictory accounts of the Colebrook Home from 1934 to 1948. For O'Donoghue, journalist Stewart Cockburn recalled that she told him during an interview in 1977 thatat Colebrook "she had a happy childhood there with 50 other part-Aboriginal boys and girls" (qtd. in Windschuttle, 328). However, her autobiography seems to contradict this "happy" memory as she notes that the days at Colebrook were preoccupied with strict rules and "many of us were very unhappy there" (3). The people who managed Colebrook believed Aboriginal children were "dirty and ignorant"; whereas for the young O'Donoghue and other Aboriginal children at the Home, the fun time was to make up Aboriginal words (which were not allowed

---

1 John Howard, the Prime Minister at the time, denied the fact of a systematic racial removal and refused to apologise on behalf of the federal government. It was not until February 2008 that then Prime Minister Kevin Rudd made an official apology to Aboriginal people and their communities who had suffered from the removal policies.

2 The edited version of Lowitja O'Donoghue's speech was published in *The Australian*,on 15 March 2001, p.13. Note that there were cases in which children were placed in the Children's Homes at the wishes of their parents. In some cases, there were signed agreements between parents and adoptive institutions, but due to the loss of witness or documented support it was often difficult to know whether the parents in each case were fully informed or truly willing to handle their children to the institutions.

there) as a mischievous action to "make fun of Matron" and to resist the monotonous institutionalized life (3).

In retrospect, the controversy concerning O'Donoghue's case is a sad story. Whether "taken" or "stolen," "happy" or "unhappy" at the Children's Home, O'Donoghue has probably stated different aspects of her childhood stories to the best of her knowledge in different contexts. The public attention to the veracity of details led to uproar and damaged her reputation. Considering the impact of public readers' preference on Aboriginal separation stories, Penny van Toorn, among others, is concerned that if "a narrow set of codifications is taken to be representative, the diversity of Aboriginal historical experiences and representational modes is likely to be suppressed" (254; see also Whitlock 31–32). Referring to Aboriginal writers who fail to live up to non-Aboriginal standards against which Aboriginal narratives are measured, Sonia Kurtzer points out that the "frustration would be better directed at the hegemonic culture which seeks to control the manufacture and public circulation of images of Aboriginality" (27–28). O'Donoghue's case displays a complex set of power relations involving Aboriginal memories of diversified separation experiences, the form of expressions and the public reception.

It is easy to assert that O'Donoghue has fudged her childhood stories. But at this point, it is worth reflecting upon the contextual factors, including the dominant discourse and social expectations, which may come into play with Indigenous personal memories. By the 1970s, many removed Aboriginal children, who were brought up during the White Australia policy and had been made to believe that the white education system had bettered them, were expected to have some positive feelings towards the days when they received the education. As shown previously, it was not rare to find Aboriginal memories of caring and close relations between the inmates at Children's Homes during this period. Hence when O'Donoghue recalled the childhood experiences in the 1977 interview, her "happy" memories did not surprise the audience at that time. From the 1980s onwards, along with the advancement of Aboriginal movements, more and more Aboriginal adults came to "regain" their Aboriginal identity that had been once "lost" or denied (Attwood 192). As they struggled to gain more rights recognised by the mainstream white society, the traumatic memories were foregrounded in the narratives of stolen children, as a tactic to make their voices effectively heard and later answered by the national project of reconciliation since the 1990s. As Gillian Whitlock summarises, "Discourses of reconciliation privilege the therapeutic paradigm" in which "the truth of suffering can be a source of regeneration, a collective catharsis and a means of creating a moral community" (35; Humphrey 9). The narratives of trauma became an empowering asset as a result of the national interest stimulated by the reconciliation project. In this context, the upsurge of traumatic texts in the forms of autobiography can offer a strategic opportunity for Aboriginal authors, like O'Donoghue, to tap into this newly formed cultural asset with the aim of empowering the wounded individual and the community to heal the pain in their collective memory.

Moreover, it is necessary to see that memories by nature are always engaged with the present whenever people reach into their past. It is understandable that O'Donoghue's later memory may incorporate her awareness of the experience of others that came to light by way of the report. "It is evident that Indigenous writers make strategic use of their opportunities to document traumatic personal histories, and it is by no means the case that they choose to tell all," as Whitlock reminds us (34). To launch the tactical attack against racial dominance, the use of timing could be seen as an attempt to reconstruct the memories of separation. The politics of memories is more a matter of a strategic investment of Indigenous cultural and political interests than a deliberate attempt to fabricate Indigenous history. In response to the credibility of Aboriginal stories, Mellor and Haebich note

> *the oral traditions of Indigenous people are the result of skills learned and passed on in a disciplined way, as a specific task. ... the recording of oral histories, personal visions and reflections is a highly significant activity, which provides not only an archive, but also a connection with culturally definitive ways of articulating heritage. (10)*

This is not to say Aboriginal people don't forget, but to remind us of the often-neglected oral traditions which have historically shaped and guided the transmission of Aboriginal memories in autobiographical narratives. By re-presenting Indigenous voices and traditions in public discourse, the reconstruction of the separation memories thus can become a transformative force to resist racial dominance tactically and effectively.

In the following discussion of Aboriginal memories, Doris Kartinyeri's *Kick the Tin* and Nancy Barnes' *Munyi's Daughter: a Spirited Brumby*, published in the same year of 2000, can be read comparatively. These two autobiographies present the different life tracks that started from the Colebrook Home. But as I will argue, both authors transform their respective childhood memories to empower themselves for the purpose of healing and to express the hope that the historical wrongs shall not be repeated.

Doris Kartinyeri, an Aboriginal woman of Ngarrindjeri heritage, had her autobiography "professionally edited, promoted and marketed" by Spinifex Press, an independent feminist publisher (Hosking 66). The book launch was held at the site of former Colebrook Home at Eden Hills in Adelaide. O'Donoghue, Kartinyeri's former Colebrook sister, came to make a speech in front of a large audience including the media. The book has a cover dominated by two colours — red and black — evocative of the colours of the official Aboriginal flag. The picture at the centre illustrates the book's title "Kick the Tin," which draws a scene of the can kicking — a game that Kartinyeri played with other Aboriginal children at Colebrook. As the word "tin" is embedded in her name (KarTINyeri), it was a poignant metaphor that Kartinyeri sees her sorrowful life like a "tin" being kicked around. On the back cover is a powerful account of Kartinyeri's tragic life:

> *The legacy of being a member of the Stolen Generations continued for Doris as she was placed in white homes as a virtual slave, struggled through relationships and suffered with bi-polar depression. ... And it is the compelling and sometimes witty story of a courageous journey into the soul of the individual to find meaning and substance after the loss of everything the rest of us take for granted.*

In her autobiography, Kartinyeri recollects the tragedies and tortures she has been through. Her mother died at the hospital when she was only a one-month-old baby. Before her father was able to take her home, the little Kartinyeri had been "stolen" from the hospital and removed to the Colebrook Home (6). Being assimilated into the white society was a nightmare for Kartinyeri when she left Colebrook in 1959 at the age of fourteen. Continuous sexual harassment and abuse, loss of dignity, and excessive alcohol led to her ruined adult life. One of her most traumatic memories was being sexually abused by the lay minister of the church. She writes, "How would anybody know what I was going through? Where is the guiding hand a child is meant to have? ... I felt these terrible experiences had ruined my life" (61–62). Kartinyeri confronts the readers with questions that interrogate the assimilation policy. Her story concentrates an enormous amount of sadness and anger, striking an emotional chord in her readers.

Kartinyeri began her journey of healing by recollecting the fragments of memory and putting them into her autobiography. The act of writing relieved her burden and sorrow, and helped her to resolve the scars left by those difficult years in the past. She writes,

> *My life has been literally kicked about, just like the tin we used to kick around. I believe that our Aboriginal brothers and sisters experienced much suffering because of the abusive behaviour of white fella governments and regimental, oppressive institutions. (2)*

Kartinyeri evokes the painful memories of those who have also been racially discriminated and oppressed. By shifting the personal reference from the singular ("my" and "I") to the plural form ("we" and "our"), Kartinyeri translates the individual misery into the collective suffering of "Aboriginal brothers and sisters." Michael Jackson argues that in Indigenous writings the "transformation of particular subjective experience into a universalized and trans-subjective category enables one to grasp and control the situation one experienced first in solitude and powerlessness" (141–142). For Kartinyeri, to identify her personal trauma as part of a collective memory can be seen as a way of self-empowerment, enabling her to face the trauma that has scarred her life and to direct this power to heal the wounded Aboriginal communities as a whole.

Kartinyeri's journey of healing re-affirms her Aboriginal identity, as she concludes, "I am proud to be a Nunga. The battles and struggles of living in two worlds that I endured throughout my life have proven my aboriginality" (135). The Aboriginality identified by Kartinyeri is an intransigent spirit, active against racial subjugation. This statement is powerful and righteous for readers who feel compassion for Aboriginal suffering. Susan Hosking comments that Kartinyeri's story "slips comfortably into the genre of battler stories that occupy so much space in the Australian psyche" (68). By identifying and embodying the fighting spirits of anti-authoritarianism which are deeply rooted in Australian national identity, to some extent Kartinyeri transforms her autobiography into a story of suffering and courage against the universal dominance and oppression. Such rebellious sentiments are not only shared by Aboriginal groups, but also can be recognised by Australian society in general. In this sense, Kartinyeri's autobiography captures the emotional and spiritual expectation of the public and effectively transforms her memory into an asset to empower herself and the Aboriginal community towards healing and restoration. Kartinyeri's case therefore shows how the tactical recollection of Aboriginal memories engages the national discourse of reconciliation to unsettle racial oppression within Australian society.

By comparison, Nancy Barnes' self-published *Munyi's Daughter* was not so lucky in terms of public acceptance; even its launch was "disquieting and uncomfortable"

(Hosking 66). The opening sentence of Barnes' life story appears inconsistent to most readers: "We are referred to as 'The Stolen Generation'. I consider myself 'Saved'" (1). To be "saved" is an unusual interpretation of the removal experience. "This is an Aboriginal autobiography that nobody wanted to publish, and few have gone out of their way to read," as Hosking comments on Barnes' book (68). Back in 1930, the two-year-old Barnes was admitted to the Colebrook Home. She was too young to know who had sent, taken or stolen her at that time, but she had contracted polio and she believed that she was *saved* by the care of Sister Rutter and Sister Ruby Hyde, and by other older Aboriginal brothers and sisters. Barnes remembered fondly her stay at Colebrook during 1930–1941. Barnes grew up to have a successful career and as noted by Hosking, she became "a fully qualified kindergarten teacher and ... the first Aboriginal woman appointed to the Aboriginal Affairs Board" (68). Barnes' success in life can be seen from her broad smile in the three photos printed on the book's cover. One of the photos was published by the *Sydney Morning Herald* when Barnes was Director of the Ida Standley pre-schoolin Alice Springs. Her confident expression sends a clear message to readers that this autobiography can be read as an inspiring story of courage and triumph.

As a *saved* child, Barnes' alternative account challenges the mainstream understanding of the child removal in history, hence it may not have been as welcomed by readers who were eager to express compassion toward others' suffering. But beyond her smile on the cover, Barnes actually tells a story of "courage and poignancy" within a larger context of racial injustices in Australian history (vi). The resisting power embedded in her autobiography stems from her courage of telling a different story compared to other separation narratives, and from her stand against racial inequality. Barnes mentions that in her early years of working for white families, once the housekeeper told her to eat alone in the kitchen and wait on table while they had meals. In a calm but determined tone, Barnes refused:

> *I quietly replied to her, that I was employed to look after the children, and that I would do to the best of my ability. But wait on tables I would not, as I did not see this as part of my duties. (59)*

Barnes' rejection of the unfair demand was done "quietly" but properly, bringing the concession from her white employer and retaining her dignity in a racially discriminated situation. Perhaps because of her illness of polio, Barnes understood how to make strength out of weakness. Barnes neither argued nor compromised in this uneven power relationship. At this point, Barnes' spirit of resistance should not be construed as anything less than other Aboriginal life stories of fighting against racial subjugation.

Barnes writes about her search for roots almost at the end of the book, without foregrounding the theme of identity like most separation stories do. She recalls the meetings with her mother whom she met only twice in her adult years. For they were not able to communicate in the same language, the estranged mother-daughter relationship turned out to be sorrowful, especially during their second meeting which was the last time that Barnes saw her mother before she suddenly passed away. The tragic sense of alienation between mother and daughter was cruel for Barnes who "couldn't face" and she sighed, "[h]ow much grief this caused Munyi [her mother], I could not imagine" (167, 169). Though these tearful moments that echoed the trauma in many separation memories only amount to a small proportion of Barnes' entire autobiography, it would be unfair to read her story as what Hosking comments "an endorsement of separation policies" (70). Rather, Barnes blamed the tragic relationship with her Aboriginal mother on the policy of separation, which not only alienated them but also destroyed the familial, language and cultural links between them: "We were both innocent victims of a Government policy that did not take into account the pain of those separated as we were" (167). Barnes stresses the devastating effect of child removal policies and by presenting a personal story of both tragedy and success, Barns' story expands the readers' understanding of multi-faceted separation experiences.

Barnes' autobiography displays the complexity of the Stolen Generations narratives which are shaped by the historical changes and the entangled racial relations in Australian society. Her story is not exceptional. As a matter of fact, it is consistent with the finding of the National Inquiry, as noted in the report:

> *The bulk of the evidence to the Inquiry detailed damaging and negative effects …. The Inquiry did receive some submissions acknowledging the love and care … However, all of the witnesses who made these points also expressed their wish that they had not had to make the sacrifices they did. (HREOC 11)*

Part of the sadness in the Stolen Generations stories, especially for non-traumatic ones such as Barnes' autobiography and probably O'Donoghue's case too, is that not all their sacrifices and suffering have been properly recognised by the mainstream society. As Whitlock observes, compared to the majority of traumatic narratives, these non-traumatized memories often receive very critical responses and "are likely to be seen as deviant and misguided" (31). The controversy caused by the minority opinions among the already minority voices of Aboriginal people exposes the apparatus of selection within the dominant discourse. Different from Kartinyeri's traumatic account, Barnes mobilizes her personal memory in an "unconventional" way. Heragency of resistance is "disguised" by her courageous and persistent pursuit of self-esteem and independence as being an Aboriginal woman with polio. Though not without denouncing the policy of separation, Barnes' autobiography contributes to an archive of the Stolen Generations narratives, which requires the readers to recognise the breadth of separation stories and to reflect on the White Australia policy in history. Only in this way can Indigenous history embodied within their memories be known by a wider Australian public, to change the stereotypical views towards the suppressed Aboriginal subjects, and to acknowledge Aboriginal people's courage, persistence, and determination in their struggle for survival.

To conclude, autobiographical narratives of the Stolen Generations document and re-present the fabrics of Aboriginal living memories of child removal. Indigenous agency in the politics of memory challenges theracial assumption that conceives Aboriginal people as a repressed subject. I do not mean that removed Aboriginal children were not victims of the separation policy. But a wide collection of autobiographical narratives manifest Indigenous agency of self-empowerment to redress the injustices inflicted upon them both historically and at present. While engaged with generic and contextual limits in the public domain, these autobiographies can be seen as a transformative force of using Aboriginal organized memories to dismantle the "organized forgetfulness" of the dominant culture and to further Indigenous interests (Fitzgerald 58).To reconstruct Aboriginal personal and collective memories is thus of historical and symbolic significance in the revelation of past wrongs and the pursuit of a possible reconciled future.

Acknowledgments:

This paper is based on part of my PhD thesis submitted to The University of Hong Kong. An earlier version of the paper was presented at *Contested Histories and the Politics of Memories* — the 3rd Foundation for Australian Studies in China (FASIC) Conference in Shanghai, 22–25 October 2015. I thank the audience and anonymous reviewers for helpful comments and suggestions.

References

[1] Attwood, Bain, and Fiona Magowan. Introduction. *Telling Stories: Indigenous History and Memory in Australia and New Zealand.* Ed. Bain Attwood and Fiona Magowan. Wellington [N.Z.]: Bridget Williams Books, 2001. xi–xvii. Print.

[2] Attwood, Bain. "Learning about the Truth." *Telling Stories: Indigenous History and Memory in Australia and New Zealand.* Ed. Bain Attwood and Fiona Magowan. Wellington: Bridget Williams Books, 2001. 183–212. Print.

[3] Barnes, Nancy. *Munyi's Daughter: a Spirited Brumby.* Henley Beach, S. Aust: Seaview Press, 2000. Print.

[4] Bolt, Andrew. "I Wasn't Stolen: Aboriginal Leader's Shock Admission." *Herald Sun* 23 Feb. 2001 : 1. Print.

[5] Certeau, Michel de. *The Practice of Everyday Life.* Trans. Steven Rendall. Berkeley, LA: University of California Press, 1988. Print.

[6] Chakarabarty, Dipesh. "History and the Politics of Recognition." *Manifestos for History.* Ed. Keith Jenkins et al. London: Routledge, 2007. 77–87. Print.

[7] Fitzgerald, Ross. "Making History." *Social Alternatives* 8.4 (1990): 57–60. *Academic Search Premier.* Web. 25 Dec. 2012.

[8] Gilmore, Leigh. *The Limits of Autobiography: Trauma and Testimony.* Ithaca: Cornell University Press, 2001. Print.

[9] Healey, Justin, ed. Stolen Generations: *The Way Forward.* Rozelle, N.S.W: Spinney Press, 2009. Print.

[10] Hosking, Susan. "Homeless at Home, Stolen and Saved: Three Colebrook Autobiographies." *Westerly* 46 (2001): 65–73. Print.

[11] Huggan, Graham. *The Postcolonial Exotic: Marketing the Margins.* London; New York: Routledge, 2001. Print.

[12] Human Rights and Equal Opportunity Commission (HREOC). *Bringing Them Home: Report of the National Inquiry into the Separation of Aboriginal and Torres Strait Islander Children from their Families.* Sydney: Human Rights and Equal Opportunity Commission, 1997. Web. 25 Aug. 2013.

[13] Humphrey, Michael. "From Terror To Trauma: Commissioning Truth for National Reconciliation." *Social Identities* 6.1 (2000): 7–27. *Academic Search Premier.* Web. 12 Aug. 2015.

[14] Jackson, Michael. *At Home in the World.* Durham: Duke University Press, 1995. Print.

[15] Kartinyeri, Doris. *Kick the Tin.* North Melbourne, Vic: Spinifex Press, 2000. Print.

[16] Kurtzer, Sonia. "Wandering Girl: Who Defines "Authenticity" in Aboriginal Literature?" *Southerly* 58. 2 (1998): 20–29. Print.

[17] *Lousy Little Sixpence.* Prod. Alec Morgan, and Gerry Bostock. 1983. Film.

[18] Mellor, Doreen, and Anna Haebich, eds. *Many Voices: Reflections on Experiences of Indigenous Child Separation.* Canberra: National Library of Australia, 2002. Print.

[19] Morgan, Sally. *My Place.* New York: Seaver Books, 1988. Print.

[20] Muecke, Stephen. "Aboriginal Literature and the Repressive Hypothesis." *Southerly* 48.4 (1988): 405–418.

[21] Nannup, Alice, Lauren Marsh, and Stephen Kinnane. *When the Pelican Laughed.* South Fremantle, W.A: Fremantle Arts Centre Press, 1992. Print.

[22] Neill, Rosemary. "Admitting Degrees of Separation." *The Australian* 22 Mar. 2001: 13. Print.

[23] O'Donoghue, Lowitja. *Lowitja.* Kingswood, S. Aust: Working Title Press, 2003. Print.

[24] ——. "Stolen, Taken or Removed, We Suffered all the Same." *The Australian* 15 Mar 2001: 13. Print.

[25] Pilkington, Doris. *Follow the Rabbit-Proof Fence.* St Lucia, Qld: University of Queensland Press, 1996. Print.

[26] Read, Peter. "Don't Turn Your Back on Me: A Bibliographical Review of the Literature of the Stolen Generations." *Aboriginal Law Bulletin* 73.3 (1995): 22-24. Print.

[27] ——. "The Return of The Stolen Generation." *Journal of Australian Studies* 22.59 (1998): 8–19. Print.

[28] Said, Edward W. "Invention, Memory, and Place." *Critical Inquiry* 26.2 (2000): 175–92. Print.

[29] Tucker, Margaret. *If Everyone Cared: Autobiography of Margaret Tucker.* Sydney: Ure Smith, 1977. Print.

[30] Van Toorn, Penny. "Tactical History Business: the Ambivalent Politics of Commodifying the Stolen Generations Stories." *Southerly* 59 (1999): 252–266. Print.

[31] Ward, Glenyse. *Wandering Girl.* Broome, W.A: Magabala Books, 1987. Print.

[32] Whitlock, Gillian. "Active Remembrance: Testimony, Memoir and the Work of Reconciliation." *Rethinking Settler Colonialism: History and Memory in Australia, Canada, Aotearoa New Zealand and South Africa.* Ed. Annie E. Coombes. Manchester: Manchester University Press, 2006. 24–44. Print.

[33] Windschuttle, Keith. *The Fabrication of Aboriginal History. Vol. 3: the Stolen Generations 1881–2008.* Sydney: Macleay Press, 2009. Print.

[34] Women of the Sun. The Special Broadcasting Service (SBS). 1982. Television.

Xu Daozhi is a PhD candidate at The University of Hong Kong. Her dissertation focuses on the postcolonial narratives in post-Mabo Australian children's literature. Her research interests also include graphic novels, cross-cultural engagement, and poetry translation. She was awarded HKU Postgraduate Scholarship (2011–2015) and University Postgraduate Fellowship in 2011. Her PhD project was awarded a research grant from the Australia-China Council under the Australian Studies 2012–2013 Competitive Projects Funding Scheme.

The "Memory" Turn: New Research Perspectives on Chinese Australian Literature

Chen Beibei

Abstract: Chinese Australian literature, as one significant part of cultural production in Australia, has been researched from various angles. Present research has shown interests in the representations of the images of Australian or Chinese characters in Chinese Australian writings; representations of cultural citizenships, cultural translation, gender issues and racism; as well as the issue of canonizing Chinese Australian literature as an independent category. Though present research has explored in depth on many Chinese Australian literary works, there are still gaps to fill. Based on the nature of Chinese Australian literature, more research should be done from the angles of memory. As a branch of diasporic literature, Chinese Australian literature writes extensively on the representations of memory, which will be a new research perspective in future studies. By using "memory" as a novel perspective, the study of Chinese Australian literature will not be confined by the "fixed" and "clichéd" notion that it is only able to tell the Western readers about the misery suffered by their Chinese characters, rather, it is a literature fitting into the larger scope of transnational literature and needs a broader sense to understand its topics, contents and aims.

Key words: "Memory" turn; Chinese Australian Literature; Identity

摘要： 经过多年的发展，华裔澳大利亚文学在澳洲已经得到了一席之地，诸多学者都就该文学中对华人和澳人的形象表现、文化翻译和文化身份问题、性别问题、种族主义问题以及经典化问题进行了深入研究。然而，作为海外华人离散文学，华裔澳大利亚文学对于记忆的表现却极少有人涉及，因此成为一个新的研究点。研究"记忆"问题，不仅仅是对母国颠沛流离的历史或者记忆的表述，更是探索该文学对澳大利亚历史和社会的窥视镜。通过这个新的角度，笔者认为华裔澳洲文学是全球越境文学的重要一支，并且也是澳洲社会重要的文化产物。

关键词： "记忆"转向；澳洲华裔文学；身份

1. Definition and Scope of Chinese Australian Literature

Chinese Australian literature is still a "new" phrase which is under the process of definition. This research defines "Chinese Australian literature" as literary works created either in English or in Chinese by authors with Chinese heritage (either first-generation Chinese migrants, or migrants with Chinese descent).

Based on languages in which the works are written, there are two categories within "Chinese Australian Literature". One refers to literary works written by Chinese

Australian writers in the English language and the other refers to literary works by Chinese Australian writers in the Chinese language. However, in the research scope of Australian literature, the latter is rarely noticeable owing to the language barrier. Because of the language and cultural representations, this category of literature plays a significant role in spreading Chinese cultures and engaging with cultural comparisons between China and Australia. Thus, this essay uses this category of literature as the research subject.

According to Ommundsen, Chinese Australian writing, in a whole, "has been recognized as an important and growing category within Australian literature since the 1990s" (85), and has already generated a sizable body of literary criticism (see for example Lee M. 1998, Khoo 2003, Lee R. 2006, Broinowski 2003, Ommundsen 2000, 2001, 2002, 2005, Madsen 2009) (Ommundsen 85).

The changing policies in the cultural environment are significant elements for Chinese Australian literature to seize the chance and develop itself. However, the writing environment has not completely changed. At the earlier stage, Chinese Australian literature as a whole, dwarfed by the urge to protect the dominant White Australian literature, was still misread and neglected. And Chinese-Australian writing still meets challenges from dominant Australian society.

Before 1983, when Brian Castro published his first novel *Birds of Passage*, there were few Chinese Australian works in English that attracted large readerships in Australia. *Birds of Passage* exerted much influence upon Australian and international readers. Brian Castro was born on a boat from Chinese Hong Kong to Chinese Macau and immigrated to Australia when he was 12 years old. He has contributed eight novels to Australian literature and many commentaries as well as literary critical essays. Yin Rui, a Chinese scholar, argues that "Chinese-Australian English-Language literature boomed after Brian Castro, who dominated the beginning period with his novels" (Yin 105). Therefore, to some extent, he is the most successful writer among several pioneers of this field. Castro's works cover many genres such as fiction, autobiography, crime, biography, drama, novella, short stories and prose. Castro's writing is characterized by elegant and sophisticated language, involvements in several cultures, and theoretical reflections mingling with narration. Though labeled as Chinese Australian writer by many literary critics, Castro's writing extends our understanding of Chineseness as a flexible term rather than fixed. His view of China and family memory in China is quite different from other writers of Chinese descent due to his cosmopolitan backgrounds.

Since the 1990s, contemporary Chinese Australian writings began to gain notice in Australian literary circle in genres of poetry, fiction, memoir and short stories.

In terms of poetry, there are several noticeable poem collections, of which *Moon over Melbourne and Other Poems* (1995) by Ouyang Yu has received sizable criticism by Australian literary circle. His poetry collections also include *Songs of the Last Chinese Poet* (1997) and *Two Hearts, Two Tongues and Rain-Coloured Eyes* (2002). Ouyang Yu is a prominent poet, critic and novelist writing extensively on the understanding of diasporic Chinese identity, racism in Australia, cultural identification with China and cultural differences between China and Australia.

In terms of fiction, many Chinese Australian writers have contributed their works to the literary cannon, *The Crocodile Fury* (1992) by Beth Yahp, *The Eastern Slope Chronicle* (2002) by Ouyang Yu, and *Love and Vertigo* (2000) by Hsu-Ming Teo. These fictions touch many aspects of life in Australia such as early Chinese settlement, migration experience, cultural identity and diasporic memories. Tom Cho is a short-story writer with Chinese descent and his best known short story collection is *Look Who's Morphing* (2009).

Besides, *Unpolished Gem* (2006) as a memoir by Alice Pung has received many literary awards including winner of "Australian Newcomer of the Year" in the 2007 Australian Book Industry Awards and was shortlisted into *Australian Biography of the Year* and *Australian Book of the Year* in the 2007 Australian Book Industry Awards. It writes biographical life stories of Alice Pung and her Chinese-Cambodian family, about how they pursue their Australian dream. Lillian Ng, on the other side, writes memoir-style fiction based on her nanny in China. She writes about how Silver as a "Comb-up" went out of her hometown and lived in diaspora.

2. Current Criticism on Chinese Australian Literature

The development of Asian Australian literature, including Chinese Australian literature, has received considerable criticism from both cultural studies and literary research. Many criticisms have opened discussions on canonizing Chinese Australian literature. There are scholarly works dedicated to promote it as part of Australian literature such as critical works by Wenche Ommundsen from University of Wollongong. Ommundsen is a prominent literary critic who has written more than 41 critical articles with particular interests in the areas of Asian Australian writing and she summarizes and canonizes Chinese Australian literature as an independent category in her edited work *Bastard Moon: Essays on Chinese-Australian Writing* (2001), which introduces a variety of creative works by Chinese Australian writers including journalism, autobiography, petitions, films, mixed-media performance, poetry and fictions.

Plus, Ommundsen observes cultural citizenship in Chinese diaspora and argues against cultural essentialism, claiming that "the literatures of diaspora deserve to be read as documents of unique and complex cultural experiences rather than mere illustrations of archetypes" (Ommundsen 101). In essays like "Transnational Literacies: Reading the 'New Chinese Literature in Australia' in China" (2011) and "This story does not begin on a boat: what is Australian about Asian Australian writing?" (2011), Ommundsen argues for a need to consider Chinese Australian literature as part of Australian literature and examines how Chinese Australian literature is read and criticized by both Chinese scholars and Australian scholars. Her critical works pave the way for Chinese Australian literature to play a part under the transnational turn in Australian literature.

Besides, works by Shirley Tucker, Tseen Khoo, Olivia Khoo and Shen Yuanfang mainly observe gendered representations in Chinese Australian novels and autobiographies. Both Tucker and Olivia Khoo observe representations of Chinese femininity in Chinese Australian women writing. And Shen, by reading earlier male Chinese Australian autobiographies, argues that these books conform to "the Confucian model of masculinity embodied in the 'Superior Man' (junzi)" (Huang 8). Issues of cultural identity, racial identity and citizenship are also the focus of current criticism on Chinese Australian writing, such as Peta Stephenson's critical essay "Where are you from? New Imaginings of Identity in Chinese-Australian Writing" (2005) in which Stephenson links Chinese diaspora with indigenous community and claims that "Chinese (and all other) migration occurs within the history of colonization, *within* rather than after the history of relations between Indigenous and Non-indigenous people" (Stephenson quoting Curthoys, "Immigration" 172) and Regina Lee's "Flexible Citizenship: Strategic Chinese Identities in Asian Australian Literature" (2006) in which Lee argues that "Asian Australian cultural production are not only deep ambivalences surrounding cultural and political citizenship, but that it is also subject to constant re-negotiation with historical and prevailing attitudes about race and culture" (Lee 213). There are also two books published in China concerning cultural identity in this category of literature: *Being and Becoming: On Cultural Identity of Diasporic Chinese Writers in America and Australia* (Wang Guanglin 2004) and *"Death" of the "Poet": A Metaphor of an Era — The Anxiety of Identity in Australian "New Chinese" Literature 1988 to 1998*[1] (Qian Chaoying 2000). Both Wang and Qian express interests in the identity politics representations in Chinese Australian literature. Especially, Wang compares this category with Chinese American literature and argues that both of these two categories represent the identity disorientation and seek for an idealized solution to find a stable sense of belonging in multicultural societies. Last but not least, representations of masculinity have also attracted attention from scholars such as Huang Zhong, who completed his doctoral degree in University of Wollongong and Ouyang Yu, the renowned "Angry Poet". Huang's Ph.D thesis aims to conduct research on how Chinese masculinity is constructed in fiction and autobiography, and further explores the theoretical and historical underpinnings behind these constructions (Huang 2012). Ouyang Yu's focus, slightly different from Huang, is representing how Chinese masculinity encounters Australian femininity by his creative works rather than scholarly research. There are also other researchers like Alison Broinowski putting their efforts on how Asian Australian literature represents Australians and Australia (Broinowski 2003). The lists go on but are not fully listed here.

3. The "Memory" Turn: New Research Perspectives on Chinese Australian Literature

Memory studies are a wide-ranging and complex field, focusing on how memory plays its socio-cultural role in public discourse, media, and academic fields, and bringing together several different disciplines. It sheds light on the revival of cultural history and researching memory in culture has become one of the international themes in academia. The "preoccupation" with memory studies is "by no means restricted to any one country, but is an international phenomenon." (Erll 2)

Recently, there are works contributing to the "global turn" on memory studies like that of Aleida Assmann and Sebastian Conrad in *Memory in a Global Age*, or *Memory and Migration* by Julia Creet. The above books notice that memory studies are under transformation period with the view that memory is now transnationally acknowledged and understood. Instead of understanding the notion of nation as a "closed" boundary of memory studies, Assmann and Conrad hold that the nation is not "natural container

1 Borrowing Dr. Huang Zhong's translation of the original Chinese title《"诗人"之"死"：一个时代的隐喻——1988—1998年间新华人文学中的身份焦虑》.

of memory debates" any more. The boom of memory studies is generally considered as one of the effects of "multiculturalism" and the migration boom. The migration groups live between the different countries or hemisphere. They build their connections with the homelands and they have gradually generated the mixed and ambivalent feelings towards the host country which provides them food, job and loneliness. As migration and multiculturalism developed, the interests of marginalized groups became visible and the voices of these people are a growing within a "multicultural" nation from diversified ethnic groups with different cultural backgrounds and traditions. These voices have brought multiple perspectives to the history and traditions of both the "home" country and the "host" country.

Hence, current criticisms haven't put much emphasis on the representations of memory and identity in Chinese Australian literature, which means that current reading of this category is incomplete. As a category of diasporic literature, Chinese Australian literature is characterized by its focus on representing memory and identity, thus it needs more criticism on how they represent themselves in memory and how diasporic memory shapes the characters' understanding of identity.

As is suggested by Shen and Edward (quoted by Peta Stephenson 108), Chinese Australian literature as the "textual production of Chinese Australian communities" can contribute towards "destablizing traditional, white versions of history" and creates "new, intra-ethnic histories into the national narrative" (Shen and Edward 5). However, for a long period of time, literary works within this category has been only read as diasporic narratives largely addressing, like Stephenson says, "'ancient' Chinese past, exotic customs and 'traditional' Chinese cultural practices" (Stephenson 112). This tendency reflects the western audience's presumption on this kind of literature. To them, Chinese Australian literature plays a role of educating them about China (Stephenson 112). By reading the writing of Chinese Australian writers, western audiences learn the "different" cultural customs and what China looks like in these writers' eyes. This may be the truth for common western readers, Stephenson makes a novel claim that Chinese-Australian writing, not only tells us about China, but also "is increasing re-imaging various aspects of Australian society" (Stephenson 112). In addition, Stephenson also notices that, "disrupting the notion that remain the 'authentic' informants of stories about abandoned homelands, Chinese-Australian authors are actively resisting the imposition of a singular ethnic identity and are consciously avoiding simplistic and stereotypical notions of Chinese migrants" (Stephenson 112). So, by analyzing texts from this new perspective, the reading of Chinese Australian literature will enlarge readers' horizon by responding to the despair, loss, and estrangement within Australia, filling the gap of the existing criticism which lays heavily on the "problems" beyond Australia (Stephenson 115).

Then why memory and identity distinguishes Chinese Australian literature from the rest of the others? Creet argues "memory is where we have arrived rather than where we have left" (Creet 6). To Creet, "migration rather than location is the condition of memory" (Creet 9). Memory, though always bonded with a specific place, is not necessarily confined to one place only. Memory travels as diaspora happens and memory travels across borders, playing multiple roles in identity forming. Because of the disaporic nature of Chinese Australian literature, the issues of memory and identity are of great concern in the literary writing and questions like "who are we" and "who can speak in this country" are often brought up in these texts.

Identity is a significant term in media, sociological study, cultural study and literature as well. Scholars are concerned about any issues related to identity at global, national, local and personal spheres. Diaspora may cause breaking-up with old communities, and it is the reason why diasporic literatures frequently narrate the problematics of "returning home" or "searching for identity". Re-settlements may have difficulty in language and culture, thus bring "identity crisis" and cultural shocks. In the course of diaspora, identity is re-made, and re-imagined, just like memory does. Identity is not a simple issue and there is no simple definition of it because it involves many aspects such as nationality, ethnicity, social class, community, gender, and sexuality, etc. These elements may contradict with each other and cause "identity confusion" or even "identity crisis".

Paul Gilroy has suggested that "identity provides a way of understanding the interplay between our subjective experience of the world and the cultural and historical settings in which that fragile subjectivity is formed" (Gilroy 301). To Gilroy, identity is always under an on-going process of changes and thus it is wrong to view it as static and stable. Similar to Gilroy, Hall argues that cultural identity

> *is not some universal and transcendental spirit inside us on which history has made no fundamental mark. It is not once-and-for-all. It is not a fixed origin to which we can make final and absolute Return ... The past continues to speak to us. But it no longer addresses us as simple, factual 'Past', since our relation to it, like*

the child's relations to the mother, is always already 'after the break'." (Hall 226)

Based on the intriguing relations between memory, diaspora and identity, and connecting with what Ommundsen argues, Chinese Australian literature tackles two poles of the diaporas. It is not only focusing on "where are you from", but also observes and reflects "where you are at". And possibly it also deals with "where you are going". Memory and identity, as the two features of this literature, show that Chinese Australian literature can stand at the world literary stage and be criticized as equally as other featured literatures. As the globe becomes more cosmopolitan, different levels of identities are deconstructed (national, ethnical, familial and personal). Chinese Australian literature is a reservoir for scholars to observe how the essentialist approach of identity is not possible and justifiable.

4. Reading Chinese Australian Fictions as "Memory" Texts

Many fictions produced by Chinese Australian writers can be viewed as "memory texts", not only because they write traumatic memories which happened in the past, but also record memories imprinted with Australian cultures. In this part, *Silver Sister* by Lillian Ng, *The English Class* by Ouyang Yu and *Behind the Moon* by Hsu-Ming Teo are chosen to show how memory is narrated as a significant part of diasporic literature.

Begin with *Silver Sister*, a memoir-style short fiction published in 1995 by Lillian Ng. This book has a translation in Chinese but unfortunately it is not well noticed either in Australia or in China. That is probably because both Australian and Chinese readers find its contents relate to a remote past, rather than a present. However, it is a book from which how wars and other traumatic national events in one country become transnational experience in the globe by linking them to diaspora and memory studies. This text allows space to view how traditional norms such as collective memory and site of memory become contested concepts. By discussing the working of individual diasporic memory, *Silver Sister* challenges the closed boundaries and opens for more intriguing debates on how diasporic memory transforms one's identity labels.

Different from *Silver Sister*, *The English Class* is a text taking a closer look at the role of language in the dynamics of cultural memory. Ouyang Yu tackles at how cultural memory crosses borders with migrants like Jing, the protagonist in *The English Class*. Under the global turn of memory, cultural memory is also through a dynamic transformation for migrants in Australia. By living apart from the institutional cultural memory, the protagonist Jing is unable to relate to his homeland memory for a sense of belonging and is unable to define himself as an authentic Australian because he is trapped in his language games and self-conscious bilingualness.

As a novel set in Australia and targeted at second-generation migrants, Hsu-Ming Teo's *Behind the Moon* is a novel representing the tests on the functioning of transgenerational memory in affecting the identity or sense of belonging of second-generation migrants in Australia. Transgenerational memory is a term coined to interpret the vertical migration of memory among people who live in diaspora, or used to live in diaspora. It is a term to understand how teenager migrants struggle to strike roots in Australia, with their parents either squeezing their cultural memory into their brain or ignoring their roots from where the second-generation could possibly relate to for a sense of belonging. Characters in this text face challenges in terms of transnational friendships in a multi-cultural society, diasporic haunting pasts, and fears of not being "Aussie" enough.

These above texts are just some of the examples to be read as "memory texts", and the new perspectives of reading them as "memory texts" allow broader exploration of the narratives, characterization and writing purposes. By linking memory to Chinese Australian literature, this category of literature is not boring; instead, it is meaningful, complicated and international.

5. Conclusion

Memory has been playing the role of influencing identity in either its formation, or its crisis. Chinese Australian literature reflects this relation and takes it further to contest essentialist understanding of both memory and identity. They are fluid, dynamic and not confined by borders or markers. When memory is disrupted, or distorted, or fragmented, identity also is problematic. Chinese Australian literature, as a literature featuring the question of memory and identity, is experiencing a new era because it shows our memorial world is defined and re-defined. Identity is lost, and re-lost in both diasporas and migration societies.

References

[1] Broinowski, Alison. *About Face: Asian Accounts of Australia.* Melbourne: Scribe, 2003.

[2] Creet, Julia, and Andreas Kitzmann. *Memory and Migration: Multidisciplinary Approaches to Memory Studies.* Toronto: University of Toronto Press, 2011.

[3] Erll, Astrid. *Memory in Culture.* Houndmills: Palgrave Macmillan, 2011.

[4] Gilroy, Paul. "Diaspora and the detours of identity." *Identity and Difference.* Ed. Kathryn Woodward. London: Sage Publication, 2002.

[5] Hall, Stuart. "Cultural identity and diaspora." *Identity: Community, Culture, Difference.* Ed. Jonathan Rutherford. London: Lawrence & Wishart, 1990.

[6] Khoo, Olivia. "Marketing Asian-Australianness: Introduction." *Australian Humanities Review* 45(2008): 97–99.

[7] Khoo, Tseen. *Banana Bending: Asian-Australian and Asian-Canadian Literatures.* Hong Kong: Hong Kong University Press, 2003.

[8] Lee, Mabel. "Chinese Writers in Australia: New Voices in Australian Literature." *Meanjin* 57.3(1998): 578–585.

[9] Lee, Regina W. *Theorising the Chinese Diaspora: Chinese Canadian and Chinese Australian Narratives.* PhD Diss. Murdoch University, 2005.

[10] Madsen, Deborah L. "Asian-Australian Literature." *A Companion to Australian Literature Since 1900.* Ed. Nicholas Birns and Rebecca McNeer. Rochester : Camden House, 2007.

[11] Ng, Lillian. *Silver Sister.* Port Melbourne: Mandarin Australia, 1994.

[12] Ommundsen, Wenche, ed. *Bastard Moon: Essays on Chinese-Australian Writing.* Melbourne: Otherland, 2001.

[13] ——. "Behind the mirror: Searching for the Chinese-Australian Self." *East by South: China in the Australasian Imagination.* Ed. Charles Ferrall, Paul Millar and Keren Smith. Wellington: Victoria UP, 2005.

[14] ——. "Birds of passage? The new generation of Chinese-Australian writers." *Alter/Asians: Asian/Australian Identities in Art, Media and Popular Culture.* Ed. Ien Ang, Sharon Chalmers, Lisa Law and Mandy Thomas. Sydney: Pluto P, 2000.

[15] ——. "Floating Lives: Cultural Citizenship and the Limits of Diaspora." *Life Writing* 1.2(2004): 101–121.

[16] ——. "From 'Hello freedom' to 'Fuck you Australia': Recent Chinese-Australian writing." *Departures: How Australia Reinvents Itself.* Ed. Xavier Pons. Carlton: Melbourne U P, 2002.

[17] ——. "Transnational (Il)literacies: Reading the 'New Chinese Literature in Australia' in China." *Antipodes* 25.1(2011): 83–89.

[18] Ouyang, Yu. *Moon Over Melbourne & Other Poems.* Exeter: Shearsman Books, 2005.

[19] ——. *Songs of the Last Chinese Poet.* Broadway: Wild Peony, 1997.

[20] ——. *The Eastern Slope Chronicle.* Blackheath: Brandl & Schlesinger, 2002.

[21] ——. *The English Class.* Yarraville: Transit Lounge Publishing, 2010.

[22] Peng, Qinglong. Trans. Chen Beibei. "Chinese Australian Literature in Thirty Years." *YiLin* 2(2009).

[23] Shen, Yuanfeng. *Dragon Seed in the Antipodes: Chinese-Australian Autobiographies.* Carlton: Melbourne University Press, 2001.

[24] Stephenson, P. "Where are you from?: New Imaginings of Identity in Chinese-Australian Writing." *Culture, Identity, Commodity: Diasporic Chinese Literatures in English.* Ed. Tseen Khoo and Kam Louie. Hong Kong: Hong Kong University Press, 2005.

[25] Teo, Hsu-Ming. *Behind the Moon.* New York: Soho Press, 2007.

[26] Wang, Liping. "A Discussion on Chinese Australian Literature." *Contemporary Foreign Literature* 3(2003):120–124.

[27] Williams, Michael. "Chinese Settlement in NSW: A Thematic History." NSW Government, Office of Environment and Heritage. 1999. http://www.environment.nsw.gov.au/resources/heritagebranch/heritage/chinesehistory.pdf, accessed on April 4th, 2015.

[28] Yin, Rui. Trans. Chen Beibei. "Chinese Australian English Literature." *Contemporary Foreign Literature* 3(2007).

Chen Beibei is a PhD candidate at University of New South Wales, Australia. Her main interest includes memory and identity in literature, diasporic literature, and cultural studies.

澳大利亚高等教育国际化政策初探

程可珺　陈　弘

摘要： 随着全球化的日益加深，教育国际化的趋势也在不断推进，澳大利亚自 20 世纪 80 年代以来，一直是推动教育出口，走向国际的一支重要力量。本文旨在回顾其在过去 30 年间的教育国际化发展路线，着重研究政府政策、学生的录取情况、国际化所带来的问题及其未来前景，并提出了针对相关问题的解决方法及其在当今世界的意义。

关键词： 澳大利亚；教育；国际化

A Preliminary Look into the Internationalization
of Higher Education in Australia

Cheng Ke-jun, Chen Hong

Abstract: With growing prevalence of globalization, the internationalization of education is also stepping up its pace. Since 1980s, Australia has been a major force in promoting the export of education. This paper is set to review the policies promoting education internationalization in the past 30 years, with an emphasis on government policies, student enrollment, the problems and prospects of the educational internationalization as well as the corresponding solutions to some of the problems and their significance worldwide.

Key words: Australian Education Internationalization

1. 概述

在全球化的影响下，教育国际化趋势在 20 世纪 80 年代后势不可挡。许多国家都采取推进“教育国际化”，作为提高国家竞争力的有效方法。其中，澳大利亚当属佼佼者。过去的三十年中，澳大利亚教育领域，尤其是高等教育领域经历了巨大发展。澳大利亚教育部最近发布的数据显示，截至 2015 年 3 月，在澳留学的国际学生已经从 1980 年的 7 500 名（William 15）上涨到 41.3 万名。中国是澳最大的留学生来源国。目前中国赴澳留学生达 15 万人，占澳外国留学生人数的 28.5%[1]。大部分中国留学生来澳是接受高等教育、强化英文以及学习中学课程等。澳大利亚政府将为中国及各国学

1 AEI.2015. “International Student numbers 2015” [EB/OL] https://aei.gov.au/research/International-Student-Data/Pages/InternationalStudentData2015/Table B.pdf

生赴澳留学继续简化学生签证申请程序，为高等教育毕业生继续提供毕业后的工作签证。留学潮带来了巨大的经济收益，所创造的利润已让澳大利亚的教育产业多年高踞为第三大出口产业。在推动教育国际化的同时，尤其是在亚太地区，澳大利亚在政府和民间层面与各个国家和地区推进发展双边关系。教育领域的国际化合作不仅仅使澳大利亚在经济和政治上获益，而且，对其合作方来说，与澳大利亚在国际教育领域的合作在 21 世纪有着新的建设性意义。一方面，引入澳大利亚教育的国家和地区可学习和借鉴澳大利亚的经验和教训，进一步推进本国和本地区的教育事业；另一方面，对于那些同样出口教育产业的国家和地区来说，澳大利亚在教育国际化进程中的得失也可以成为其发展教育国际化的建设性先例。

本文旨在通过研究 30 年澳大利亚“教育国际化”进程的演革，探讨其发展轨迹和特点，细致分析澳大利亚政府的教育政策，研究其国际化教育的成果。

2. 高等教育发展的历史回顾

2.1 从教育援助到教育贸易

20 世纪 50 年代，以奖学金为基础的科伦坡计划（Colombo Plan）吸引了一大批国际学生赴澳求学。作为该项目的一部分，澳大利亚政府为来自南亚和东南亚的学生提供奖学金资助。正是由于这种激励机制，在 1955 年，大约有 10 000 名国际学生赴澳学习，其中一半是中国学生（Lowe 22）。就此，科伦坡计划开启了政府教育资助的先河。1974 年，澳大利亚联邦政府取消了包括海外学生在内的所有学生的学费，到了 1979 年，海外学生费用委员会决定向海外学生征收 30% 的额外费用，自此，教育贸易化模式在 20 世纪 80 年代正式开启。

20 世纪 80 年代早期，由于经济危机的影响，对于在澳开展教育国际化运动的看法也分成了截然不同的两派。其一认为，教育国际化应延续其教育援助的方式持续下去，另一种观点认为，应该正视教育，将其纳入经济活动的范畴。为了更好地进行权衡分析，澳大利亚政府分别成立了格尔德林（Goldring）和杰克逊（Jackson）委员会，分别研究对于在澳留学生的教育政策和对于在澳留学生的教育援助政策。1984 年，这两项研究分别正式公布。格尔德林委员会主要负责对整个教育政策的评估，杰克逊委员会发布了《澳大利亚在亚太地区进行培训和研究活动的经济价值评估》（Fraser 25）。格尔德林报告反对对教育国际化政策的商业化改革，而杰克逊报告则支持了这样的变革，认为这将能够极大地促进澳大利亚经济的发展。杰克逊认为澳大利亚应该将教育国际化进行产业化变革，让各教育机构能更积极地参与国际竞争，吸引更多的国际学生。他认为，国际学生应支付全额学费。有了这些收入，学校就有了资本，可以为学生提供更好的留学服务。他提出应将教育国际化政策进行“经济合理化”的认知。最终，澳大利亚政府采纳了他的想法，并开始对在澳留学生进行“录取、分配、资助政策的经济合理化”（杨 60）考量，并制定和实施了相应举措。这些举措为政府和高等教育机构带来了巨大的经济利益。

当时，在澳留学生主要来自中国香港、马来西亚和新加坡，学习的专业主要有机械二程、自然科学、技术、经济和商业（Fraser 25），大部分人都在完成学业之后回国工作。留学生分布的学校也不平均，但以新南威尔士大学和莫纳什大学为较多。

1985 年，澳大利亚政府正式实施“教育出口”政策，各教育机构向在澳留学生收取全额学费，并允许学校将学费收入部分留成，以进一步营销推广，提升留学生课程的质量。与此同时，对于在澳留学生的援助没有被完全废弃，如对于全额支付学费的学生，澳政府提供更宽松的移民政策。在这些政策的推动下，全额支付学费的机制正式确立。

2.2 教育国际化的贸易阶段

1987 年，澳大利亚就业、教育、培训部（Department of Employment, Education and Training, DEET）部长约翰·道金斯（John Dawkins）对澳大利亚高等教育进行大规模的改革。他鼓励强化大学和学院的管理，并赋予管理人员更多的权利，进行类似企业董事会式的运作。在高等教育领域，应高效、全面利用来自个体和私人教育机构所产生的经济收益，来帮助政府缓解经济压力。约翰·道金斯呼吁社会，应该视教育领域的新政策为国家经济政策中不可或缺的一部分。他指出，如果要使国家更加兴盛，就必须在态度、时间等各方面都作出改变。教育，尤其是高等教育，应成为推动这些改变的核心力量（Dawkins 11）。道金斯的政策具体表现在 1987 年，将就业、教育、培训部取代联邦第三级教育委员会（the Commonwealth Tertiary Education Commission, CETC）。联邦第三级教育委员会于 1977 年成立，主要负责高等教育领域。基于道金斯的重组政策，该委员会被废弃，国家就业、教育与培训委员会（National Board of Employment, Education and Training）成立，取代了联邦第三级教育委员会的顾问角色。就业、教育、培训部则负责高等教育领域的规定制定功能。从此以后，就业、教育、培训部就取代了联邦第三级教育委员会来直接管理教育机构的活动。

除此之外，道金斯还主张废弃双轨机制，并实施高等教育供款计划（Higher Education Contribution Scheme）。通过前者，澳大利亚建立了一个统一的国家高等教育系统，合并了诸多学院和机构到大学中去。后者引入了一种新型资助方式，使在澳留学生可以申请到贷款来帮助他们完成高等教育。虽然高等教育供款计划没有直接帮助到在澳国际学生，但是这种用户支付的方式也帮助了在澳的国际化教育。这些政策都推动了教育资源的优化和教育机构的强化管理。

在这些政策出台之后，澳大利亚的教育市场急剧扩大。在没有限制学生数目的情况下，大量的国际学生蜂拥而至，其中的大多数仍然来源于亚洲。而他们中的大多数享有比之前更大的资金援助。通过研究发现，他们所选择的专业包括工程机械、商业研究、计算机科学、科学和数学的师范教育和亚洲研究等等（荣，李 154）。在此之后，教育产业愈来愈成为澳大利亚一大出口产业。

随着赴澳留学生越来越多，1990 年，政府推出一项全新的政策，要求所有留学生支付全额学费。这一项政策标明澳大利亚政府正在重新考量他们的国际化教育政策。因为在此之前，所有在澳的留学生通过三种方式支付学费：1. 由澳大利亚发展援助局全额资助；2. 支付部分学费，并同时由海外学生办公室分担一部分；3. 自己全额支付。自 1990 年政策出台以来，所有国际学生都需支付全额学费至国际教育机构。随着政府资助数量的减少，大学和其他教育机构开始不断扩大国际学生的招生量，这不仅带来巨大的经济收益，同时也提升各类学校在国际上的地位。

2.3 从教育贸易化走向教育国际化

随着国际学生数量的大幅增长，人们对于澳大利亚国际化教育的质量也开始有了顾虑，各种各样的问题一一浮现，诸如安排不合理的课程、非法移民，以及发展国际化教育事业和推动教育产业化之间存在模糊的界限等等。为了防止在亚太地区留学市场的缩减，澳大利亚公平竞争暨消费者委员会（Australian Competition and Consumer Commission, ACCC）在 1990 年开始致力于提升高等教育质量，为国际学生建立"行业道德实施准则"。为了确保支付学费的国际学生与教育机构本身都能实现其应有的价值，政府也支持了这样的行业道德标准的确立和实施。

为了达到这个行业道德标准，教育机构必须保证教育的营销推广与教育质量均达到同样的水平。通过这样做，不合格的教育机构被排除在外，而国际学生的利益也受到了保护。

政府还推出了另一项政策，在 1991 年设立了海外学生教育服务法案（ESOS Act 1991），在这项法案之下，国际学生在某种程度上被视为客户，他们的法律权益受到保障。这项法案旨在强化政府对国际化教育提供方的管制。在任何国际化教育提供之前，相应机构必须在澳大利亚联邦政府招收海外学生院校及课程注册登记（Commonwealth Register of Institutions and Courses for Overseas Students, CRICOS）中登记。只有在获得各州及领地的认可之后，才能提供国际化的教育服务。这项法案是澳大利亚政府保护留学生利益的先驱，也是国际上第一个保护留学生学费的法律框架（丁 167）。这表明澳大利亚政府愈加重视从保护学生利益的角度推动国际化教育的发展，这些都为后期的进一步国际化运作奠定了坚实基础。

3. 高等教育国际化在 21 世纪的进程

进入 21 世纪以来，澳大利亚在推动教育国际化的过程中，一直处于领先地位，有活跃的师生流动，国际化的课程设置，大量的海外交流项目和国际间的协作。学科设置的国际化在内容、研究方法、外语学习中都一一得到实现。其中，由于政府在推广营销、立法和质量保证方面的大力支持，以国际学生的招募和海外项目的开展最为卓越。

3.1 政府政策

3.1.1 推广营销

为了进一步推广国际教育市场，澳大利亚政府采取了一系列的措施来积极推动品牌壮大和国际合约的建立。

为了更好地参与品牌营销，政府全面利用了其在国际上的各种关系，来提供专业性的顾问咨询和建议。在政府的支持下，各机构每年都参与了在海外的教育巡展和新闻发布会，例如，“在澳大利亚学习”活动已经持续举办多年，从2009年起又注入了新的内容和形式。许多家长和学生所关心的问题都被提上议题，并且针对性地提出了解决方案。其他更具体的方案包括：① 对澳大利亚六大留学生来源国学生提供额外的经济资助；② 在相关网站提供更细致的调研结果；③ 更好的培训和信息的获取通道；④ 举办一系列产业峰会。同时，在亚洲全面进行介绍，宣讲澳大利亚的教育优势和科研优势，尤其是六大合作国家，包括中国、印度、韩国、印度尼西亚、马来西亚和泰国。除此之外，澳大利亚政府还提供多种多样的奖学金给国际学生，包括澳大利亚发展奖学金，澳大利亚领导力奖和奋进奖，而奋进奖是在2009年纳入整个奋进奖学金系统的，且专门针对亚洲学生。有了这些奖学金的吸引，澳大利亚高等教育得以更加加强了其国际化的趋势。

政府还通过有效利用一些组织来帮助提高其教育推广进程。很典型的例证便是1994年，澳大利亚国际教育组织（Australian Education International, AEI）成立。澳大利亚国际教育组织致力于在全球推广教育产业，推进与政府间的合作。该机构对市场的调研和数据的分析为政府作出正确的决策提供重要的支持。

进入21世纪以后，政府更加重视与各国之间的协作。政府与美国、泰国、新加坡签订了《自由贸易协定》，与新西兰签订了《澳新更紧密经济关系贸易协定》。因教育贸易也是《自由贸易协定》和《澳新更紧密经济关系贸易协定》中的重要一部分，签订这样的条约不仅消除了不同国家之间的障碍，同时也为澳大利亚的教育服务提供方带来更多的便利。

3.1.2 立法支持

1991年所推出的海外学生教育服务法案在当时推动了澳大利亚教育国际化的进程，但是同样也滋生了一定的问题。由于一些教育机构被授权自主招生并收费，他们开始自主不断扩大国际学生的招募，无限制地帮助学生获取签证来谋取自身利益。有的国际学生在澳逗留超过法定时间。由于没有政府相关的法律政策的限制，无法遏制这种非法行为。因此为了保证澳大利亚教育质量，也防止学生签证的肆意发放，澳大利亚政府重新拟定了《2000年海外学生教育服务法案》，该法案：第一，用特定的方法保证国际学生的资金；第二，强化了对学生信息的管理；第三，对于违反规定的做法设定了严厉的惩罚。

在《2000年海外学生教育服务法案》之后，许多其他的相关政策也已被通过和修订，包括如2000年《海外学生教育服务法案（保证金贡献）》，2001年《海外学生教育服务法案》修正案等等，都促成了保障国际学生教育服务的法律系统。

3.1.3 教育质量保证

为了保证国际化教育的质量，澳大利亚政府建立了一个完整又灵活的框架机制。在1995年1月，澳大利亚学历资格框架建立（Australian Qualifications Framework, AQF），覆盖高等教育、职业教育、中小学教育的16种学历。该框架对于澳大利亚政府来说十分重要，因为这确保了其教育的质量，而且这些指导性策略不仅适用于学历教育，同时也适用于国内外课程的提供。该框架共有10级，1级为最低。16种学历的确定将由学生在教育和培训阶段所获的成绩决定。

在2000年，澳大利亚大学质量署（Australian Universities Quality Agency, AUQA）在维多利亚州成立。这是一个非营利组织，独立于政府和教育机构而存在。它的一项职责是每五年通过审查和到校访问来审核在澳大学和海外大学的学术质量。这些审查结果公布在网络上，所有人都能将之作为指导来评估。在2002年到2007年，AUQA开展了两轮评估。根据第一轮评估的结果，他们确立第二轮的审查的主题就是“国际化”。该机构同时也审核联邦、各大州和当地的教育机构，以确保其工作也符合《国家高等教育许可程序议定书》。

3.2 录取国际学生

3.2.1 学生数目

2012年3月至2015年3月不同类别国际学生数目

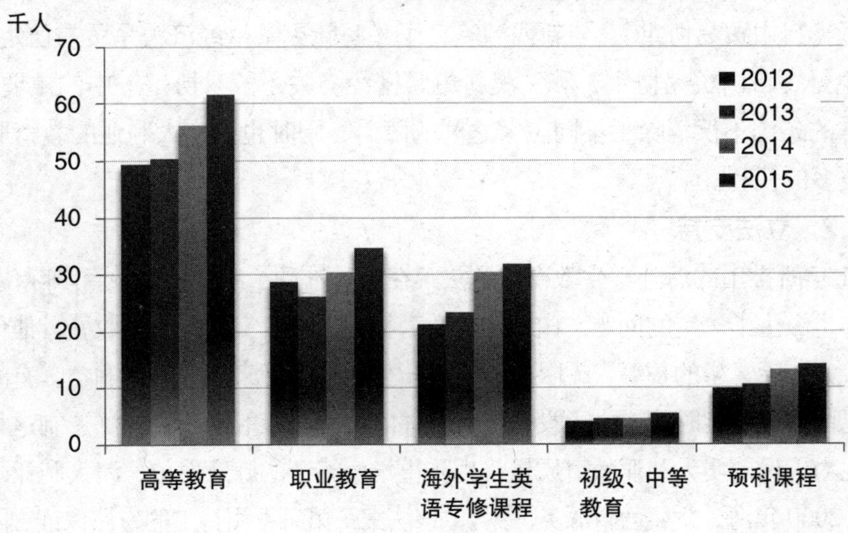

澳大利亚高等教育阶段的国际学生在21世纪全球化的浪潮下不断增长。截至2015年3月，共有413 032名在澳全额支付学习的国际学生，比2014年同期上涨了11.5%。截至2015年3月，共招纳146 964名新生，比2014年同期增长9.3%，比过去10年的平均值高出5.3%[1]。

根据上图，在2012至2015年间，国际学生的录取量总体态势保持不断上涨。其中，高等教育吸引的留学生数目始终为四项教育类别之首，且在2014至2015年保持高位增长。生源吸收能力位居第二的职业教育领域，也保持4年内稳步增长，除了在2013年有小幅回落。值得注意的是，海外学生英语专修课程作为第三大热门板块，在2014年以及之后都收获了大幅度增长，足见澳洲在吸引国际学生研修英语方面不断增强的竞争力。

具体看各个教育类别在各个国家分布状况，按照AEI的国际学生录取情况月度总结（截至2015年3月）（Monthly summaries of international student enrolment data by March 2015）[2]，数据如下：

截至2015年3月，高等教育领域共拥有最高比例留学生数目，高达52.6%。学生总人数和录取人数相比2014年同期分别增长10.1%和9.4%。其中，中国和印度学生总数分别占据35.4%和11.7%。截止到2015年3月，研究型硕士录取人数小幅下跌了0.7%，但非研究型硕士仍以年增率4.2%的速度增长，学士录取人数年增长率高达18.1%。

职业教育领域共吸引22.5%的国际留学生，总人数及新录取人数都比去年同期增长了15.5%和13.4%，其中印度学生的比例最大，高达18.3%，中国位居第二，达8.2%，韩国为第三，达8.1%。

就海外学生英语专修课程而言，共占国际学生总数15.8%，录取人数占比21.5%，分别比去年同期增长8.7%和4.6%。其中，中国学生为该领域的主要成员，总人数占比高达25.5%，新录取人数占比也位居第一，达22.2%。其次为巴西（8.5%）、泰国（7.7%）和哥伦比亚（6.8%）。

初级、中级教育领域共拥有3.6%国际留学生，比去年同期增长13.5%，值得注意的是较去年同期，录取率增长了23.6%。其中中国和越南学生为主要部分。

预科课程的国际学生总数也获得了15.7%年增长率。其中，中国（29.0%），美国（14.0%）和巴西（11.1%）为三大主要来源国。

---

1 AEI 2015 International student enrolments in Australia 2012–2015 [EB/OL] https://aei.gov.au/research/International-Student-Data/Pages/InternationalStudentData2015.aspx

2 AEI 2015 International student enrolments in Australia [EB/OL] https://internationaleducation.gov.au/research/International-Student-Data/Documents/Monthly%20summaries%20of%20international%20student%20enrolment%20data%202015/03_March_2015_MonthlySummary.pdf

3.2.2 主要的学生来源

主要的学生来源于亚洲国家，在最近几年，来自亚洲的学生人数迅猛增长，且长踞第一名。在亚洲，这些生源国的分布均匀，许多国际学生来自于东北亚，以及东南亚地带。

截至 2015 年 3 月，在澳大利亚生源地中，中国内地、印度、越南、马来西亚和韩国，都实现了逐年增长的学生输出率，这五大生源地占据了澳大利亚所有国际生源的 52.5%。

澳洲留学生 5 大来源地留学生人数占澳洲总学生人数 52.5%

国家和地区	至 2014 年 3 月	至 2015 年 3 月	年增长率	所占比例
中国内地	102 277	115 311	12.7%	27.9%
印　度	35 521	46 367	30.5%	11.2%
越　南	19 406	20 038	3.3%	4.9%
马来西亚	16 609	17 701	6.6%	4.3%
韩　国	17 076	17 153	0.5%	4.2%
其他国家	179 683	196 462	9.3%	47.5%
所有国家汇总	370 572	413 032	11.5%	100.0%

除了这五大生源地之外，还有其他国家和地区，出现了巨大的增长，如下图 [1]

录取率超过两位数增长的国家和地区（除前五大来源地）

——生源总数超过 4 000 名

国家和地区	录取人数 截止到 2015.3	年增长率	排　名
泰　国	14 421	11.7%	6
尼泊尔	13 444	18.3%	7
巴基斯坦	10 849	19.3%	10
中国台湾	7 042	29.1%	15
斯里兰卡	4 871	17.4%	19
意大利	4 720	34.8%	20

1 AEI.2015. “International Student numbers 2015” [EB/OL] https://aei.gov.au/research/International-Student-Data/Pages/InternationalStudentData2015/Table B.pdf

在2002年到2009年间，来自中国内地的学生量位居所有国际学生总量之首。印度生源的录取率自2002年以来平稳增长，到2008年达到峰值，但在2009年之后，没有继续增长。在2006年之前，新加坡一直在生源国的前十之内，但是之后被巴西取代。同样的，尼泊尔在2008年也取代了美国进入前十，沙特阿拉伯也取代中国香港，在2009年荣登前十。在1989年之后，来自中国香港的在澳学生一直保持高速增长。但自2004年之后，中国香港的生源数开始减少。

3.2.3 主要学习的专业

主要学习的专业在21世纪也发生了改变。在20世纪90年代，所选择的专业主要集聚在商业管理和经济学领域。有关市场营销、财务会计等学科在国际学生中十分热门。第二大热门学科是科学，而相对冷门的专业有兽医学和法律。自2001年，管理和商业成为了亚洲学生的热门选项。第二大热门专业从科学改变为信息技术。学科兴趣在地理上也有很大的不同，东南亚学生更热爱工程机械，而南亚、中亚、东北亚学生更喜欢信息技术。

4. 高等教育国际化所面临的问题

虽然在21世纪，澳大利亚教育已经发生了重大变化，但仍然存在诸多问题，影响其进一步的发展。

第一个问题是过分关注国际教育出口的利润。在过去的十余年，澳大利亚教育从来没有掉出过全国出口产业前四。相较于教育出口产业的巨大回报，政府的资金支持相对来说却十分微薄，这使得教育机构尽量从教育出口中谋取更多的利润，从而造成负面的后果。因为资金的问题，很多教育机构开始不断扩大招生数目，而不考虑其本身的接纳能力。这样的现象的直接后果就是，教育的质量被忽视。许多赴澳留学生发现，所学课程削减了，但价格依旧昂贵。这样会使澳大利亚教育质量整体的名声被破坏。同时，一些教育机构通过给学生提供学生签证来牟利，这也导致了非法移民问题的产生。

第二大问题在于澳大利亚高等教育在国际化浪潮中的优势相对减弱。澳大利亚教育的优势体现在两方面，一为学术优势，另一为非学术优势。就学术优势而言，澳大利亚过去一直因其强大的学术水准享誉世界，根据《泰晤士报高等教育高校排名》（*Times Higher Education*）和澳大利亚教育国际开发署（IDP）的排名数据显示，在2005—2006年度评选出的全球200强大学中，澳大利亚大学占其中17位，从第19名排列至第166名，其综合排名仅在美国和英国之后。这体现了澳大利亚教育的综合实力在全球的地位十分领先。但在2008—2009年度，澳大利亚有9所大学入围前200强，排名从第16名到第182名。在最新的数据中，2013—2014年度，澳大利亚共有

7 所大学进入前 200 强，排名从第 34 到 114 名。从排名上的下滑可以清晰地看到澳大利亚的学术优势正在减弱。其学术实力下滑的另一个表现在于其国际化后的课程设置也显得更缺少竞争力。

究其原因，不充足的政府财政支持是主因。没有充足的财政支持，使得许多教育机构开始将重心从提高教育质量转移到追求既得利益，这对澳大利亚教育发展的未来潜力造成损害。随着欧美国家不断强化自身实力，以及其他亚洲国家教育事业的蓬勃兴起，澳大利亚需要考虑如何重新强化其教育实力。

除了学术方面的竞争实力下滑之外，非学术领域的竞争实力也在下降。这些因素包括社会的安全问题、生活成本问题等等都成为了国际学生考虑是否赴澳留学的主要因素。2009 年发生的袭击印度学生事件，使印度学生对于澳大利亚的安全性产生巨大怀疑。

同时，澳元的升值以及上涨的生活成本都削弱了澳大利亚在亚洲留学生心目中的吸引力。

第三大问题在于对于亚洲认识的局限性。21 世纪也被称为亚洲的世纪。亚洲在各方面都达到了长足的发展，其教育事业也蒸蒸日上，但澳大利亚一直视亚洲为其教育出口产业的目标市场，却从没有意识到两国教育产业之间的互相学习交流的必要性。澳政府对于亚洲语言和文化学习和交流的资助颇少的现状正是这种现象的例证。亚洲学生的英语水平参差不齐，也给后期亚洲学生学习课程和融入澳大利亚社会提供较大困难。

5. 总结

澳大利亚的高等教育开始走向国际化，经历了从教育援助转向教育贸易，进而发展到教育国际化的成熟阶段。教育市场不断壮大，国际学生人数的剧增，使得政府制定和出台各项相关法律、标准、条例，以解决教育国际化中出现的问题，确保国际教育稳步发展。

亚洲国家一直以来都是澳大利亚留学生的最大生源输出国。热门学科已转变至管理、商业和信息技术，这符合 21 世纪的发展趋势。

我们可以看到，澳大利亚教育国际化的成功有着重要的经验：

（1）为了发展高等教育，必须大力关注高等教育的国际化发展。在澳大利亚，教育国际化是发展其国民经济和外交的方式。澳大利亚正是认识到了这一点，才使其能更有效地实施教育国际化策略。

（2）在发展教育国际化的进程中，政府应保持其引领地位。在澳大利亚教育的国际化发展中，政府的作用功不可没。正是由于政府不断地调整其战略中心，并适时解决教育领域中出现的新问题，而且在各个方面，包括市场推广、立法和质量保证等领域的不懈引领和支持才使得其教育事业不断发展。

（3）在发展教育国际化的进程中，必须合理地给予教育机构自主权，使之能更好地应对教育市场的变化。在澳大利亚，政府和教育机构各司其职，政府致力于打造良好的政策条件和外部环境；教育机构通过自主地控制自己的运作和管理，因而按照自己的规划发展教育事业。同时自主性也不能过度，以防出现不必要的问题。

（4）在发展教育国际化的进程中，需要建立一个严格有效的质量保证系统，来进一步推进高等教育的发展。澳大利亚教育质量保证系统发展得比较健全，保障了赴澳留学的国际学生的权益。澳大利亚学历资格框架（AQF）、澳大利亚大学质量署（AUQA）都为教育质量的保证提供了制度上的依据。

针对澳大利亚教育的问题，政府并不仅仅重视经济利益，而是通过增进外交和民间关系，提升教育质量和学生的学习体验。同时政府也加大财政支持，来减少教育机构面临的资金压力。除了直接的资金补助，政府也引导教育机构寻找合理的方式去获利。为提升澳大利亚教育的优势，澳政府提供长期稳定的资金支持，增进学术交流和合作，加强质量保证系统都对澳大利亚教育业裨益颇多。对于非学术领域的优势，有必要为国际学生营造安全体制，减少其生活成本支出，提供更好的学生签证服务等等。目前，澳大利亚政府正推出“新科伦坡计划”，鼓励和支持更多的澳大利亚学生前往亚洲求学，以更加积极的态势进入亚洲时代。

参考文献

[1] AEI. “International student enrolments in Australia 2012–2015.” 2015. [EB/OL] https://aei.gov.au/research/International-Student-Data/Pages/InternationalStudentData2015.aspx

[2] AEI. “International Student numbers 2015.” 2015. [EB/OL] https://aei.gov.au/research/International-Student-Data/Pages/InternationalStudentData2015/Table B.pdf

[3] AEI. “International students in Australian universities.” 2015. [EB/OL]. https://aei.gov.au/research/Research-Snapshots/Documents/International%20students%20in%20Australian%20unis%202015.pdf

[4] Dawkins, Hon J.S. “Higher Education: A Policy Discussion Paper.” Canberra: Aust. Govt. Pub. Service, (1989): 11.

[5] Fraser, Stewart E. “Overseas Students in Australia: Governmental Policies and Institutional Programs.” *Comparative Education Review* 28.2(1984): 25.

[6] Lowe, David. “Canberra’s Colombo Plan: Public Image of Australian Relations with Post-colonial South and Southeast Asia in the 1950s”. *Journal of South Asia Studies* 25.2(2002): 22.

[7] Williams, Sir Bruce. *Overseas Students in Australia: Policy and Practice.* Canberra: International Development Program of Australian University and Colleges Limited, 1989.

[8] 丁丽军．基于 AUQA 的澳大利亚高等教育质量保障模式研究．南昌：江西人民出版社，2012 年．

[9] 孔令帅．析澳大利亚高校课程国际化．世界教育信息 .2005(06): 10–12.

[10] 荣军、李岩．澳大利亚跨国高等教育发展探析．教育探索 .2012(1): 154–156.

[11] 沈雕．新时期澳大利亚高等教育国际化的特点评析．重庆高教研究 .2013(05): 92–102.

[12] 王留栓、褚骊．澳大利亚高等教育国际化概述——从发展教育出口产业谈起．复旦教育 .1999(2): 40–44.

[13] 杨舒．澳大利亚高等教育国际化的发展和启示．煤炭高等教育 .2008(7): 60–62.

[14] 曾满超、王美欣、蔺乐．美国、英国、澳大利亚的高等教育国际化．北京大学教育评论 .2009(4): 91–98.

程可珺，华东师范大学澳大利亚研究中心研究生，主要研究方向澳大利亚教育。

陈弘，华东师范大学澳大利亚研究中心主任，副教授，主要研究方向澳大利亚文化。

澳大利亚与 1945 年形成的区域格局
——当代战略的久远历史

尼克·比斯利

摘要： 本文探讨了战后协议在澳大利亚国际政策中的重要地位。本文尤其关注美国在二战后的各个条约中的区域领导地位和经济优势是如何融入澳大利亚国际事务的根基之中及其长远影响。本文的第一部分阐释了美国是如何渗透其在澳大利亚国际事务中的影响以及这种影响对于澳大利亚当前政治困境的重要意义。本文的第二部分讨论了 1945 年区域战略条约的基础构架从关注东北亚地区到聚焦澳大利亚政策的转变。文章最后反思了澳大利亚对于美国能长期处于世界首要地位的极大信赖，及其基于这种信赖对其战略未来所做出的选择。

关键词： 澳大利亚；战略方针；同盟；澳美关系；中澳关系

Australia and the Region that 1945 Created:
The Long History of Contemporary Strategy

Nick Bisley

Abstract: This paper examines the importance of the postwar settlement to Australian international policy. In particular, it considers how the postwar settlement of American regional primacy and economic dominance became built into the foundations of Australian international engagement and its long-term consequences. The first part of the paper explains how this occurred and why it is so important to Australia's current policy dilemmas. The second part of the paper examines how changes to the fundamental structures of the 1945 regional strategic settlement, focusing primarily on Northeast Asia, are driving shifts in Australian policy. It concludes with a reflection on the choices Australia has made about its strategic future as it is heavily invested in the belief that U.S. primacy can endure over the long term.

Key words: Australia; strategic policy; alliance; Australia — U.S. relations; Australia—China relations

一、引言

2015 年是极具纪念意义的一年。这一年，人们会见证两德统一 25 周年、越南战争结束 40 周年和维也纳会议闭幕 200 周年。当然，这一年也是二战结束 70 周年。但是对于澳大利亚而言，这一年中没有任何其他纪念活动比庆祝第一次世界大战中澳新军团在加利波利半岛登陆 100 周年的纪念日更为重要的了。

在澳大利亚成为英联邦的殖民地国家之后，悲剧很快就深深印刻在了澳大利亚的国家神话（Brown 2014）之中。尽管国家主义和与之相关的一些悲剧性事件在当代政治和澳大利亚民众心中扮演着举足轻重的角色，比如灾难性的达达尼尔战役（一战中，以英国为首的协约国企图从当时的奥斯曼帝国手中抢夺达达尼尔海峡，并由此引发战役）就对澳大利亚有着非凡的意义，但相较之下，太平洋战争的结束以及这场战争之后所形成的世界格局却在澳大利亚产生了更为深远的影响。

如果说 1915 年使得澳大利亚人认识到其在国际舞台上的位置，那么 1945 年则为其创造了一个全新的世界。也正是在这样一个新世界里，澳大利亚第一次在国际事务中行使了自己的权利。同时，澳大利亚在新的世界格局中的表现也显示出其应对国际新形势的政策方针与堪培拉的国际政策之间深厚的渊源。

二战后所形成的世界格局对于澳大利亚的发展极为有利。但是当国际环境发生变化的时候，有关澳大利亚战略方针中的一些基本设定的问题也就被不断提出。这些问题的核心都围绕着以中国经济的腾飞为代表的东北亚的飞速发展，而有关澳大利亚未来发展的政策性辩论也是愈演愈烈（Bisley, "Australia" 297–318）。尽管如此，从本质上看，澳大利亚两党对于未来的规划都建立在 1945 年后形成的世界基本战略格局在中长期里将保持不变这一前提之上。

本文就 1945 年对于澳大利亚战略性方针长期以来留下的阴影展开了探讨。本文的前半部分着重关注澳大利亚的战后移民问题并阐释了其是如何转变了澳大利亚与世界的联系，并就移民问题为澳大利亚国际方针的基本构建所带来的重要改变展开研究。文章在这一部分还关注了美国主导地位的优势以及澳大利亚战后移民的演变过程。本文的后半部分则探讨了地区秩序的转变以及澳大利亚对于这种转变的认知和应对。文章最后反思了澳大利亚对于美国能长期处于世界首要地位以及美国领导下的区域秩序长期维持不变的极大信赖，以及基于这种信赖所选择的政策方针长远的发展方向和这种选择的前景展望。

二、面对新世界

1. 澳大利亚政策的基本构建

在 1901 年澳大利亚联邦成立之前，澳大利亚大陆上的各个英属殖民地虽然规模较小，但却以其独特的身影活跃在国际舞台之上。1788 年最早的一批欧洲移民开始定居在澳大利亚，而之后澳大利亚殖民地的繁荣也正源于这批移民的勤劳与智慧。19 世纪由羊毛、黄金（最为重要的商品）带来的国际贸易帮助欧洲移民在澳大利亚大陆上生存并创造繁荣（Madsen 29–51）。作为大英帝国的一部分，生活在澳大利亚的各移民社会都参与了当时很多的大事件。澳大利亚各殖民地的军队也投入到大英帝国的对外战争中去，比如英帝国在苏丹的战役、布尔战争，甚至他们还加入了镇压中国义和团运动的八国联军，不过澳大利亚军队参与八国联军侵华的历史现在已鲜为人知。但即使是在各殖民地统一为独立的澳大利亚联邦之后，澳大利亚也没有得到过国际社会的正式认可。因此，虽然澳大利亚在第一次世界大战中为协约国阵营立下汗马功劳，也声势浩大地出席了巴黎和会，但是其并未能凭此制定出独立的外交和防务政策。而无论是在经济还是军事方面，澳大利亚与外界的一切往来都仍处在英国的控制之下。

尽管澳大利亚联邦宪法把发展对外关系明确地视为这个新成立的联邦政府[1]的一项权利，澳大利亚事实上却在很长一段时间里都没有能力和权力去实施其外交策略。澳大利亚的外交部规模很小，甚至当时在伦敦都没有设立任何澳大利亚的外交代表机构。作为英联邦的一个自治领地，[2]澳大利亚在 1923 年正式参与到国际社会的活动中来，但是在威斯敏斯特政体于 1942 年被正式采用之前，澳大利亚议会一直对其母国（英帝国）唯命是从。尽管在二战之前（Meaney 1976）的国际关系之中已能隐约察觉到澳大利亚独特的身影，但是直到 1945 年轴心国战败、新的国际秩序被确立之后，澳大利亚才开始真正独立地实施其外交与防务政策。

那么澳大利亚又是从何时开始全面地参与到国际事务中来的呢？二战后，很多澳大利亚曾经熟知的规则与秩序都不复存在了。大英帝国已日薄西山，而二战中曾经缔结并战胜轴心国的大同盟内部也开始分裂，在 1948 年便为冷战冲突所取代。与此同时，新的世界秩序逐渐形成。当欧洲各国忙于自身的战后重建之时，生活在其各个殖民地上的人民也在探索建立属于他们民族自己的国家。英国绝不是当时唯一一个深陷危机的帝国，事实上，1945 年标志着一个帝国时代的终结。

澳大利亚抓住时机在全球范围内建立外交机构，发展自身的国际政策。澳大利亚的外交部培训了一支专业的外交队伍，将澳大利亚大使馆迅速地建立在了全球的各个主要首都城市里。直到 1939 年，全球还只有伦敦有一个澳大利亚的外交代表机关。但仅仅一年之后，澳大利亚大使馆便出现在华盛顿、努美阿、渥太华和东京。1941 年，澳大利亚大使馆开到了重庆、帝力和新加坡；1944 年，澳大利亚又在惠灵顿和新德里新建了大使馆。至二战结束，澳大利亚已经与所有关键区域的伙伴——中国、日本、新加坡、新西兰和印度（Gurry 12）互通外交往来。澳大利亚在外交领域的迅猛发展不仅发自其对于独立处理自身事物的强烈愿望，更源于其对于当时风云变幻的世界的认知。

澳大利亚在参与国际事务时，认为世界永远处在一种剧烈动荡的状态之中。正如一位前高级官员，澳大利亚罗伊研究所所长阿伦 . 金杰尔所说，这种看法“反复体现

---

1 Commonwealth of Australia, *Commonwealth of Australia Constitution Act 1900*, Sect 51, xxix.

2 The term given to self-governing, white-dominated settler societies in the British Empire, such as South Africa, Canada and New Zealand.

在澳大利亚人民的世界观之中。因此，这种看法自然不断地出现在澳大利亚的政界人士与官员的话语中，比如，在一位澳大利亚外交部长向议会做的首份报告之中就流露出这种看法……”（Gyngell 2004）世界在澳大利亚人眼中之所以永远这么风云变幻，主要是因为澳大利亚政策的诞生与发展的环境总处于迅速而广泛的变革之中。二战后10年，从堪培拉到德里，甚至漂洋过海到日本，许多国家和地区的政治地位都发生了变化。而当时爆发在印度尼西亚、朝鲜半岛和越南国土之上的战争，使得澳大利亚的邻近区域成为了冷战时期伤亡最为惨重的战场。即使是在国际关系趋于缓和的时期，也不时爆发出各种危机，如20世纪70年代的石油危机，随时存在的新冷战威胁，旷日持久的战争草草收尾，再加之全球化的进程和诸如恐怖主义和传染病之类的跨国界威胁，处于这样的国际环境之中的澳大利亚决策者和分析家总有一种不安定的危机感也就不足为奇了。

1945年国际形势的转变在澳大利亚国际政策中遗留下的另一主要后遗症在于澳大利亚对于其国际地位长久以来的一种焦虑感（Burke 2008）。生活在这样一个人烟稀少而资源丰富的大洲之上，澳大利亚人总为来自外部世界的种种威胁感到惴惴不安。而在19世纪，澳大利亚与大英帝国在地理位置上的距离，也使得澳大利亚始终受制于欧洲列强的战略阴谋。当欧洲大陆对殖民地展开种种争夺之时，澳大利亚感到其自身也被卷入这些纷争之中。随着金矿的发现，澳大利亚成为了当时大英帝国最为富庶的一个属地，但澳大利亚人的恐惧也随之加剧，因为这些刚刚被开采出的金矿可以轻而易举地被德国、法国甚至是美国掠夺。人们很容易遗忘悉尼港的军事防御直到19世纪60年代一支美国舰队的突然驶入之后才真正建立，显然，经历了内战洗礼的美国绝不会成为英国及其任何殖民地的盟友。

2. 美国的主导地位

1945年，英国世界强权统治的终结，让澳大利亚的国际政策和策略展望受到了最为深远的影响。随着英国的实力和战略意志明显地日渐式微——这一点在整个二战过程中是很明显的，且在亚洲地区的战后合约里也得到了证实，为此澳大利亚面临着要寻求一个新的安全保障国的需求。澳大利亚是曾经世界上处于支配地位的海上霸主——大英帝国的属地，因此曾有个实力强大的安全保障国。澳大利亚的地理环境——疆域广阔以致人口分布稀疏，意味着这个国家要通过提高其海上优势入手来保障其地缘政治安全。英国海军曾经的霸主地位为它无疑提供了保障。

但日本帝国的军队轻易压垮了英国在亚洲地区的防线，尤其是新加坡的沦陷，给了澳大利亚决策者们一个重要的教训。这之后，日军紧接着于1942年对澳大利亚达尔文展开了空袭——虽然这是日军在二战期间对澳大利亚本土进行的唯一的直接攻击，这场进攻也迫使澳大利亚人意识到了自己的战略弱点以及在失去强有力的不列颠帝国这一后盾的情况下寻求国家生机的必要性。幸运的是，代替英国在西太平洋地区统治地位的是一个和英国语言、政治价值观、历史文化纽带有共同之处的国家：美国。

澳大利亚决策者们开始在二战期间将目光转投美国。之后成为总理的约翰·柯廷的著名讲话中明确表达了这一转向。他发表声明说："澳大利亚指望着美国，这对我们与联合王国的传统血肉关系丝毫也没有损害。"[1] 但是由于如今澳美两国之间长期稳固的关系，让人很难想起事实上美国起初是拒绝为澳大利亚提供安全保障的。澳大利亚转向美国的背后有几个动机。其中最明显的是澳大利亚希望可以借强国之力在遭遇袭击时进行防御，同时能威慑潜在进攻者。澳大利亚当时认为，战后的区域格局不稳，对于实力较弱的国家生存而言很有挑战。眼看日本军国主义势力很可能复苏，澳大利亚对日本重整军备再度崛起产生强烈恐惧。同时随着中国共产党取得解放战争的胜利，这个富有的白人民主国家对共产主义心怀无限忧虑。此外，二战结束不久，中南半岛、荷属东印度群岛以及马来半岛的殖民地独立高潮迭起，影响着地区稳定。这些都让澳大利亚执政者们意识到寻求一个强大的盟友来保障国家安全迫在眉睫。

澳大利亚寻求与美国建立紧密关系的第二个目的是增强澳大利亚国家影响力。一战期间，澳大利亚积极参战且伤亡相对惨重。有超过 38% 的成年男性入伍参战，约五分之一阵亡，在所有参战国中伤亡率相当惨烈（Higgins 1988）。然而澳大利亚的政治家和军事领导人却在战略决策制定这一环节上毫无发言权，在二战中也同样遭此待遇。正是感到本国在权力核心中影响力的缺乏使得澳大利亚政治领导人寻求与美国建立联系来结束这一局面。澳大利亚人并非想当然地认为自己能以此左右美国的政策制定，他们只是强烈地希望在战略对话中享有自己的发言权。

为实现上述目标，澳大利亚政府认为需要得到美国有力的公开承诺。最为首要的是与美国签署条约，得到美国正式声明的保证，即澳大利亚享有美国保护。不过，美国政府并不愿意做出此类保证，也绝不会轻易对此做出任何正式的承诺。自 20 世纪 40 年代后期，美国战略制定偏好采用非正式的形式来实现其安全承诺。很明显美国之前意图减小其在当时亚太地区力量的实力和规模，但后来打算维持其在太平洋地区的势力。

朝鲜半岛战争的爆发带来了美国政府对其在亚洲的长期战略所持的态度的转变。因为这场战争中显现的冲突证实了美国的担忧，同时欧洲冷战已开始全面影响亚洲。对于澳大利亚而言，朝鲜战争对其战略政策的长远方向产生了至关重要的影响，这主要是因为以下关键两点：首先，澳大利亚经慎重考虑，以领先其他国家向美国为首的联合国部队派遣陆军为策略来彰显其对美国的重要价值和忠诚度（O'Neill 1991）。这

1 John Curtin Prime Ministerial Library, Records of the Australian Broadcasting Corporation, John Curtin's speech to America, March 14, 1942, JCPML00434/1.

一战略手段影响了美国政府，尤其是很关键地引发了国会中关于美国对澳大利亚建立条约层面保护的讨论。第二个原因是，澳大利亚给了美国一个潜在提示，即要在亚洲地区扩张战略存在。正如朝鲜战争的爆发所显现的那样，战后时期亚洲的区域安全秩序是动荡不安的。

当时澳大利亚不仅希望能得到以条约形式建立的安全承诺，而且为了实现这份承诺澳大利亚希望得到一个更为明确的集体安全承诺。[1]1949 年北大西洋条约开创了组建集体安全的先例。条约的第五条申明：对于一个缔约国的武装攻击，应被视为对所有缔约国的攻击。[2] 澳大利亚领导人，尤其是外长佩西·斯彭德，希望在后来成为“澳新美安全条约”的条约中确立相似的缔约。但这一条约遭到了美方代表的拒绝。因为美国不想过紧束缚自己的手脚，何况考虑到它在亚太地区正在进行与日本和韩国条约协定以及其他事务安排，美国有更多方面需要顾虑。华盛顿政府不想在亚太地区给自己设下羁绊，这一来会限制住它的政策选择，二来会带来将它卷入冲突的风险。此外，美方代表告诉澳方代表，条约的签订还要考虑到美国参议院的态度，且他们认为如北大西洋第五公约类似的构建集体安全的内容不大可能被国会通过。[3]

1951 年，澳新美条约作为亚太地区战后“安排”的正式确立在旧金山签订。这份条约中包含的外交安排并不像那天签订的其他条约一样属于被视作美国为确保地区格局稳定而建立的更大战略系统一部分的附属条约。作为一个在当时刚获得能制定独立外交政策的国家，澳大利亚不仅出色地组建了外交使团并完成了重要的外交任务，它还连同整个亚太地区找到了一个新大不列颠。

国际大环境同样对澳大利亚的经济概况起到支持作用。战前澳大利亚的主要经济伙伴是英国和整个大英帝国——澳大利亚经济在很大程度上受到了英国在一战和二战期间建立起的最惠国制度影响，然而在二战后它不得不寻觅新的市场和合作伙伴。当时的美国无论在亚太区域还是在全球范围都对澳大利亚的利益有所帮助。它成为了对澳投资的主要来源以及澳大利亚对外出口的主要市场。且当时的国际贸易环境建立在由美国承担以官价兑换黄金的义务、美元起着世界货币作用的“布雷顿森林体系”之上，该体系使得澳大利亚有机会发展新的贸易关系。澳大利亚开始大量出口至亚洲，尤其是韩国和日本来满足朝鲜战争引发的需求。[4] 虽然美国并未像在安全领域里那样在

---

1 On these motives see the, at times self-serving, memoir of the period by then Australian foreign minister Percy Spend, *Exercises in Diplomacy* (Sydney: Sydney University Press, 1967).

2 NATO, North Atlantic Treaty, Washington, D.C., April 4, 1949, http://www.nato.int/cps/en/natolive/official_texts_17120.htm.

3 Some think that this was a polite way of refusing the request, see J. G. Starke, *The ANZUS Treaty Alliance* (Melbourne: Melbourne University Press, 1965), 45.

4 On the role of the Korean War in jumpstarting economic growth in East Asia, see Richard Stubbs, *Rethinking the East Asian Economic Miracle* (Basingstoke: Palgrave Macmillan, 2005).

经济方面起到和英国的相同作用，但它对失去了英国市场和投资的澳大利亚在找到成功的经济发展道路上起了至关重要的作用。

紧随战后的一系列安排并非就此定格。由于地区地缘政治不稳定，战后格局在很多方面不尽如人意。朝鲜半岛和中南半岛的大规模冲突和有关殖民地独立的较小规模的冲突引起了人们对东亚地区长期安全和稳定的怀疑。战后战略格局最重要的发展发生在 20 世纪 70 年代中期。在这之前，由于亚洲几个关键国家都不愿接受战后地缘和政治格局，使得该地区成为冷战爆发的上半战场。朝鲜半岛和中南半岛爆发的战争不仅是由本土环境直接所致，同时也是因各方势力意图改变战后格局。20 世纪 70 年代中期发生的根本性转变就是以外交手段结束了亚洲几个大国对战后地区格局性质和遵循的秩序产生的重大分歧。

中美外交关系的正常化改变了亚洲的战略格局。本来该地区特点是受到了两次大战和无数小冲突的影响，现因和平稳定受到瞩目。亚洲各国之前已同意了美国及其盟国于 1945 年确立的国际秩序规划。但是中美之间这场地缘政治的发展为日后改变亚太地区及全球的经济加速化铺平了道路。

从二战中走出的澳大利亚具备新获的权利来开创一片自己的外交政策前景。它眼前的世界和 1939 年前它所了解的世界已截然不同。澳大利亚领导人敏锐地意识到了美国在亚太地区和全世界扮演的举足轻重的角色，他们着手将自己国家未来的安全和这个新兴的区域超级大国捆绑在一起。澳大利亚预料美国可能成为的大国角色得到了印证，尤其是在 20 世纪 70 年代中期战后国际秩序得到巩固之后。美国在亚太地区占据的首要地位成为了东亚战略平衡的基石。鉴于所有重要国家，即便有些许微词，也都接纳了美国的重要地位，以及当时亚洲各国很大程度上因渴望将本国社会同新兴全球经济的至少一些方面联系起来而选择着力发展国内经济，美国所处的地位尤具影响力。

直至 20 世纪 70 年代中期，战火纷飞中形成的新世界对澳大利亚是极为有利的新布局。通过和美国结盟，澳大利亚得到了安全保障，威慑了潜在的进攻者。中美两国签订的条约也为其提供了更为重要的地区安全利益。最后，从亚洲发展中经济体的兴起之中，澳大利亚也在经济上有所获益。确实，与美结盟以及美国军事力量支撑着的区域框架对澳大利亚的战略政策和贯穿该政策的思想产生了意义深远的重要作用。

三、亚洲的转变

1. 中国的回归

对于该区域的大部分国家而言，中国经济的快速增长已成为澳大利亚所处国际环境之中的最大改变。澳大利亚由此面临着双重挑战，一方面是与中国贸易投资关系更加紧密，而另一方面，又对中国的战略信心及其对当前区域秩序的挑战怀有不安。

中国经济增长的传奇已闻名于世，20 世纪 70 年代后期开始的现代化进程促成了一段令人瞩目的经济改革期，使中国融入世界经济（Lardy 1994）。不到两代人，中国就已从一个糊口度日的封闭之国转变为世界上最大的混凝土、钢铁和消费品制造商。从购买力平价来看，中国已成为世界最大的经济体之一（Bird 2014），即使近期经济增长速度有所减缓，中国仍是世界经济发展的重要原动力，也是继美国后的世界第二大石油消耗国。[1] 中国经济的发展对于澳大利亚来说至关重要，因其对大量商品供应的总需求显著增长。1972 年时，中澳两国间贸易总值还仅停留在 8 600 万澳元（Yu 2012）。自 2007 年以来，中国已成为澳大利亚最大双边贸易伙伴。2013 至 2014 财政年度间，澳大利亚对中国出口增长了 28%，总价值超过 1 000 亿澳元，占澳大利亚总出口的 36.7%。[2] 而中澳的双边贸易总价值约 1 500 亿澳元，占澳大利亚贸易值的近 30%。中澳贸易关系的增进也映现了中国的飞速发展。商品货物仍占贸易量的首位，铁矿所占比例至今仍最大。民间关系也是建立贸易关系的重要支柱，国际教育就是一个重要的资源，其价值可称得上是与煤炭出口相同。中国向澳大利亚输送了大量留学生，其数量较之他国可谓遥遥领先，中国更是赴澳旅游的第二大国。

贸易仍是中澳经济往来之中最为重要的部分，不过投资也开始日益成为一大重要元素。中国一向被认为是澳大利亚的第八大投资国。源于中国的投资往往从其他国家或地区引入澳大利亚，如荷兰、中国香港以及避税港加那利群岛。需要强调的是，虽然就像中国对待其他全球外商一样直接的投资额并不高，但澳大利亚一向是中国资产流出的首选国度（Ferguson and Hendrischke 2012）。

因而中国的崛起对澳大利亚来说十分有利。这个商品资源富足的国度，属于那极少的几个没有因近期经济危机而陷入萧条的经济合作与发展组织成员国，相反，它正步入第 24 个经济持续增长的年头，这也是其历史上最长的一次持续增长阶段。20 世纪 80 年代和 90 年代的一系列自由化改革是促成这些瞩目发展成就的重要因素，而与中国的往来更是关键因素。然而中澳之间的联系也带来了一系列挑战，其中最显著的问题就是关于澳大利亚战略和防御政策。这是澳大利亚历史上第一次与一个在历史、价值观及联盟关系上无共同立足点的国家成为首要经济合作伙伴。尽管中国超越日本成为澳大利亚第一贸易伙伴，但由于日本与美国的密切联系，中澳贸易的紧密并未带来潜在的安全隐患。

正因如此，澳大利亚内部就其与中国经济的密切往来以及其与美国的战略联系之间所存在的冲突展开了激烈辩论（Thayer 20–26）。正因为中美两大国之间日益弥生的

1 Energy Information Administration, "China Country Analysis," http://www.eia.gov/countries/country-data.cfm?fips=CH.

2 One hundred billion AUD is worth approximately 78 billion USD. Data from DFAT, "China Fact Sheet," December 2014, http://www.dfat.gov.au/trade/resources/Documents/chin.pdf.

竞争关系，这一冲突较难化解。辩论的主线将取决于中国利用经济力量来转变澳大利亚政治策略的程度，以及堪培拉身处华盛顿与北京之间尴尬位置的前景。中国的经济发展使澳大利亚面临国际政策调整的挑战，中国的高经济增长及其对澳大利亚的重要性将影响澳大利亚外交策略以及中短期的国际立场选择。中澳经济上的相互依赖明显地改变了关于澳大利亚外交和国防政策更广泛的辩论方向，即使并没有真正意义上地改变任何政策。但正是在中国崛起的更广泛战略层面上，澳大利亚面临其最大的挑战。由于中国的复兴，自20世纪70年代中期以来盛行的亚洲地区政治、军事及经济格局正开始瓦解。

正如琳达·雅各布森所说的，中国的核心利益在于其政治体系的稳定、领土完整安全和以经济为主的战略，这是自中华人民共和国成立以来都不曾改变过的（Jakobson 2014）。然而，中国对其核心利益的维护并不仅仅可能改变地区平衡，促进国防现代化的发展（Liff and Ikenberry 52-91），同时也对该区域的现状有所影响，还将影响战后秩序的核心原则和地缘政治现状，即美国的首要地位及其维护的现状。美国已明确表示反对改变现状，并反对一切影响各地区对美国的依赖性的行为以及对美国首要地位的挑战。由此，澳大利亚迎来了自1945年以来针对其国防安全最大的挑战，澳大利亚需一方面考虑中国给世界主导秩序带来的影响，另一方面又因在保持其与崛起大国的关系的同时来应对这种挑战。

2. 美国的信誉

战后和解，尤其是在70年代整合后的稳定局势，最关键的是依赖于美国的首要地位以及几乎所有核心大国对此的认同。70年代以来，人们对战后和解的第一支柱——美国能长期保持地区主导地位的能力产生质疑，而近期这种质疑的声音又日趋增多。主导地位是指美国能够保持作为重要政治和经济力量，能阻止其他大国的战略行动，并果断塑造对其有利的战略设置。[1] 主导地位最重要的实际功能取决于他国的看法，即占主导地位的国家是否能保持其影响力和公信力。地方国际政治正步入一个新阶段，人们对两种特性的质疑声不断增多。很显然，目前对美国主导地位的挑战主要来源于人们的观念而非实质，而在国际政治中，人们的主观看法影响极大。

在奥巴马政府下，美国外交政策重新转移至亚洲。[2] 其政策的主要有两个目

1 For the seminal discussion of the concept of international primacy see Samuel P. Huntington, "Why International Primacy Matters," *International Security* 17.4 (1993).

2 The pivot has been explained by senior policy officials at length in many forums, the two key ini-tial statements were: White House, "Remarks by President Obama to the Australian Parliament," Canberra, November 17, 2011, https://www.whitehouse.gov/the-press-office/2011/11/17/remarks-president-obama-australian-parliament; and State Department, "Secretary Clinton on America's Pacific Century," Speech to East West Center, Honolulu, November 10, 2011, http://fpc.state.gov/176998.htm.

的：第一，将美国的战略重点从亚洲西南部以及伊拉克和阿富汗战争转移，并刻意朝着亚洲长期优先地位努力。第二，是给所有利益相关者一个信号，亚洲将成为全美首要战略重点。像美国这样在全球范围内公开的国家，优先级设置是至关重要的任务，一方面要考虑内部资源分配问题，并尽可能多地寻求外部国家支持。因此，这样的转变需考虑很多，特别应将欧洲这样长期重要性较低的地区纳入考虑范围。

这一核心策略的主要问题是显而易见的：它在很大程度上还只是一个外交信号而并没有任何新的实质性的战略承诺。高级官员们明显地表露出对地区问题的担忧，他们认为有必要抓住每一个机会重申美国战略核心的真实性以及美国会付诸实际的行动力。[1] 然而如果美国确实能做到，那么这些反复的陈述就根本无必要。因此零星的怀疑声开始出现，这在以前却是从未出现过的。

美国的自信心缺失与其短期和长期趋势都密切相关。华盛顿认为伊拉克和阿富汗战争已经扭曲了美国的战略重点，并且使美国的规划和资源远离亚洲。然而在这两方面的冲突中，美国显然没有实现其战略目标。更重要的是，这些战争，尤其是伊拉克战争中，美国政治、经济及军队的损耗似乎明显体现了美国使用武力的意愿较以往下降。奥巴马政府对持续的叙利亚流血冲突和俄罗斯入侵克里米亚的态度，反映出美国犹豫的心态加强。尤其是叙利亚战争中美国不惜代价地划“红线”，可见其承诺的可信度已不同于以往。近期，美国的战略行为预示着美国可能会谨慎地使用武力，即使决定参与武装冲突，也无法保证美国一定能用军事力量来达成其政治目的。

对该地区的忧虑也与美国区域性战略金融及政治可持续性的问题相关，频繁出现的政府停摆现象，以及美国政府长期面临的金融挑战，都或多或少体现了美方政治的疲软状态，同时也给美国区域军事主导地位的持久度打上问号。随着亚洲国家的逐渐富强，美国越来越难以承担主导该地区所需花费的政治或经济力量。在那些怀有这种顾虑的人看来，到 2040 年美国就很难维持其今天的区域主导地位了。不过很显然，不是所有人都持有这一看法，比如澳大利亚就认为美国的首要地位能长期或至少是中期维持下去。同样，该地区较弱势的国家诸如越南和菲律宾，也在与美国发展更紧密的关系。

需要重申的是，尽管对于这一地区的忧虑已浮出水面，但现在还未对整体战略平衡构成威胁。不过这些担忧的存在确实反映了二战后建立的区域秩序基本结构上的一个重要变化。

1 For example, Chuck Hagel, “United States Contribution to Regional Security,” Speech Delivered to Shangri-La Dialogue, 2014, May 31, 2014, https://www.iiss.org/en/events/shangri%20la%20dialogue/archive/2014-c20c/plenary-1-d1ba/chuck-hagel-a9cb.

四、澳大利亚对美国主导地位“双倍下注”

亚洲地区秩序的基本特性正在发生变化。毫无疑问，中国作为经济强国的重新崛起可以说是世界历史上一件意义重大的事件。曾经有利于澳大利亚参与国际事务的一系列环境正悄然变化。那个兴起于 1945 年又巩固于 20 世纪 70 年代的世界格局已经气数将尽。对此，澳大利亚采取了一系列决定性的战略承诺。尽管学术界及公众辩论提供了各种各样的政策选择，澳方政府已经对于澳大利亚的战略性未来有了决断：澳大利亚将密切保持和美国的盟友关系，并且相信亚洲地区秩序的远景将取决于美国一贯保持的主导地位。与期待澳方政府会在一定程度上保持与美方政府的战略距离的舆论截然不同，澳大利亚选择了将其和美国的未来捆绑在一起，而堪培拉与华盛顿之间的联系也的确是前所未有的紧密（Bisley, “Ally” 403–418）。

自从世纪之交以来，澳大利亚政府就已经煞费苦心地探寻澳大利亚战略命运和美国之间更为紧密的联系。这一阶段的澳大利亚政策开始于保守党总理约翰・霍华德执政时期，正是他使澳大利亚卷入同伊拉克和阿富汗斯坦的冲突之中。霍华德执政时期还签署了同美国的贸易协定，试图解决长期困扰盟国的贸易纠纷的“临界线”问题。近来，工党延续了这种亲美趋势，并从 2009 和 2013 的国防白皮书中都不难发现澳大利亚长期以来对美国的密切关系。澳大利亚政府以最简单明白的语言表明了其对美国将长期扮演地区内中坚力量的深信，并笃信中美有能力应对他们的差别。2013 年的白皮书提到：“澳大利亚所预见的未来是一个中美在竞争与合作中保持建设性关系的未来。”[1]2013 年上任的阿博特政府已经拟定新的白皮书，其预计在 2015 年发表并被认为将保持这种更广泛的战略眼光。

澳大利亚的长期战略政策包含以下三个关键因素。第一，致力于与美国的同盟是其国防政策的基石。澳大利亚相信美方政府将继续是该地区内举足轻重的存在，并且可以对澳大利亚的国防提供一如既往的保障和帮助。第二，澳大利亚认为地区秩序从 20 世纪 70 年代中期以来已经成型，以美国为主导的该秩序将再持续至少 30 年。就本质而言，澳大利亚的高层决策者认为在战略回归中美国将长期保持其从 20 世纪 70 年代开始就占据的区域主导地位。第三，也可能是最关键的一点，澳大利亚认为日益强盛的中国将被囊括到现有局势下。正如 2013 年的白皮书所言，尽管竞争激烈，但从大局而言，中国在现行秩序中已经寻得一席之地。不过澳大利亚对于美国主导地位下如此大的赌注是否真的明智呢？

澳大利亚政策的三核心要素中，第一个似乎是最可靠的。美国一直视其在亚洲的前沿部署具有关键的战略意义。美国总统奥巴马的接任者，无论来自哪个党派，都可

1 Department of Defence, *Defence White Paper 2013* (Canberra: Commonwealth of Australia, 2013).

能加强美国在亚洲地区的部署。虽然有人质疑美国该政策的财政可行性，但鉴于美国目前投用国内生产总值的 4% 在国防上，完全足以支撑该政策，特别是再考虑到美国政治系统对该政策的重视。在相信美国有能力并将成为澳大利亚政府所中意的盟友这一点上，澳大利亚的政治家们是完全正确的。

然而，关于第二个要素——美国能否在接下来的数十年中继续保持主导地位却并非如此确定了。或许最重大的问题是军事力量主导的政策在未来能否继续稳定该地区。在过去，美国的存在的确延滞了其他国家使用武力达成自身目的的行为，但是这种阻挠是否会在未来持续有效呢？这是不可知的。然而，只有不断依靠盟友日本，美国才能在亚洲地区得以存在，并且制衡其他国家，这样的假设是高风险的。除非日本成为灵活的战略强国并忠实于和美国的盟友关系，那么这种假设才是有理有据的。问题是无论是从政治上还是经济上这都不可能发生。同样地，军事上日益强大的日本将触发其他预见了不平衡发展形势的国家破坏地区稳定的举动。另一个对美国地区政策的更为长期的挑战是政治方面的。目前，所有大国在政治上都会承认美国的主导地位，但是亚洲各国未必会满足于生活在一个由华盛顿政府主导政治的世界里的。

这使我们不得不谈到中国。澳大利亚对于中国的政策看起来是异常乐观的。但是中国也在积极通过自身影响改变国际形势。亚洲基础设施投资银行的建立就是最好的说明，还有很多其他领域中也可以证明，如中国在上海合作组织的领导地位，以及其参与六方会谈和其他区域性的倡议（Bisley, “Real” 2014）。中国明白：现行秩序的规则，价值观和制度是由他国建立，反映了他们的某些利益，随着时间的推移、国际环境的改善，将更好地体现自己的利益和价值观。

无论是现在或在未来 10 至 20 年内，中国不想也不会寻求与美国的公开的军事竞争。但是，不能因此就认为没有明确的军事争端意味着中国将单纯地接受现行的所有条规。事实上，中国已经意识到现行的安排是不利于其发展的，这使得改变现行国际形势下的某些要素势在必行。而正是这一点，澳大利亚与其最重要的战略合作伙伴和其最大贸易合作伙伴的价值和利益的冲突，使得现在的澳大利亚战略政策制定者面临着前所未有的最为棘手的国际形势。

1945 年以后，澳大利亚凭借高明的外交政策登上世界舞台，并借此重新构建了其价值观并充分获取了利益。特别是 20 世纪 70 年代中期，澳大利亚更是受益于中国和美国建立的外交关系。这些政策充分考虑到澳大利亚的文化，自然禀赋和地理位置，让澳大利亚获益良多。但是，实际情况正在发生变化，文化、利益和价值观的取向也不比从前。未来的 70 年在方方面面都将与过去的 70 年大相径庭，而澳大利亚那依然停留在过去之中的现行政策似乎已不再能把握未来时代的命脉。

参考文献

[1] Bird, Mike. "China Just Overtook the U.S. as the World's Largest Economy." *Business Spectator* October 8, 2014. http://www.businessinsider.sg/china-overtakes-us-as-worlds-largest-economy-2014-10/#.VP5g8WSUdFA.

[2] Bisley, Nick. "An Ally for All the Years to Come: Why Australia is Not a Conflicted American Ally." *Australian Journal of International Affairs* 67.4(2013): 403–418.

[3] ——. "Australia and Asia's Trilateral Dilemmas: Between Beijing and Washington?" *Asian Survey* 54.2(2014): 297–318.

[4] ——. "The Real China Challenge: Beijing's Blueprint for Asia Revealed." *National Interest* October 24, 2014. http://nationalinterest.org/feature/the-real-china-challenge-beijings-blueprint-asia-revealed-11550.

[5] Brown, James. *ANZAC's Long Shadow: The Cost of Our National Obsession.* Melbourne: Black Ink Books, 2014.

[6] Burke, Anthony. *Fear of Security: Australia's Invasion Anxiety.* Cambridge: Cambridge University Press, 2008.

[7] Ferguson, Doug, and Hans Hendrischke. "Demystifying Chinese Investment: China's outbound investment in Australia." KPMG and the University of Sydney China Studies Centre. August 2012. http://www.demystifyingchina.com.au/reports/demystifying-chinese-investment-2012.pdf.

[8] Gurry, Meg. *Australia and India: Mapping the Journey.* Melbourne: Melbourne University Press for the Australia India Institute, 2015.

[9] Gyngell, Allan. Introduction. *Changing Utterly? Australia's International Policy in an Uncertain Age.* Ed. William Tow. Sydney: Lowy Institute for International Policy, 2004.

[10] Higgins, Matthew. "Australians at War." *Yearbook Australia 1988.* Canberra: ABS, 1988.

[11] Huxley, Tim. "Response to PacNet#35 United States 1 China 0." *PacNet 35R* June 12, 2012. http://csis.org/files/publication/Pac1235R.pdf.

[12] Jakobson, Linda. *China's Unpredictable Maritime Security Actors.* Sydney: Lowy Institute for International Policy Research Report, 2014.

[13] Lardy, Nicholas. *China in the World Economy.* Washington, D.C.: Peterson Institute for the International Economics, 1994.

[14] Liff, Adam, and G. John Ikenberry. "Racing Toward Tragedy? China's Rise, Military Competition in the Asia-Pacific and the Security Dilemma." *International Security* 39.2(Fall 2014): 52–91.

[15] Madsen, Jakob. "Economic Growth and its Drivers since European Settlement." *The Cambridge Economic History of Australia.* Ed. Simon Vile and Glenn Withers. Cambridge: Cambridge University

Press, 2014: 29–51.

[16] Meaney, Neville. *The Search for Security in the Pacific, 1901–1914.* Sydney: Sydney University Press, 1976.

[17] O'Neill, Robert J. "The Korean War and the Origins of ANZUS." *Munich to Vietnam: Australia's Relations with Britain and the United States since the 1930s.* Ed. Carl Bridge. Melbourne: Melbourne University Press, 1991.

[18] Thayer, Carlyle A. "China's Rise and the Passing of U.S. Primacy: Australia Debates its Future." *Asia Policy* 12(July 2011): 20–26.

[19] Yu, Chang Sen. "Sino-Australian Economic Relations." *Australia and China at Forty.* Ed. James Reilly and Jingdong Yuan. Sydney: Newsouth Publishing, 2012.

尼克·比斯利（Nick Bisley），澳大利亚拉筹伯大学亚洲事务委员会执行主任，拉筹伯大学国际关系学院教授。研究领域主要包括亚洲国际关系研究、全球化和大国外交。澳大利亚国际关系研究领域历史最悠久的学术期刊——《澳大利亚国际事务杂志》主编；澳大利亚国际事务协会理事、亚太安全合作理事会成员、国际战略研究所的高级研究员和华盛顿东西方中心（EWC）的访问学者。

（赵雅君　高方方　龙冰淳　史李丹　译）

中国与澳大利亚青年创意市集之比较研究

庄　瑜　秦艳龙

摘要：青年创意市集，代表着民间创意，它立足于日常生活，又依靠市场内生动力生长，在凝聚城市创意力量、营造城市创新氛围方面起着积极的作用。作为青年创意市集的主要组织者，高校也肩负着大学生创新教育的责任。本文通过比较中澳两国的青年创意市集，基于对青年创意市集概念、现状、类型、典型案例的分析，探索这股民间力量对大学生创新教育的启发。

关键词：创意市集；创新教育

A Comparative Study of the Youth Creative Markets
in China and Australia

Zhuang Yu

Abstract: Youth creative markets, as a representative of folk creativity, origins from the daily life and develops based on the commercial market, which takes effect on the creative force in the cities as well as constructs inventive circumstance. The universities and colleges are the main sponsors to organize the youth creative markets and have the responsibilities for the students' innovation education. This research explores how the innovation education evolves from the youth creative markets in China and Australia with the analysis of the market's concept, situation, types and typical cases.

Key words: creative market; innovation education

一、研究缘起

2015 年 9 月新上任不久的澳大利亚总理特恩布尔在 12 月 7 日正式宣布启动“国家创新与科学计划”，他表示应该释放创新和想象力，迎来“思想繁荣”，以此推动政府创新并促进创业文化。澳大利亚的下一个繁荣，不是矿业繁荣，而是可持续的繁荣，被喻为从 mine 到 mind 的转变。早在 2009 年，澳大利亚政府继 2001 年颁布的创新行动计划后颁布了又一个十年改革方案：《强大的理念——面向 21 世纪创新方案》（*Powering Ideas, An Innovation Agenda for the 21st Century*），这是一个指导澳大利亚创新体系发展的政策框架，目的是使澳大利亚更富有生产力与竞争力（段 44–46）。澳大利亚政府深知，要保持生产力的平稳和有价值的生活方式，必须建立强大的国家创新体系。同样地，2014 年，李克强总理于夏季达沃斯论坛上就提出要在中国掀起“大众创业”、“草根创业”的新浪潮，形成“万众创新”、“人人创新”的新态势。2015 年，李克强总理在政府工作报告中指出要把“大众创业、万众创新”打造成推动中国经济继续前行的“双引擎”之一。[1] 两个国家都在实施并积极推进以“创新”为核心的国家战略，对于高校而言，这也推动着大学生创新教育的持续深入。青年创意市集，代表着民间创意，它立足于日常生活，又依靠市场内生动力生长，与文化创意产业、创意经济大潮、青年创业相联系，在凝聚城市创意力量、营造城市创新氛围方面起着积极的作用。作为青年创意市集的主要组织者，高校也肩负着大学生创新教育的责任。创新教育是以培养大学生创新意识，提高创新能力和创业能力为目的的一种教育方式（王 117-118）。本文从青年创意市集的研究出发，通过比较中澳两国青年创意市集概念、现状、类型、和典型案例，探索此类民间创意及文化创造力对大学生创新教育，特别在营造创新氛围、开设创意课程、挖掘创业潜能方面的启发。

二、青年创意市集的概念

创意市集是指在特定时间、场地展示、售卖个人创意性产品的活动，简而言之，就是拿着自己做的东西去赶集。与一般市集不同的是，创意市集上的商品主要是富有个性和原创性的产品（龚 14）。青年创意市集指以青年人为主举办的创意市集，是传统市集在当代的一种新形态。“创意市集”的概念最早由台湾女设计师王怡颖于 2005 年提出，她采访了伦敦 Spitalfields 市场里 16 位设计师和艺术家，采访稿集结成册时，在市场前加了“创意”二字，并出版《创意市集——伦敦市集 16 位艺术家 / 设计师访谈录》一书，就此“创意市集”的概念在国内传播开来。

在澳大利亚，创意市集更多地融合在传统的市场或市集中，以售卖原创艺术品、手工制品为主。悉尼的帕丁顿周六市场（Paddington's Saturdays Markets）、堪培拉的旧公车站集市（Old Bus Depot Markets）、墨尔本的坎伯威尔星期天市场（Camberwell Sunday Market）和码头区星期天市场（Docklands Sunday Markets）、布里斯班的贵族区发电厂市集（Powerhouse Farmers Market）、达尔文的米切尔街夜市（Mitchell Street Market）、珀斯的亿谐德市场（E-Shed Markets）等不只是城市的文化地标，也是艺术家的聚集地，各类创意作品随处可见。

中国大陆第一个青年创意市集由广州《城市画报》主办，市集定位于“年轻人与城市”，取名“iMART”，寓意既有“Idea-Mart”（头脑创意市集）之意，也有“I am Art”（人人都是艺术家）的内涵。举办至今，形式多样，包括 iMART 创意产品展、iMART 互动加法创作、不插电音乐表演、主题派对等多种活动。之后，青年创意市集的概念席卷全国及海峡两岸，北京、上海、深圳、杭州等城市陆续举办 iMART 市

1 国务院 *http://www.gov.cn/xinwen/2015zccfh/content_2827683.htm*

集，并开始拥有城市品牌的青年创意市集项目：如北京的“南锣鼓巷创意市集”、上海的“上海湾—ONE 创意市集”、深圳的“OCT-LOFT-T 街创意市集”、杭州的“西湖创意市集”、香港的“Nomad Nomad 创意市集”、台湾的“西门红楼创意市集”。

三、中澳两国青年创意市集的现状

1. 传播途径：熟人圈 + 社交网络 + 旅行 app

青年创意市集以青年人为主要载体，因此市集的信息来源主要依靠熟人圈的“口口相传”，各类社交网络的发布及旅行 app 介绍。在中国，公众微信号、新浪微博、豆瓣网是三大主要发布创意市集信息的社交网络工具。“中国创意市集”（cnimart）是依托 www.cn-imart.com 网站的公众微信号，致力于全国创意市集信息的收集和原创品牌设计师的收录信息汇总，每隔两到三天就会发布全国各地创意市集举办的主题、时间和地点等信息；新浪微博以发布市集里的创意品牌为主，例如 @ 超模小熊桃妃-原创手工玩偶熊、@ 慕容九的手作珠宝、@Mr_Reber 手工皮具、@zookeeper- 手工日记本等，他们既是市集的参与者，同时经营着原创品牌，用微博作为宣传和交流的窗口；豆瓣同城是豆瓣网中提供各城市当地所有音乐、戏剧、讲座、聚会、旅行、集市等线下活动的资讯频道，在“聚会”一栏中设有“集市”板块，公布各类集市的信息，以青年创意市集为主，并附“我有兴趣”和“我要参加”等预估按钮，以此对市集参与度作初步估计。在澳大利亚，许多市集具有多年的历史，已成为当地的重要文化地标，是当地市民及游客的常往之地，且时间较为固定，多开设在周末，传播的方式以口口相传或旅行 app 为主，例如澳大利亚的 Australia Travel app。此外，在中国的蚂蜂窝、穷游、携程等旅行 app 上也能搜索到澳大利亚的市集信息。

2. 举办形式：地摊 + 实体店 + 网店（龚 119–125）

地摊模式是青年创意市集最基本、最普遍的形式，不同于普通游商小贩，创意市集地摊是需通过向市集坐办方或协办方申请经过一定程序方可开设，有室内室外两种类型。室外的场所包括广场、公园、创意园区、社区空地等。例如，澳大利亚的布里斯班贵族区发电厂市集坐落在贵族区 New Farm 的布里斯班发电厂内、布里斯班的博格路市集（Boggo Road Market）建在监狱旧址上、墨尔本失物招领复古市集（Lost & Found Market）曾一度开设在一家废弃的酒吧内。中国则有北京海淀公园的 iMART 创意市集 × 迷笛、杭州西湖广场的文化创意市集、天津民园西里的“赶巷子”创意夜市等等。室内的场所包括购物中心、商务楼、老建筑、废弃的工厂或店铺、博物馆等。比如北京大悦城商厦的“糖果小镇”创意市集、上海 1933 老场坊的 1933 创意市集、成都银石广场购物中心的创意市集、上海当代艺术博物馆的鹦鹉螺美学生活市集。实体店和网店模式的青年创意市集是地摊模式的演变与延伸。实体店模式的青年创意市集是指在固定的经营场所集中销售创意产品的模式，天天开集。例如，台湾花莲创意文化园区内有一个固定室内场所，被分割成若干区域，每个区域归属一个文化创意品牌销售自已的产品，消费者不但能直观产品，且场地固定，能让品牌更拥有足够的忠实度。而澳大利亚布里斯班的帕丁顿复古市集（Paddington Antique Market）（张，程 168–185）从建筑的外观开始就充满着复古且炫彩的式样，例如嫩黄墙体配上草绿栅栏，店内则荟萃着各个年代的珍品。网店模式的青年创意市集随着网络技术的发展、WEB2.0 的普及应运而生，指在某个网络平台上聚集一定数量的创意品牌，品牌拥有者通过网络平台推广与销售，购买者通过网络平台进行了解和购买，例如以疯果网（www.fengguo.com.cn）和哇噻网（www.wowsai.com）为代表的专属网站、米墨乐品为代表的淘宝店铺等。

3. 主办方类型：媒体 + 文化公司 + 高校

青年创意市集的主办方呈多样化形态：媒体、文化公司、高校、政府、社会组织、慈善机构等。其中媒体、文化公司和高校是举办国内青年创意市集较为活跃的主体。媒体主办者因为拥有自己的渠道，因此在发布、宣传开集信息上具有传播快、影响力大的优势。例如广州的《城市画报》是大陆首个创意市集 iMART 的发起者，后继还在北京、上海、深圳、重庆等地推广创意市集的理念和活动形式。文化公司一般拥有较厚的经济实力，还能举办现场演出等文化艺术活动，以增加市集的吸引力。例如上海的鹦鹉螺市集多以复古、创意为主题，还会配有运动派对、城市嘉年华等活动形式。高校举办创意市集有的是以本校艺术类专业展示原创作品为主的单个高校市集，例如台湾师范大学表演艺术系因开设文化创意产业课程而设立学生创意市集，将学生的创意向公众开放，集市共 72 个摊位，分别以孔子的 72 个弟子的名字命名（肖 80–81）；有的是以展现大学生创意思维与才华的高校联合市集，例如由《浙江日报》和浙江理工大学艺术与设计学院共同举办的杭州大学生创意市集，引来了中国美术学院、浙江工商大学、浙江中医药大学、浙江传媒学院、杭州电子科技大学、杭州师范大学等多所在杭高校学生的积极参与，成了一次学生创意作品展示的欢乐派对（张等 9）。

四、青年创意市集的典型案例分析

1. 原创理念型创意市集

原创理念型创意市集指赋予市集一定的主题，且展示或售卖的物品以原创为主。墨尔本的失物招领复古市集以“失物招领”替代“老物件”的概念，展示的都是 20 世纪 40 年代到 90 年代的物品，有历史穿越的复古感。上海的怀旧跳蚤集市（Dreams

Factory Asia）以“怀旧”为主题，要求参与者带二手杂货或手工创作来摆摊或者交换，活动宗旨以拥抱怀旧为乐趣。香港的小生活市集（A nice place to）每个月都有一个主题，使市集添了更多趣味。例如二月是“成双成对”，三月是“三人行必有我师”，五月市集则以“五感生活”为主题，希望每天忙碌于工作的人，能用第五感去欣赏他人的创意，从而丰富自己的生活经验。此类市集以主题的形式既能让市集里的原创物品得以分类，合并同类项的方式使同类创意产品可形成系列，产品背后的理念得以在同一时间进行呈现；又能通过主题，使产品的概念和原创者的经营理念回应社会议题。

2. 分享 + 交换型创意市集

分享 + 交换型创意市集是指在市集上分享各自创意的来源、同时交换技能的市集，经常以举办工作坊、小课堂、现场展示的方式开展交流互动。上海柯勒的二十四节气市集，每月举办两次“手艺课堂”，内容有木刻水印、瓷刻、黄草编、蓝印花布等，参与者可借着手工及各种工艺，了解传统手艺技能。北京南锣鼓巷市集是南锣鼓巷胡同节的重要组成部分，市集上有各种老北京传统非遗项目的现场展示，如彩塑兔儿爷、北京料器邢、京派内画鼻烟壶、北京宫灯等。此类市集的作用在于给予有创意想法的青年一个面对面交流的平台，让他们的作品得到赏识，获得市场的肯定，同时在宽松灵活的环境下学习传统手艺并交流技能，使文化与手艺得以延续和传播。

3. 鉴赏 / 生活型创意市集

鉴赏 / 生活型创意市集是指以生活为主旨的市集，美食是生活的主要组成部分，它也有“创意”的一面，让来访者有不同的视觉 + 味觉体验。阿德莱德的中央市集（Adelaide Central Market）里，常常会摆上近百种乳酪，让访客试吃的同时还会开设鉴赏课程，为食物赋予庄重的地位。布里斯班的博格路市集的书摊上，也会摆上几袋圣女果与几瓶番茄沙司，并注明书与食物间的共性：“给人们提供新鲜的补给”。布里斯班的北街周日有机市集（Northey Street City Farm Sunday Organic Market）会开设关于“活力生活”的课程介绍，教授如何种植健康的蔬菜、如何拥有一个菜园、如何饲养家禽等（张，程 168–185）。此类市集以美食为主，但不乏传播对美食的鉴赏和对健康生活的态度，是对创意生活理念的传递，也预示创意可以遍布生活的每个角落。

4. 创业 = 兴趣型创意市集

创业 = 兴趣型创意市集是指以兴趣为导向、以创业为目的的市集。台湾桃园龟山私立龙华科技大学三创（创意创新创业）中心每三个月举办一次创意市集，产品来自学生个人兴趣出发的物件，有口味特别的食品、生活创意手工、自创魔术等，旨在透过市集平台，学生能改善产品的特色，推动产品的商品化或产业化。广州红专厂创意市集，坐落于红专厂文化创意园区，园区里聚集了百余家设计师工作室、文创企业及创意体验区等，市集口号是："如果你有创业激情或者你是创意达人，请来红专厂亮出你的新奇想法"。此类市集能使参与者将兴趣与创业结合，在市集上提早接受市场考验，累积经验与自信心，有助于日后的顺利创业，同时挖掘新生代创意人才，促进新产品的产业化，发挥创意实践和创新转化的双重功能。

5. 摆摊 × 表演型创意市集

摆摊 × 表演型创意市集是指市集除了摊位摆放，还包括原创乐队表演、街头舞蹈、涂鸦 SHOW、行为艺术等多元表演形式的市集。墨尔本的维多利亚女王市场（Queen Victoria Market）虽然被认为是南半球规模最大和最古老的市场，街头艺人的表演仍旧是市场里一支独特旋律。荷伯特的萨拉曼卡市场（Salamanca Markets）同前者一样，售卖玻璃工匠、制陶师、木工或画家独特作品的同时，地下音乐人也以另一种艺术形态与他们同台展现。深圳的 T 街创意市集每月第一和第三个周末举行，市集上有街头艺术家行为表演、小型乐队表演、滑轮、单车等时尚新潮表演。北京的草莓音乐节创意市集是草莓音乐节中的一个板块，音乐节的参与者同样也是市集的消费者，时装展示、游戏互动、摇滚乐队表演成为创意市集的风景线。此类市集将"创意"的概念从物件扩大到表演形式上，让每一种创意通过不同的表达形式得以表现，跨界的表现手法能促发灵感的碰撞与激发，给予参与者发散性的启示，也让创意市集更充满青春时尚的气息。

相较两国的青年创意市集，中国的创意市集较为独立，访客多为青年人，他们抱着好奇、革新的心情投入其中，把参加市集活动作为一种时尚行为，高校是创意市集的重要推手，创意市集成为大学生创业的展示窗口。澳大利亚的创意市集多隐藏在各大已成规模且具有历史积淀的平民综合市集里，生活元素较突出，能在平凡的事物中开创新的吸引力，尤其在传统手工艺中挖掘创新力，市集的生命力旺盛，有可持续性。两国都偏好摆摊 × 表演型的创意市集，通过各种表现形式，不但提升了市集的关注度，且丰富的艺术表现本身也是"创意"的一部分。

五、对大学生创新教育的启发

1. 创建高校创意市集群，营造校园创新氛围

高校是青年创意市集的主要发起者，部分高校已集结成群。例如，杭州下沙高校园区的大学生创意市集是由浙江理工大学自发的小范围活动发展而来，后在园区的支持下，每天下午五点半开放。北京大学生创意市集自 2011 年举办首场活动以来，以

每年一场的速度发展着，参与学校从 20 余所到现如今的 30 多所，集市上有上万件展品，种类涉及平面艺术、服装服饰、插花装饰、金工、雕塑和小发明等。不过，大部分高校的创意市集仍以单打独斗为主。上海的东华大学已连续举办七届创意市集；广西艺术学院大学生创意市集创办于 2007 年，已连续举办十四届；也有一些高校零星地举办过 1—2 次创意市集。尝试将高校创意市集形成群落，有利于不同高校不同专业的同学互动交流与学习，无论是师生、生生或是参加集市的路人之间，都可交流创意的来源与创作的感受，使创意气氛环绕于学生周围，满足了校园原创设计师们对一个开放、多元创作生态的渴望。对于高校而言，举办创意市集是大学生创新教育的尝试，是第二课堂中培养学生创新思维和创新能力的民间力量。市集展现的作品不但包括如手绘工艺、传统技艺、时尚生活、原创设计等物质类，也可包括如原创音乐、原创舞蹈、原创魔术、原创话剧等非物质类面向全体的作品形式。

2. 促进高校与校外机构合作，开设创意实践课程

高校开设创意市集，多源于艺术或设计类专业学生的作品展示。事实上，寻找创意并制作成品并非艺术或设计类专业学生的专利，面对现代社会的急速发展，无论是有形还是无形，人们每天都需要应对不同程度的变化，创新思考的能力与积极探索的态度才是应对变化的重要抓手。青年创意集市里怀揣创意甚至后来拥有独立创意品牌的人大都来自多元的专业领域：Mary Sanver 原本从事法律事务，后成为“Mary Sanver”品牌女性家居服的创意设计人，她的设计中没有任何两件完全相同的产品（王 124–129）。“芸香堂”的掌门人多年经营着一家互联网软件开发公司，却因为对香的热爱转而投身于这份全新的事业。他另辟蹊径从事制香、焚香，自立门户、自产自销，全然一副雅士风范[1]……为使高校开设的创意实践课程更符合市场规律和需要，高校可尝试与校外机构合作，推动课程的建设与发展。例如，台湾中正大学紫荆书院的“创意思考与实践”课程是“面向全体”的选修课程，前半段主要从创造心理学的角度出发，强调“思考”的内涵，配合各种跨领域的案例佐证，让学生了解创意的内涵并能鉴赏一个好的创意，后半段的课程则是强调“实践”，通过期末作业的实践环节，结合理论与实务。[2] 墨尔本大学的“墨尔本模式”则要求学生在结束学业前，能将所学用于现实，通过实地考察、基于项目的学习等方式进行实践（李，陈，张等 97–100）。基于校外创意市集的特色，高校可与“分享 + 交换型创意市集”中设立工作坊、手艺课堂的校外机构合作开办沙龙、工作坊、小课堂，借助机构的资源为学生开拓眼界，以开办“手艺课堂”闻名的文化机构上海柯勒的课堂教师就有非物质遗产文化传承人、

1 芸香堂官方微博 http://weibo.com/611231015

2 台湾中正大学紫荆书院 http://www.ccuelite.ccu.edu.tw/home.php

工艺美术师、书画协会会员等，成为传承“理论”的重要支撑。作为知名独立书店代表，西西弗书店也是重庆创意市集的主办方，辖区是入住师生最多的大学城，书店本着“灵感可以交流，创意可以分享，可以因创意而丰富生活的理念”为大学生提供创意展示空间，亦能成为课程“实践”的场地。

3. 搭建高校与市场交流平台，挖掘学生创业潜能

在澳大利亚，创业型大学（Entrepreneurial University）已有10多年的建设历史，兴起于莫纳什大学，许多大学纷纷效仿，在全国掀起一股高校创业的热潮。（荣，李 113-116）创业型大学积极培育高校内部的创业文化，形成高度凝聚力，促使学生们为着同一创业目标而努力。同时，创业型大学努力创办自己的企业，依托学校的人才优势，将创新成果转换为成熟的商品。在中国，2015年5月，国务院办公厅颁布《国务院办公厅关于深化高等学校创新创业教育改革的实施意见》（国办发［2015］3号），特别指出[1]：“探索建立校校、校企、校地、校所以及国际合作的协同育人新机制，积极吸引社会资源和国外优质教育资源投入创新创业人才培养。”以高校创意市集的方式带动学生进行原创品的开放，给学生搭建与市场交流的良好平台，为学生的未来创业做好前期市场铺垫和商业行为演练，并累积经验和信心，为今后的创业和品牌创立打下基础。高校创意市集相对其他主办方组织的市集，能促进学校创意与发明成果商品化或产业化，强化师生的创新能量，提升创业产出，并提供创意实践、创新转化和创业辅导三大功能。当然，针对创意市集的发展规律，如果要在高校进行基于创意市集的创业平台的建设，在布局上必须进行多角度、系统化的思考，特别是创意市集产业链的拓展与整合。创意市集产业链属于创意推动型的产业链，产业链的拓展中知识产权保护是核心，大学生的创意产品有“投入成本高，复制成本低”的特性，容易遭到抄袭与复制而失去原来的优势建设独立创意品牌，相关的知识产权保护是前提和基础（杨 63-66）。产业链的整合主要指各环节的优化和环节关系的梳理，包括产品和创意的完善、外包量产的质量管控、渠道的拓展、市场营销、自身知识产权体系的完善等。这也需要高校拥有专业的创业指导团队，协助学生理顺各环节的工作，这与《国务院办公厅关于深化高等学校创新创业教育改革的实施意见》（国办发［2015］3号）所提出的：“……探索建立跨院系、跨学科、跨专业交叉培养创新创业人才的新机制，促进人才培养由学科专业单一型向多学科融合型转变……”相一致。

青年创意市集这股民间力量能凝聚城市的创意力量，为营造城市创新氛围起着积极作用，也为大学生的创新教育改革的持久战注入活力。

---

1 国务院 *http://www.gov.cn/zhengce/content/2015-05/13/content_9740.htm*

参考文献

[1] 段慧兰 . 澳大利亚创新政策及其启示 . 湖南社会科学 .2010(3): 44–46.

[2] 龚小凡 . 创意市集：民间创意来力量的集合地 . 北京：九州出版社，2013 年 .

[3] 李红宇、陈强、张毅等 . 澳大利亚墨尔本大学“墨尔本模式”改革初探 . 清华大学教育研究 .2008,29(6): 97–100.

[4] 荣军、李岩 . 澳大利亚创业型大学的建立及对我国的启示 . 现代教育管理 .2011(5): 113–116.

[5] 王娜 . 大学生创新教育初探 . 教育探索刊 .2007(2): 117–118.

[6] 王怡颖 . 创意市集——伦敦市集 16 位艺术家 / 设计师访谈录 . 北京：三联书店，2005 年 .

[7] 肖潇 . 台湾创意市集地摊达人的狂欢盛宴 . 新经济导刊 .2008(2): 80–81.

[8] 杨从锋 . 基于创意市集产业链的高校创业平台的搭建 . 浙江工贸职业技术学院学报 .2014(1): 63–66.

[9] 张进步、程园园 . 市集 . 北京：中信出版社，2015 年 .

[10] 张力等 . 创业创新从创意开始——杭城大学生创意市集火爆异常 . 杭州日报 .2008–4–24(9).

庄瑜，博士，华东师范大学外语学院讲师，主要研究方向包括思想政治教育、学科教育。

秦艳龙，助理研究员，北京大学信息科学技术学院。

“触摸奉献”

——《窗口：当代澳大利亚诗歌——中英双语选集》[1]序言

Jen Webb and Paul Hetherington

（陶乃侃 译）

一、出版目的

近期在堪培拉大学成立的国际诗歌研究所（International Poetry Studies Institute）旨在建立世界范围的诗人与诗歌研究的联系。该研究所以促进诗歌研究的新方法为宗旨，兼顾协助新诗的创作与发表，促进对诗歌的新阐释，刺激各式各样的诗歌品种杂交，同时致力于协助诗人更为自信地表达自己的心声，更为频繁地以跨文化的方式表达，并与世界各地的艺术家形成更为频繁的互动。

陶乃侃向我们提出汉译澳大利亚当代诗歌的建议时，我们立即同意了。这是一种开展诗人与汉语诗歌读者以及（主要是）与澳大利亚各界的诗歌读者之间“对话”的新方法——一种不是只限于文化界空谈而毫无结果，而是付诸于实现的文化交流的方法。其困难不仅在于语言各不类同，而且可预见不同文化的接受与再现也各不相同，以及不同语言的遣词造句、文法排列亦各不相同。如墨西哥诗人奥克塔维奥·帕兹（Octavio Paz）所言：“每一种语言都是一种世界观，每一种文明都是一个世界。阿兹台克诗歌赞美的太阳不同于埃及颂诗中的太阳”（153）。

但是翻译旨在两种语言、两种文化、两种语境之间构建桥梁；因此这个项目尝试通过每位参与者的专长、文化通识与习性通力协作建立起这样的桥梁。陶乃侃作为译者是从汉语的视角来处理这些作品，同时他也熟悉澳大利亚的文化与习俗。我们俩作为编辑是从澳大利亚的视角，以及由阅读英译中国诗歌而对其产生的钦佩，加之我们对中国诗歌传统的博大丰富亦有所认识来实现这个项目。

入选如此一部诗集的诗人并非全都是人们期待的名字（尽管许多“期待的”名字已经在别的诗集中出现过），然而他们中的许多人，尽管作品卓越，却鲜为境外人士所

1 该书即将由上海三联出版社出版。

知。但是他们全是献身于诗歌创作的实践者，全都有表达自己的趣味盎然的方法。我们决定在这部诗集再现二十位诗人，其中包括一些相当有成就的诗人，一些相较尚在创作初期的的诗人，以及一些一直坚持创作且目前在各自作品中发展个人品位的诗人。

他们全都是澳大利亚生机勃勃的诗人社群成员，不过有一两个还算不上老“澳洲人”，近期才移居这个国家。但是这些诗人要么是澳洲人要么与澳洲密切相关，大致如此。他们在澳大利亚的诗歌社群及其传统中占有一席之地。澳大利亚的诗歌传统可以追溯到几千年前，追溯到澳洲土著居民以歌谣、诗、故事为形式的口头文学传统。一些民间文学已经译成英语并出版为多种诗集，其中包括 T. G. H. 斯特雷罗（Strehlow）选编的《澳洲中部诗歌》、罗纳德·伯恩特（Ronald Berndt）选编的《阿恩厄姆地区的爱情歌谣》、马丁·杜威尔（Martin Duwell）和 R. M. W. 迪克逊（Dixon）合编的《月光小溪旁的小伊娃》以及其他澳洲土著的歌谣选集；2014 年斯图亚特·库克（Stuart Cooke）编辑出版了《乔治·迪昂盖延的布鲁之歌：金柏利西部组诗之一》。澳洲土著的口头文学传统仍然作为当代土著文化和诗歌的重要部分在继续。

较为近代的诗歌传统始于 1788 年，即英国人移居到澳大利亚的历史时刻，同时带来了英格兰的、爱尔兰的、苏格兰的以及其他诗歌形式。林地民谣和叙事诗是 18 世纪晚期至 20 世纪初期最为典型的诗歌形式，亨利·罗森（Henry Lawson 1867–1922）和班卓·帕特森（Banjo Paterson 1864–1941）也许是这一漫长时期最著名的澳大利亚诗人。时至 20 世纪 30 年代，现代主义运动开始在澳大利亚产生重大影响，正如那场两大诗歌运动间的著名争执所佐证。金迪沃罗巴克派（Jindyworobak）企图发现任何“别具澳大利亚特色”的内容（Gifford 1944），并要表达“本土的”澳大利亚文化和语言；而“愤怒的企鹅”一派则相反，抵制本土题旨，更加青睐具有某种欧洲意味的、澳大利亚之外意味的内容（Harris 1939）。继现代文学文化中的这次争执之后，澳大利亚诗歌已经发展成一种深深渗透国际潮流，尤其是国际大都市潮流影响的独特的本土话语，同时保持着对当地问题、当地环境与当地文化语境的关注。时至 20 世纪中期朱迪斯·莱特（Judith Wright 1915–2000），肯尼思·斯莱瑟（Kenneth Slessor 1901–1971）、A. D. 侯珀（A. D. Hope 1907–2000）、罗斯玛丽·道伯森（Rosemary Dobson 1920–2012）等澳大利亚诗人在传承他们各自的浪漫主义传统的同时给本土诗歌带来一种明显的智性。而杰克·戴维思（Jack Davis, 1917–2000）、乌捷如·农努科尔（Oodgeroo Noonuccal 1920–1995）、鲍比·赛克思（Bobbi Sykes 1943–2010）以及其他诗人则给澳大利亚的主导文学话语引进了关注土著人民对人权的诉求，这是一种承认历史事实的表达，也是对传统土著价值的重申与重新激活。这些诗人的创作有助于为本世纪形成高度多元折中的诗歌写作实践格局打下了基础。

当今澳大利亚的诗歌虽然拥有广阔的诗学形式，但大多情况是由一些小出版社和设于大学的文学杂志来支持。典型的例子是《米安津》（*Meanjin*，墨尔本大学）《南风》(*Southerly*，悉尼大学)和《西风》(*Westerly*，西澳大学)。此外还有《夹克2》(*Jacket 2*，与诗人约翰·特伦特尔(John Tranter)协作)、《尤尔克街》(*Eureka Street*)等众多发表网络诗歌的杂志。支持诗歌评论的机构有《澳大利亚图书评论》(主编长期由诗人彼特·罗斯担任)、《无烟火药诗歌评论》(*Cordite Poetry Review*)等。澳大利亚诗歌选集也定期出版，近期引人注目的例子有《最佳澳大利亚诗选系列》，每年由布莱克出版公司出版。此外有约翰·金瑟勒(John Kinsella)2008年出版的《澳大利亚诗歌企鹅选集》。出版澳大利亚诗人个人作品选集的文学期刊、选集和出版社支持着形式多样、风格多变的诗歌创作。田园诗可见于诸如莱思·玛雷(Les Murray)或者约翰·金瑟勒的作品；费·兹维基(Fay Zwicky)、罗伯特·格雷(Robert Gray)等的城市抒情诗不断扩展国际都市诗的界域；而多萝西·珀特(Dorothy Porter)和斯蒂文·赫瑞克(Stephen Herrick)则使韵文小说更为流行。此外有喜爱试验诗歌的诗人，其中有海索尔·史密斯(Hazel Smith)和艾尼亚·沃维克兹(Ania Walwicz)，还有一群热情的追随者，诸如奥玛·缪塞(Omar Musa)和皮·欧(Pi O)热衷表演的"敲打"诗人。同时有一些诗人既依靠他们的亚洲背景又依靠他们的澳洲背景探索合适的诗歌表达方式，并形成一种迅速发展的趋势，其中有亚当·艾特肯(Adam Aitken)、欧阳昱、米歇尔·凯希尔(Michelle Cahill)。这部选集旨在重现正在丰富的澳大利亚诗歌传统中创造的二十位诗人的作品，包括一些鲜为人知的心声，并为读者提供一部具有当代澳大利亚诗歌的多样性与总体诗歌意味的选集。

二、翻译途径

我们选择了入选该诗集的诗人，每位诗人挑选一定数量的诗作供翻译选用，再由陶乃侃选定可译的作品。毕竟如沃尔特·本杰明(Walter Benjamin)所指出，并非所有诗歌都是可译的。通过跟陶乃侃谈论这个项目、讨论选译作品的原则等，我们开始较为认真地考虑翻译艺术，以及沃尔特·本杰明称之为翻译之"方法"(70)；考虑译作如何可以为人理解，翻译如何可能有所变形。

文学理论对翻译本身颇有焦虑，尤其是诗歌翻译。"翻译"一词本身与问题相当无关，英文这一词来自拉丁词"translatio"，意为"带过去"或者"带过来"(Kasparek 83-87)。然而这个词趋向传达背叛的意思。在某些罗曼语中翻译一词演化自拉丁词"traduco"(领过去)，这个词对母语为英语的人而言传达的是诽谤的概念。此外还有"优秀"的翻译与忠诚的联系，这又导致背叛与真实等相关概念。

约翰·德莱顿(John Dryden)于1697年对翻译者阐明几个要点，并写明三种方法：

- "直译"(metaphrase)——一种"仆人式"的、"教谕式"的而又非常忠实于某一作品，将某一作者的作品逐字地、逐行地由一种语言翻译到另一种语言；

• “意译”（paraphrase）——译者关注原文的意思而非保持忠实于原文的实际词语；

• “模仿”（imitation）——译者能抑或不能以忠于原文的方式翻译词语或意思之处，取而代之制作出一个实际上由原文萌发的作品。（17–18）

德莱顿像许多翻译家一样力图在前两种方法间领航一条道路并抵制第三种方法的诱惑。对他而言，翻译一篇文本的要领在于将其译得易懂、典雅并能吸引当代读者。因此论及他翻译的维吉尔诗歌时德莱顿写道：“我已尽力让维吉尔说这样一种英语，假如他生在英国长在这个当下时代好像他自己就会说的英语。”（26）

当然这绝不是一个简单的运作，而且许多评论者坚持认为这几乎是不可能的，尤其是涉及诗歌翻译。奥克塔维奥·帕兹，像德莱顿一样也是一位诗人兼翻译家，就提出诗歌不能翻译的观点，他说诗是由“回音编织而成，是有意义的声音的互动和反射，是一幅蕴意的织品”（155）。德莱顿也阐明相似的意见：“诗是如此微妙的美酒，从一种语言倒到另一种语言时，将全都挥发掉。”（20）然而，这两位翻译家也都摒弃了这一顾虑；帕兹的理由是每一种西方语言中许多最好的诗歌是翻译的诗歌，而德莱顿的理由是假如诗歌翻译仅只模仿词语，那将是失败的，但是假如诗歌翻译表达原文作者的思想与情感，那将是成功的。

在实践中，凡翻译作品都含有失败的因素，同时也往往含有成功的因素。任何一种语言凡诗皆无法全部“阐释”为另一语言但大多容易接受“带过去”的某些形式。既然诗歌的首要意义总是趋向难以捉摸，趋向多意，也许我们应该不去过多质疑翻译。玛丽·安娜·考斯写道“像翻译者一样准确地意识到作者自己可能并没有抓住意思对我们多么有用，好像一大堆杂乱的非确定性的东西就会涌现出来就集聚在翻译这一概念四周”（54–55）。

然而翻译往往成功地传达原作的本意，有时还传达原作的基调感，甚至原作者的意图。而且有据可辩的是虽然并没有成为非常成功（就忠实或准确而言）的译作，有的诗歌翻译就诗艺而言甚至胜过原作一筹。无论情况如何，最引人注目的诗歌翻译自信地以诗歌的身份在新的语言中存在下去，同时本质地传达原作的内容、基调以及原作称之为观点的方面。

更有甚者，有的译作从声称再现的原作中获得自己的生命。就英语而言，艾兹拉·庞德（Ezra Pound）的《华夏集》就是显著一例。《华夏集》并没有十分忠于汉语原作（这并不奇怪，因为庞德当时还不能阅读汉语），但这是因他爱慕这些诗而使然。这将我们引导至有关翻译的一个中心问题。诗人都会同意，理想的情况下，任何诗歌翻译应该能使他们的诗成为成功的诗篇，披着它们的新外衣发挥作用，即已经穿上的新语言衣服的原作。但是，至于多大程度上诗人愿意自己的诗作被直译、多大程度上他们愿意被意译，将莫衷一是。

有的译者欣赏“模仿”的主意因为它可导致新的诗歌从被“翻译”的原作突现出来，并且最成功的范例是以许多译作不具备的活力发挥诗歌的功能。以英国诗人罗伯特·洛维尔（Robert Lowel）的诗集《模仿集》（*Imitations*）为例，洛维尔并没有以表现原作的精神或者卓越的诗艺为主，而是突出原作的感染力以引起读者的注意，同时基于原作创造出他自己的新诗。他对此评道：“这些诗并不是完全准确的翻译，而是对原作进行诗歌式的诠释。”（Fuller 33）他之所以如此诠释是为赞誉他在其他诗人——包括兰波和萨福——不同的诗歌中的新发现，并以此提醒我们注意，这些诗人的原作，无论如何，并不是它们原初的样子。由于他们最初写作的语言已经改变，由于产生这些诗歌的时代精神已经更改，这些诗歌也随之早已被无数读者或多或少地“再翻译”或“再诠释”（re-translated）。例如，我们不能完全理解历史遥远的萨福的时代，也不能理解那个时代的诗歌理论与文化理论，而且我们也不能追溯出萨福诗歌残片保留的那种语言的微妙，但是我们能用我们自己的理解与欣赏来赋予它们新的形式，这样，我们便以最好的方式赞誉这些诗作可爱的复杂性。

任何情况下，翻译许诺将某一首诗的某一思想传达给一群新读者，他们将以不同的语言和文化理念来理解这首诗，但仍然可能从阅读中获得许多乐趣。以此而论，翻译往往是一种跨文化相遇的形式，往往向我们提出诸如意义转换、语言运作、基调、声音等问题。许多例子说明，很多具有价值的内涵可以从一个世界、一种语言翻译到另一语言和世界。

参考文献

[1] Benjamin, Walter. “The task of the translator.” *Illuminations: Essays and reflections.* Ed. Hannah Arendt. Trans. Harry Zohn. New York: Schocken Books, 1968.

[2] Caws, Mary Ann. “When is losing finding? Translating Surrealism.” *On translating French literature and film II.* Ed. Miriam Salama-Carr. Amsterdam: Rodopi, 2000.

[3] Dryden, J. “On translation.” *Theories of translation. An anthology of essays from Dryden to Derrida.* Ed. Rainer Schulte and John Biguenet. Chicago: University of Chicago Press, 1992.

[4] Fuller, John. “From “Trade Winds.” *Robert Lowell: interviews and memoirs.* Ed. Jeffrey Meyers. Michigan: The University of Michigan Press, 1988.

[5] Gifford, Kenneth, ed. *Jindyworobak: Towards an Australian Culture.* Melbourne: Jindyworobak

Publications, 1944.
[6] Harris, Max. "An approach to Australian poetry." *Jindyworobak Quarterly Pamphlet* 1.2(1939):9–15.
[7] Kasparek, C. "The translator's endless toil." *The Polish Review* 28.2(1983):83–87.
[8] Paz, O. "Translation: literature and letters." Tans. Irene del Corral. *Theories of translation. An anthology of essays from Dryden to Derrida.* Ed. Rainer Schulte and John Biguenet. Chicago: University of Chicago Press, 1992.

Jen Webb, 澳大利亚堪培拉大学创意及文化研究中心主任、杰出教授。
Paul Hetherington，澳大利亚堪培拉大学副教授、国际诗歌研究所所长。

《外长日记》[1] 简评

戴　宁

《外长日记》(*Diary of a Foreign Minister*) 一书的作者为前澳大利亚外长鲍勃·卡尔(Bob Carr, 1947–)。卡尔先生是澳大利亚老牌政治家，16 岁即加入了工党，先后担任新南威尔士州工党支部主席和工党全国青年部主席，从 1988 年开始担任新南威尔士州反对党领袖，并于 1995 至 2005 年担任新南威尔士州州长，是澳大利亚连续担任州长时间最长的人。在此期间，他进行了许多大胆的改革，在推动经济发展、保护环境方面都取得很多成就，颇受民众欢迎。卡尔在 2012 和 2013 年间出任澳大利亚联邦政府外交部长，《外长日记》正是这一时期的记载。目前，卡尔先生受聘于悉尼科技大学澳中关系研究所，担任所长职务，同时也是多所中国大学的客座教授。他所发表的关于中澳关系的言论(包括担任外长期间)见解独特，在中国颇具影响力。

卡尔的《外长日记》主要记录了他从 2012 年 3 月被吉拉德总理任命为外长，至 2013 年 9 月以陆克文政府外交部长身份出席圣彼得堡二十国集团(G20)领导人峰会为止，这十八个月外长生涯的全部重要活动、立场、观点及其变化，并与读者分享了一位政治家的个人生活经历、喜怒哀乐、心路历程。日记基本沿着两条主要线索交叉进行：一是作为外交部长，代表澳大利亚处理各种对外关系，二是作为澳大利亚联邦议会参议员及重要内阁成员，参与制定并执行工党政府政策，并参与包括选举在内的工党各种活动。

作为外长，卡尔亲身经历了那一时期的重大国际事件，并参与了涉及澳大利亚的重要外交活动，他从历史、价值观、现实利益等多种角度讲述了澳大利亚外交政策的形成背景、出炉经过和深远影响，其中涉及澳中关系、澳美关系、澳大利亚与亚洲关系以及其他地区性和全球性关系。与传记和回忆录的不同之处是，《外长日记》使用了大量真实材料，包括外交电报、参阅材料、与全球高级领导人私下交流记录、与澳大利亚执政及在野领导人、外交家、学者的私人谈话。由于《外长日记》完成时间很近，所涉及的诸多重大国际事件和外交关系仍处在发生发展过程中；所涉及重要人物仍活跃在各自领域，所以具有重大现实意义，为研究当代澳大利亚外交政策提供宝贵的一手资料。

同时，作为一名资深政治家，卡尔先生又是联邦政府一名重要的内阁成员，处在澳大利亚政坛核心位置。他的日记也详尽讲述了两党斗争、工党内部派系之争的来龙去脉、贯穿始终的竞选活动，以及最终的政府更迭。《外长日记》中使用涉及国内外政策制定与修改的政府活动记录，包括内阁会议、各种委员会会议、议会党团会议、参议院听证会、质询时间等。同时，作者对澳大利亚政坛存在的各种现实问题（工党与自由党之争，工党内部派系之争，吉拉德与陆克文领导权之争，媒体与政治关系，政府更迭）有尖锐而深刻的分析与评价。为读者了解研究澳大利亚政治体制（议会制政府的构成及运作、政党理念、议会党团在制定政策上的核心作用，乃至民主政治、选举政治的实质等大话题）提供了最直观、最生动的具体资料。

在所有国际关系中，不管是全球的还是地区的，双边的还是多边的，自始至终困扰外长的问题是中国的崛起和在处理澳中、澳美关系上的不同理念和声音。他一直试图追根寻源，理清头绪，采取恰当政策，目的是“保持更健康和平衡的澳中关系”。在《外长日记》一开始，卡尔外长就介绍到：

> 澳大利亚如何对待中国和美国也是我们领导层中争议较多的问题。三位前总理，即弗雷泽、霍克和基廷，以及一些商界人士和学术评论家都表示，澳大利亚在2011年偏离了中国。这个话题是我们这一地区国家所讨论的更大话题的一部分，即在中国重新崛起的时代背景下，我们将如何调整自己。与此同时，中国重新崛起的话题又是更大话题的一部分，这个更大话题就是我们要把经济影响力和战略重心转移到亚洲。

作为西方政治家，卡尔无时无刻不流露出对美国自由开放价值观的青睐。他说澳美关系是“基于我们对共同价值观和共享利益广泛而长期的承诺，而且，也正因如此，我们成为‘如此愉快的同盟’。”但难能可贵的是，他能够冷静思考，对美国外交实质，以及澳美关系走向做出超越意识形态和个人喜好的客观判断。“我喜欢美国人，但我仍然对美国人的判断力感到担忧，担心他们在焦虑和偏执驱使下是否有能力与中国打一场冷战……他们在911之后已经草率地发动了两场战争——这也是我所担忧的。”他也从美国领导人和学者论述中总结出原因，比如就在9·11发生前几天，比尔·克林顿曾在悉尼对他说：“我们国家有些人认为美国必须永远拥有敌人。”1995年，美国作家诺曼·梅勒对他说，“冷战结束，弥漫在空气中的硝烟尚未散尽，美国人就不得不开始寻找新的敌人来取代苏联。是苏联让他们同仇敌忾，团结一致，让他们充满活力。”这些话题在他心中引起共鸣，以致他写了一篇博文，论述了美国人世界观中的病态，“看着这个帝国深陷泥潭，而且拒不从越战中吸取教训，使我对它的喜爱多了一层谨慎。”此外，卡尔外长也多次提到他对美国新保守主义者和极端保守主义者的深恶痛绝：“是他们一手制造了伊拉克乱局以及（我现在想到的）阿富汗乱局。”他甚至说：“所有那些新保守主义者，以及像拉姆斯菲尔德那样的极端分子，都应该受到审判。”

卡尔对待中国关系的基本理念和努力也可以从他和总理吉拉德的工作讨论中看到。（2013 年 1 月）“她强调要将中国作为实现战略对话的主攻方向，‘这将是一个醒目的外交政策成就。’的确如此。”而卡尔外长最根本的国际政治理念是，“上周日……在记者招待会上，我竭力反对各种遏制中国的设想。我对媒体说，我们可以与中国和日本都改善关系，这一点没有问题。我说：‘国际关系不必非得是一场零和游戏。’”他与新加坡外长多次探讨中国关系：

> 归根结底：澳大利亚的梦想是看到一个良好的美—中关系。新加坡也是如此。如果美国与中国双边关系破裂，这将是我们的噩梦。假如这种情况发生，那对我们，对新加坡，对整个世界，我想都是一场噩梦。中国与美国的关系是世界上最重要的双边关系。对我们如此，对整个世界亦是如此。

卡尔外长对中国关系的把握，应该说在一定程度上取决于他对中国的了解认识，这种了解认识在他上任后也经历了变化。

> 中国城市的现代化程度十分惊人，令我猝不及防，大跌眼镜。中国西部四川省省会成都完全没有我们想象中的那种贫困和挣扎。（我们乘火车到达）重庆，也没有我想象中那么灰暗，污染。就像我对海伦娜说的，这里不比新加坡差多少。这些城市有高楼大厦、公园绿地、购物中心……

随着对中国感性认识的加深，加上情感上的偏爱，他对中国文化有了较大的兴趣和深刻的理解。“接着，我们到了福建，这里是海伦娜祖父母的故乡。我们快速走访了三个城市：福州、泉州、厦门。海伦娜开心极了……泉州……这里更突出了中国的核心道德：和睦相处。”卡尔外长有历史专业背景，而且阅读涉猎广泛，使他对中国历史文化有较全面的了解。

《外长日记》所记录的最后一次出访是 2013 年 9 月在圣彼得堡，给他留下最深刻的印象是，“二十国集团领导人峰会结束后，我们来到康斯坦丁诺夫斯基宫的大台阶上。中国外长王毅与我道别。他已经知道我的位置将由别人取代。他大声说：‘你……

是……朋友。'" 这其实是外长先生为自己在澳中关系上所做努力的总结，反映出他对获得中国方面认可的满足。上述日记摘抄和分析显示，卡尔外长在复杂的澳中关系和澳美关系上，在美国重返亚洲的背景下，秉持工党长期的独立外交传统，而不是基于价值观的保守主义政策，致力于与大国保持一个健康平衡的关系，以最大程度维护澳大利亚利益。

除了大国关系之外，《外长日记》还记录了卡尔外长参加的所有地区及全球不同层次的会议和论坛。他不断出席或举办各种早餐会、午餐会、晚宴，甚至睡前酒会。“身为外长，我相信我的判断力，我选择恰当的词汇，吸收各种知识，为我所用。我超脱了平庸，为我的国家尽职尽责。人们相信我。这个感觉好极了。”出身卑微的卡尔外长，经过几十年的政坛磨练，不断自我修炼，为自己在这个位子上的表现深感自豪。“我有时候会问自己：这是我吗？是我在主持一个联合国论坛吗？我，一个来自马特拉维尔沙丘的孩子？”

在主持英联邦国家会议时，面对 54 个国家外长或官员代表，面临着最终落实英联邦章程的重任，

> 我决定速战速决，干净利索完成所有议题，就像我主持工党青年团会议一样，就像我主持金斯福德·史密斯选举委员会会议和州内阁会议一样。我知道，人们希望遇到一位行事果断，具有魄力的主持人，能够不断推进议程。我做到了！午餐前结束会议！他们纷纷祝贺我只用了规定时间的一半就圆满完成了任务。

在其他会议场合，他同样显示出优秀政治家的本色：

> 在整个会议过程中，我一直因势利导，循循善诱，随时捕捉大家能够一拍即合，达成共识的契机。我及时打断不实之词，或引起众怒的话题。我不时委婉提醒大家加快速度，然后让他们各抒己见，并畅所欲言。我是最出色的会议主席。这一点我毫不怀疑。

《外长日记》记录了他与全球外长俱乐部同事之间公开的和私下的交往，其中包括他与印尼外长马蒂、斯里兰卡外长佩里斯和新加坡外长尚穆根的多次会见、交谈，乃至私人通信。卡尔外长具有很现实的考虑，“外长的责任并非天下头等大事，比如避免战争发生，避免国家主权沦丧。外长工作的内容之一就是与外长们建立友好关系，以便在某一天需要打个电话时，你能够打通这个电话。”正是通过与圈子里的同事热诚相待，精心培育融洽的私人关系，他疏通渠道，多次解决了官方渠道

无法有效解决的外交难题，如遣返难民，打击人口贩子，鼓励民主、开放，解决领事案件等。

卡尔外长十分重视21世纪澳大利亚与东南亚的关系，因为这个世纪被认为是亚洲世纪，他希望成为东南亚与欧洲之间的桥梁："出访印度尼西亚之后，我去了文莱，参加一连串的东亚峰会会议。在这些会议上，我总是想，在我们北方，有这十个繁荣发展、充满活力的东盟国家是符合澳大利亚利益的……欣喜地看到东盟世界所有国家都对我们抱有好感。"外长希望看到的正是澳大利亚与东盟建立务实关系："……一圈繁荣的、有活力的东南亚国家对澳大利亚至关重要。他们的超市会摆满我们的产品。我们的年轻人可以到彼此国家上大学。他们的国防力量在我们北方接受培训，他们的公司通过在澳大利亚投资成为跨国企业。"

卡尔外长努力改善与东盟各国的关系，与阿拉伯国家的关系，以及与拉美国家和南太平洋国家的关系，并终于收获了进入联合国安理会的重大成果，展现了其谨慎的思考和灵活的外交手段。对善于学习、注重提升个人能力的卡尔外长个人来说，不断的接待和出访活动也让他感觉收获颇丰，"周五时，我对所罗门群岛的情况尚一无所知；而现在，我对它的历史有了基本了解，对这里的特色也有了一些感受。这就是为什么我特别珍视这份工作。"

作为一个16岁就加入工党，一辈子以参选议员，为公众服务为理想的卡尔先生，于2012年，在退出政坛六年后，再度出山，接受工党政府总理吉拉德邀请担任了联邦政府外交部长。卡尔担任外长的初衷也很自然，"我一直秉持人活一世，学无止境的理念，所以这次求之不得的机会岂能错失。"在澳大利亚政治体制里，卡尔外长本身作为参议员，要在堪培拉参加所有议会会议，履行议员职责。同时，作为内阁重要成员，他也得在堪培拉和悉尼履行政府官员职责，参加各种会见活动，完成连续的出访活动。同时，作为一个积极活跃的政治家，他不辞劳苦，充满热情地参加所有工党筹款活动，为工党候选人竞选拉票。"我认为这是我应尽的义务。随时随地，有求必应。"

他对领导人的忠诚并不是一成不变的，对国家利益和道义原则的忠诚导致他与吉拉德产生矛盾，乃至针锋相对。他在《外长日记》写道："对个人的忠诚要服从对政党的忠诚。"此事涉及在联合国关于巴勒斯坦地位问题上的表决。"在与总理的这场争执中，我必须取胜，因为她已经被来自墨尔本的亲以色列集团所左右……我说，如果澳大利亚允许一小撮墨尔本企业家否决我们的中东政策，那简直太可怕了。"从外长的角度来说，他发现澳大利亚甚至不能对以色列定居点政策"表示关切"，更不能批评、谴责，因为任何对以色列的批评都会被总理办公室驳回。"这件事说白了就是把我们的外交政策分包给了工党捐助人。看起来就是这么回事。这让所有前景都变了味儿。"

为了在国际上与广大国际社会站在一起，在国内赢得阿拉伯人和穆斯林的选票，他执意在联合国表决问题上改变以往的反对态度，改为投弃权票。而在决定外交政策的内阁会议上，总理特权和吉拉德的执著使他无法完成自己的计划，于是他决定通过议会党团的压力迫使吉拉德改变决定。《外长日记》使用政治家之间的邮件、短信、电话记录等，对此发难的前前后后，对所有相关人员的点滴表现，进行了戏剧性的详尽描述。我们看到，他动用了所有资源，使出浑身解数，经历了“惊心动魄的12小时”，终于迫使总理接受他的建议。这是澳大利亚做出了顺应时代潮流的决定，也为澳大利亚赢得了国际社会的尊重。在这段记录中，我们可以清楚地了解到内阁政府的运作、原则、纪律以及议会党团在澳大利亚政治中的决定性作用。

在短短18个月的外长任期内，卡尔时刻想着工党的命运，因为这也直接关系到他的个人命运。他哀叹自己时运不济，“要是能在一个正常的，享有议会多数的政府里担任外交部长该多好啊。要是摊上一位有意思，有权威，在所有民调中都能轻松领先的总理，而且首轮计票能拿下45%，那该多好啊；要是能一口气干五年外长该多好啊。”如果工党政府有望连任，他就有时间制定宏伟计划，放开手脚大干一番了。随着工党支持率不断下滑，工党众多席位岌岌可危，为了能将工党损失降到最低，他转投了陆克文阵营，并在陆克文政府里完成了最后几个月的外长职责。《外长日记》记载了他与政府领导人，工党派系大佬的频繁交流。

卡尔始终对工党的命运充满担忧，

> 澳大利亚工党是否已经同其他社会民主党派一样，陷入了长期的结构性衰落。我们这个政党已经没有什么活力了，只是一息尚存而已。有时候，我觉得睁睁看着澳大利亚工党气数已尽。但再想想，我发现工党一直是这副模样，一直处于疲于奔命，苦苦挣扎的状态。如果恰好领导人有创造性思维，还能勉强支撑，但如果支持率下降，则朝不保夕，命悬一线。

这正好生动体现了澳大利亚政党政治，选举政治的现实。

《外长日记》是一本鲜活的澳大利亚政治教科书，涵盖了当代政治领域的诸多话题。他对近年来活跃在国际舞台上的重要角色都有介绍与描述，为读者提供了一副国际舞台众生相。同时，《外长日记》在严肃的思考和尖锐的观察之外，还有穿插了外长先生幽默风趣、谈吐直率的故事和八卦，他不无调侃地与读者分享了他的真实心理活动，以及生活习惯和喜好。他博览群书，好学不倦，《外长日记》就记录了大量他阅读的书籍，观看的电影戏剧。读者或哑然失笑，或不以为然，或吐槽不断，或击掌叫好，但一定会掩卷而思，重新认识一些现象和问题。

戴宁，北京外国语大学英语学院澳大利亚研究中心副教授，研究兴趣为澳大利亚政党和政治体制。

本书由外语教学与研究出版社出版，2015 年 11 月 22 日在北京外国语大学首发。

北京外国语大学 澳大利亚研究中心

中心概况

北京外国语大学澳大利亚研究中心始建于 1983 年，是国内最早建立的澳研中心之一。澳研中心在 1988 年成功主办了中国首届澳大利亚研究国际研讨会，并发起成立了中国澳大利亚研究会，胡文仲教授担任会长至 2000 年，杜学增教授从 2004 年至 2010 年担任会长，李又文副教授从 2004 年至 2014 年担任研究会秘书长。目前李又文担任中国澳大利亚研究会副会长，李建军担任北外澳研中心主任、中国澳大利亚研究会秘书长。

北外澳研中心的主要任务是澳大利亚研究方向的硕士生教学和培养，是国内目前师资最多、课程开设最齐全的澳研中心之一。中心教师都有在澳大利亚著名大学学习和研究的经历，中心的研究生多次获得澳中理事会资助赴澳进行学术研究，并有机会参加中澳校际交流学习。目前澳研中心有 8 名专职教师、5 名荣誉 / 客座教授和 23 名在读硕士生。

目前澳研中心开设的课程有：澳大利亚历史、澳大利亚文学、澳大利亚社会与文化热点问题、澳大利亚民族主义、澳大利亚政治体制、澳大利亚政府管理、中澳关系、当代澳大利亚政治热点问题、澳大利亚性别研究、澳大利亚语言与社会、澳大利亚经济与投资政策、澳大利亚经典阅读、澳大利亚电影等。

师资队伍

姓　名	职　称	研究领域
马克林	荣誉教授	中澳关系、当代澳大利亚政治
李又文	副教授	澳大利亚电影、文化理论
夏玉和	副教授	澳大利亚社会与文化、民族主义
戴　宁	副教授	澳大利亚政治体制
陈兰芳	副教授	澳大利亚历史

（续表）

姓　　名	职　　称	研　究　领　域
李建军	讲　师	澳大利亚文学
窦　薇	讲　师	澳大利亚性别研究
周杜娟	讲　师	澳大利亚媒体、跨文化交际
胡　丹	讲　师	澳大利亚经济、中澳经贸关系
李　尧	客座教授	澳大利亚文学翻译
大卫·卡特	客座教授	澳大利亚文学、文化
马克·费南	客座教授	澳大利亚历史、司法
韩　锋	客座教授	澳大利亚对外关系

在研项目

澳大利亚电影中的华人形象
澳大利亚粤裔华人参政
中国现代文学在澳大利亚的翻译与接受情况
新环境下澳大利亚华人华侨中华文化传承与传播研究
SBS 电视台与多元文化主义话语的构建
澳新华文媒体与华人社会
澳大利亚性别研究
澳大利亚投资政策研究
澳大利亚文学在中国的出版和传播
周思小说研究

学术交流

澳研中心与格里菲斯大学、昆士兰大学、阿德莱德大学、拉筹伯大学、西澳大利亚大学、西悉尼大学、堪培拉大学等澳大利亚多所大学保持密切的关系，与澳中理事会、澳大利亚驻华使馆和国内兄弟院校的澳研中心保持良好的关系。澳中理事会资助建立的中国北方澳大利亚研究资料中心设立在北外图书馆。

澳研中心近年承办了 2013 中国—澳大利亚跨文化研究论坛、2014 马克林教授在华任教 50 周年暨西方的中国研究研讨会、2015 北外澳研高端教学论坛。2015 年 8 月，澳研中心 5 位教师受在华澳大利亚基金会的资助赴墨尔本大学、拉筹伯大学、莫纳什大学和迪肯大学访问交流，加强了双方的联系。2015 年 11 月，北外澳研中心将主办 2015 中澳关系暨跨文化研究论坛，来自西澳大利亚大学、阿德莱德大学、昆士兰大学、、悉尼科技大学、伦敦大学、清华大学、华东师大和北外等国内外知名高校的学者将参会交流。

澳研中心师生庆祝马克林教授来华任教 50 周年（1964—2014）

2015 北外澳研高端教学论坛与会者合影

2015 年 8 月北外澳研中心教师访问拉筹伯大学

联系方式

通讯地址： 北京海淀区西三环北路 2 号北京外国语大学英语学院澳大利亚研究中心，100089

电子邮箱： australianstudies@bfsu.edu.cn

中心网页： http://ausc.bfsu.edu.cn

本辑澳研学人

胡文仲，北京外国语大学英语教授，博士生导师，《外国文学》主编。1935生于天津，祖籍江苏，1954年北京外国语学院毕业后参加工作，1979—1981年在澳大利亚悉尼大学进修，获得文学硕士学位，回国后继续在北京外国语学院英语系任教。曾任北京外国语大学副校长、国务院学位委员会外文学科评议组成员、国家教委外语专业教学指导委员会主任、中国英语教学研究会会长、中国跨文化交际研究会会长、中国澳大利亚研究会会长等。

胡文仲教授长期从事英语教学与研究、跨文化交际研究和澳大利亚文学研究，共出版专著9部、教材5种、编著15部、译著5部，在国内外学术刊物上发表论文70余篇。专著包括：《英语的教与学》（外语教学与研究出版社，1989年），*Encountering the Chinese*（与Neal Grove合著，美国Intercultural Press, 1991年），《澳大利亚文学论集》（外语教学与研究出版社，1994年），《外语教学与文化》（与高一虹合著，湖南教育出版社，1997年），《跨文化交际学概论》（外语教学与研究出版社，1999年），《超越文化的屏障》（外语教学与研究出版社，2002年），《超越文化的屏障（修订版）》（外语教学与研究出版社，2004年）等；主编《中国英语教学（三）》、《大众英语》、《公务员英语》、《文化与交际》、《跨文化交际面面观》、《英美文化辞典》、《跨文化交际与英语学习》、《跨文化交际学选读》、《澳大利亚研究论文集（一）》、《和胡老师谈学英语》等。

胡文仲教授曾在澳大利亚悉尼大学、墨尔本大学、美国宾州州立大学、威斯康星大学、日本青山学院大学任客座教授；在英国兰卡斯特大学、澳大利亚国家图书馆任客座研究员；1987年被评为国家级有突出贡献的中青年专家，1990年被悉尼大学授予名誉文学博士学位，1996年获得澳中理事会文学翻译奖，1999年获得澳中理事会突出贡献奖；2015年获得许国璋外国语言研究奖：中国外语教育终身成就奖。

《澳大利亚文化研究》稿约

《澳大利亚文化研究》是一本综合性的学术研究论丛，收集关于澳大利亚文学、文化、语言、历史、哲学、经贸、政治、外交等学科的中英文研究文章，为从事澳大利亚问题研究的学者提供交流学术成果的园地，以适应我国日益深入的澳大利亚研究的需要。

本研究论丛目前暂设“学者访谈”、“作家作品”、“文坛纵览”、“社会文化”等栏目，还会根据实际需要增加“理论前沿”、“作家谈文学”、“好书共享”等栏目，此外还特设“澳研中心一览”与“澳研学人”，向读者介绍国内有影响力的澳大利亚研究中心与澳研学者。

本研究论丛欢迎全国各地从事澳大利亚研究的学者批评指正或来函来稿，中文稿件以 8 000 字左右为宜，英文稿件宜不超过 6 000 英文单词。来稿请用 Word 软件编辑，第一页请附作者简介，包括作者姓名、性别、年龄、工作 / 研究单位、职称、研究领域及近期成果、联系方式。中文稿件应包含标题、摘要、关键词、正文、参考文献等部分。文中若引用前人研究成果，请用文内夹注的方式标注文献来源，不用脚注。夹注中所引用或参考的文献，应在文后“参考文献”部分详细列明，一般应包含作者名、文章名、文章出处（如报刊、文集等）、出版社、出版时间、版本、页码等，网络文献应该标注链接地址，“参考文献”宜详尽准确，以便读者可据此追溯该文献所引原文。英文文献格式参考 MLA，中文文献参考《外语界》格式。

本研究论丛接受电子邮件投稿，不必另行寄送打印版稿件，稿件请发送至 adlywhyj@163.com，请在邮件标题中注明“澳大利亚文化研究稿件”。

编辑部主任： 周小进
电 子 邮 箱： adlywhyj@163.com
地　　　址： 上海市松江区文翔路 1900 号
邮　　　编： 201620